CW01467033

PROFESSIONAL SECURITY AGENT
BASIC TRAINING

PALMETTO
PUBLISHING

Charleston, SC
www.PalmettoPublishing.com

Professional Security Agent Basic Training
Copyright © 2021 by Robert Nile Nolan

All rights reserved

No portion of this book may be reproduced, stored in a retrieval system, or transmitted in any form by any means–electronic, mechanical, photocopy, recording, or other– except for brief quotations in printed reviews, without prior permission of the author.

Hardcover ISBN: 978-1-63837-863-1
PaperbackISBN: 978-1-63837-864-8
ebook ISBN: 978-1-68515-078-5

PROFESSIONAL SECURITY AGENT BASIC TRAINING

1ST EDITION

ROBERT NILE NOLAN

Shadow Security LLC
907 Mill Seat Lane
Allardt, Tennessee 38504
716 848-9696   931 879-7610
ShadowSecEP@gmail.com

"Training is the sacred responsibility of Professional Security Agents at all levels.

Let no security agent ever fail because that agent was not properly trained "

Robert Nile Nolan

CONTENTS

FROM THE AUTHOR

Today's security agent responsibilities require professionals who are trained and certified in many aspects of protecting people and property. *Professional Security Agent Basic Training* promotes professionalism by providing new security agents with a *standardized basic training program.* This training enables the new security agent to better serve his or her client, thus enhancing the image of the professional security agent community. It also provides a foundation to build upon prior to attending professional security academies and online training.

Competition for employment as a professional security agent is very intense. The new security agent needs to have a basic understanding of what is expected of a professional. This book standardizes what employers should expect of professional security agents beginning their careers. Study the information contained in this book. Having this knowledge will help you toward starting your journey to become a true professional security agent.

Welcome to the professional security agent community!

Robert Nile Nolan

PROFESSIONAL ETHICS

Insist on honesty, integrity, and fairness, and be strongly committed to upholding and promoting the highest ethical professional standards in all aspects of our profession.

Recognize that corruption and anticompetitive measures distort markets and hamper economic and social progress. It is therefore essential for members of our profession to avoid such practices.

Support efforts by international and national authorities to establish and enforce high ethical standards for our profession.

Comply with applicable competitive legislation. Honest competition must be based on integrity, product quality, price, and customer service.

Do not accept soliciting or bribes in any form.

Always make professional decisions based on objective reasons and criteria, and avoid conflicts of interest between private activities and the conduct of our profession.

SECURITY AGENT CODE OF CONDUCT

1. Respond to employer's professional needs.

2. Exhibit exemplary conduct.

3. Protect confidential information.

4. Maintain a safe and secure workplace.

5. Dress to create professionalism.

6. Enforce all lawful rules and regulations.

7. Encourage liaison with public officers.

8. Develop good rapport within the profession.

9. Strive to attain professional competence.

10. Encourage high standards of officer ethics.

SECURITY AGENT TRAINING AND CAREER DEVELOPMENT

Training is a necessity if individual performance is to be enhanced to any appreciable degree. The training process is complex and will be addressed in the following areas:

- the role of training in a security professional's development

- different development methods and their benefits

- the relationship between a professional's development and nonprofessional development

- the role of the individual in his or her career development

THE ROLE OF TRAINING IN A SECURITY PROFESSIONAL'S DEVELOPMENT

To explain the role of training in a security professional's development, a clear definition of the word *training* is established as those activities which are designed to improve human performance on the job the employee is presently doing or is being hired to do. Advancement as a security professional must include training, education, and development. Training (the physical part) includes hands-on training, such as weapons, driving skills, people skills, and so on). Education consists of those human resource development activities that are designed to improve the overall competence of the employee in a specified direction and beyond the job now held. Development prepares the employee so that he or she can move with the organization as it develops, changes, and grows through the efforts of employees and applied technology. It also creates growth in the organization through the combining of training, education, and new opportunities.

Training, education, and development have their own place within the human resources development process, and although all are related to each other, each is a separate, distinct entity. Training will have a measurable impact on job performance, provided the training is given properly and directly affects an organization's development, whereas education will change attitudes and outlooks.

DIFFERENT DEVELOPMENT METHODS AND THEIR BENEFITS

Development methods vary and include lectures, videos, training exercises, on-the-job training (OJT), and tests. Lectures are sometimes used as an instructional technique. A key note for giving a lecture is to remember that a lecture is to establish a common base of knowledge when this base does not exist. Lectures can also be used to assess learners, what they know, and how they feel about certain topics. Lectures differ from demonstrations in that demonstrations explain what is to be accomplished beforehand and teach proficiency through the use of hands-on training. The benefits of different development methods include the following:

- increased job efficiency where specific job tasks are performed better

- better relations between security agents and management

- enhanced professional identity by security agents who see growth within themselves

- pride and job satisfaction

- increased loyalty to the employer who has shown an interest in the security agents by providing training for them

- decreased turnover, as there are fewer situations that make the security agents feel uncomfortable and incompetent

- fewer mistakes

- decreased number of accidents

- improved discretionary judgment with better decisions being made

- protection from allegations that the professional security agent is negligent in performance of his or her duties

When the professional security agent learns as much as he or she can about learning theory and instructional techniques, performance will improve. All persons involved in the training process will develop their own career aspirations and increase their value to themselves, their families, and their employers.

THE DIFFERENCE BETWEEN PROFESSIONAL AND NONPROFESSIONAL DEVELOPMENT

Professional development creates growth for the security professional and the organization through the combining of training, education, and new opportunities. Experience eventually becomes the catalyst in developing the security agent and the organization. When an employer maximizes professional development by using the security agent in the most efficient and cost-effective manner possible, the organization will develop through the efforts of the professional security agent.

Nonprofessional development is the assignment of mundane daily tasks, such as walking a post day after day or standing a post on a daily basis. The only development a security guard gets is learning a new task, such as a change in the route of travel or change in static placement. This guard serves a minimal purpose and often is not prepared to effectively deal with the public and perform duties to maximum efficiency.

THE ROLE OF THE INDIVIDUAL IN HIS OR HER CAREER DEVELOPMENT

The professional security agent seeks avenues and opportunities to broaden his or her skill sets and competencies to meet current and future job demands. This may be accomplished through incentive programs, coordination through local colleges, seminars, or any other method that encourages individual professional development.

PROBLEM SOLVING AND DECISION MAKING PROCESS

In your position as a security agent, you may be called upon to solve problems and make final decisions. This can be very stressful, and you may sometimes question whether you are making the right decisions.

There's a process that can help you make these decisions and remain confident that you've made the best decision you possibly could. It's called the *Problem Solving and Decision-Making Process*. There are five steps to this process consisting of the following:

1. **Recognize and define the problem**. Clearly state exactly what the problem is.

2. **Gather all essential information**. Is this something that is within your capability to handle yourself, or do you need assistance? If you need assistance, your first avenue should be to consult your coworker. If you need more assistance, your next avenue should be to consult your immediate supervisor. Answer the following questions: who, what, when, where, why, and how.

3. **Develop possible solutions**. There are sometimes seemingly thousands of ways of solving a problem. Do some investigating. Gather as much information about the problem as you can. Write down every solution you can think of.

4. **Analyze the solutions**. In order to solve the problem or make a decision, are there necessary logical steps that must be taken? Prioritize the criteria into a logical sequence (i.e., step 1 must be completed before you can go on to step 2 and so on).

5. **Select the best solution**. Evaluate all of the possible solutions based upon the results of your investigation. Gathering information about the problem will result in your final decision being an "informed"

decision. Choose what you think is the best solution. Implement your decision, and *supervise* the implementation. You must ensure that the final outcome is how you predicted. Lack of supervision may result in an outcome that reflects a perception different than yours. However, it will be *you* who is ultimately responsible.

Note: *Throughout the problem solving and decision making process actually put pen to paper, and write down all of the criteria in each step. Looking at the information in writing will make it easier to analyze exactly what you are doing. This will help you have confidence that you have accomplished the best job you possibly could.*

THE BACKWARD PLANNING PROCESS

You will often have specific things to accomplish throughout your shift. For example, you have to be at a certain place at a certain time. Maybe you have to have an entryway sealed by a specific time, but you are busy elsewhere, and you feel you can't be in two places at the same time. Using this process may help you to achieve your goal on time and not miss important items. Write down the following steps at the beginning of your shift, and stick to the schedule you have set up for yourself.

> **Step 1:** Write down your ultimate goal. What specifically do you want to achieve and by what time?

> **Step 2:** Ask yourself what milestone you need to accomplish just before that, in order to achieve your ultimate goal. What do you have to do, and by when, so that you're in a position to reach your final objective?

> **Step 3:** Work backward some more. What do you need to complete before that second-to-last goal?

> **Step 4:** Work back again. What do you need to do to make sure the previous goal is reached?

> **Step 5:** Continue to work back, in the same way, until you identify the very first milestone that you need to accomplish.

When you read a backward plan, it doesn't look much different from a traditional forward plan. However, creating a backward plan is *very* different. You need to force yourself to think from a completely new perspective to help you see things that you might miss if you use a traditional, forward-looking chronological process.

RISK MANAGEMENT

During your assignment at your post, the one asset you will use the most is your power of observation. It is your responsibility to be aware of your surroundings. Your success as a professional security agent depends on it. You must constantly be aware of potential hazards in your area of responsibility and exercise corrective measures to minimize anyone getting hurt. Utilize "Risk Management at a Glance" to ensure nobody gets hurt.

The risk assessment does not need to be a lengthy ordeal. Follow the criteria listed under "Risk Management at a Glance." This will help you decide if you can complete the project without anyone getting hurt.

RISK MANAGEMENT AT A GLANCE

Risk Management identifies and controls hazards before they become accidents.

Risk Management applies to all tasks at all times.

The following *five steps* are applied:

1. Identify the hazard or risks. What is or is not risky? Consider all aspects of current and future tasks, environment, and known risks.

2. Assess the hazard or risk: How big is the risk? Label it from "low" to "extremely high." How likely will the hazard occur? If the hazard does happen, how bad will it be?

3. Develop controls and make *risk* decisions: What can stop or reduce the hazard? Create controls to reduce the hazard until the lower risk outweighs the potential damage.

4. Implement controls: Make sure everyone knows—and uses—the controls you created.

5. Supervise and evaluate: Visit the people doing the work. Do the controls work? Supervise and revise until they do.

CONFLICT RESOLUTION

In your position as a security agent, you may be called on to resolve conflicts, squash arguments, and maintain order. When order gets out of hand, chaos ensues. Immediate control is necessary; however, the control needs to be applied in a diplomatic way so as not to add fuel to the fire. Use these ten go-to phrases to defuse potentially volatile conversations.

1. **"Thank you for your opinion. I'll think about it."** When you receive unsolicited advice at a meeting or event, respond with this casual conversation terminator. The goal is to be polite and end the conversation. There is no need to be defensive or rude.

2. **"Is this a good time for you?"** Whenever you want someone's full attention for a conversation, ask this simple question. If the response is no, ask, "When would be a better time?" Agree on another time, and a fight is avoided.

3. **"Would you like my thoughts?"** One of the biggest complaints people may have is that they are constantly receiving orders and judgments. If you are confronted with an angry response ("Who made you the authority?" or "It's none of your business"), you might benefit from trying a different approach. Ask if the person wants to hear what you have to say. If he or she says yes, it means he or she is ready to listen. If the person says no, then try a different approach.

4. **"Why don't we get the facts?"** Some people who come to meetings tend to argue about anything and everything, including things that can be easily resolved. If you find someone in a dispute, state this one-liner so you can move on from the discussion before it spirals into a fight.

5. **"I need your help. Can you please…?"** If someone is not assuming his or her share of responsibility, rather than accusing the person of being lazy or inconsiderate, ask him or her for what you want, and be specific. People are not mind readers.

6. **"Let's wait on this until we have more information."** Know when to table a discussion. At times, it's important to remind yourself and your conversation partner that it's too early to discuss the issue. Preferences will change over time, as will facts.

7. **"What did you mean by that?"** Sometimes asking the right question is all it takes to avoid an argument. We all make assumptions about other people's intentions. Asked in a genuinely interested (and not passive-aggressive) way, this question allows your conversation partner to explain him- or herself before you jump to conclusions. Only then should you offer your response.

8. **"I don't like that, so why don't we do this instead?"** This is how to complain with impact. Rather than nagging about a problem, focus on finding a solution for the future.

9. **"I'm sorry you're upset."** When you find yourself frustrated with someone who didn't take your advice, you desperately want to say something like "I told you so" or "That was a dumb thing to do." Don't. Dishing out criticism won't change a thing. A compassionate response will help you both move forward.

10. **"Let me get back to you."** Everyone needs a prepared comment to delay a response when he or she is put on the spot. Keep this line handy at all times. If you don't know the answer or don't want people to feel as if they are being dismissed, give them a time when they can expect a response, and then make sure that you do respond.

MASLOW'S HIERARCHY OF NEEDS

Your assignment as a professional security agent will most certainly require you to interact with people of different cultures, opinions, and personalities. Abraham Maslow (1908–1970) was an American psychologist who was best known for creating a theory of psychological health predicated on fulfilling innate human needs in priority, culminating in self-actualization.

What does this mean to you? It means that *all* people have certain needs. If you can address these needs, you will have a better chance of creating an atmosphere where nobody gets hurt. You're not expected to help someone reach self-actualization, but you are expected to resolve tense situations. Maslow's hierarchy of needs is a tool that may help you in your interaction with others.

Maslow stated that people are motivated to achieve certain needs and that some needs take precedence over others. Our most basic need is for physical survival, and this will be the first thing that motivates our behavior. Once that level is fulfilled, the next level up is what motivates us, and so on.

1. **Physiological needs**—these are biological requirements for human survival (e.g., air, food, drink, shelter, clothing, warmth, sex, sleep). Don't worry, if you don't provide these needs; they will provide them for themselves.

2. **Safety needs**—protection from elements, security, order, law, stability, freedom from fear

3. **Love and belongingness needs**—after physiological and safety needs have been fulfilled, the third level of human needs is social and involves feelings of belongingness. The need for interpersonal relationships motivates behavior. Examples include friendship, intimacy, trust, acceptance, receiving and giving affection and love, and affiliating, being part of a group (family, friends).

4. **Esteem needs**—Maslow classified these into two categories: (i) esteem for oneself (dignity, achievement, mastery, independence) and (ii) the desire for reputation or respect from others. This is where a pat on the back in front of others comes into play.

5. **Self-actualization needs**—these include realizing personal potential, self-fulfillment, seeking personal growth and peak experiences, a desire "to become everything one is capable of becoming." It is said that self-actualization is never truly obtained because once a person has become everything they thought they could be, they set new goals for themselves.

KEEP-IN-MEMORY TRAINING

Learning Objective: Security agent will train using the keep-in-memory training technique.

Keep-in-memory (KIM) training has been used for years in military units and police forces around the world. KIM training will help to train the mind to prepare for an event where the guard will need to recall and recount certain events and to assist in surveillance detection.

Practical Exercise
One security agent will take ten random objects and place them out of sight of the guard. The security agent being tested will have thirty seconds to look at the items and then one minute to write down as much detail as possible about the items viewed.

PROACTIVE COUNTERMEASURES

Learning Objective: Security agent will know the proactive counter-measures to combat terrorist targets.

These proactive countermeasures will be explained in more depth in this section:

Vigilance
Observation
Targeted questioning
Careful searches
Comprehensive employee awareness

Vigilance: Alert security can prevent or mitigate a suicide or homicide attack.

Observation: Keen observation of people and vehicles for signs of suspicious behavior is critical to early detection of an attack.

Targeted questioning: Making eye contact and polite inquiries demonstrate that security personnel are alert. Verbal exchanges also allow the trained officer to assess nonverbal indicators.

Careful searches: If reasonable suspicion merits a search, be very careful not to detonate an IED.

Comprehensive employee awareness: Vigilance is enhanced if guards and local employees are involved and listen to each other. Intelligence is a vital part of surveillance detection.

CONFRONTING A COMPLIANT SUSPECT

Learning Objective: Security agent will know the steps to take when confronting a compliant suspect.

- Issue verbal commands in a very loud, firm voice.

- Clear the area of all nonessential personnel.

- Direct the suspect to show hands, palms up.

- Direct the suspect to place any carried items on the ground and then move two steps away from them.

- Direct the suspect to remove outer clothing and place the garments on the ground.

- Direct the suspect to lie face down, with arms outstretched, palms up, face turned away from you.

- Do *not* approach the suspect. Wait for the arrival of your supervisor or a police officer.

ESCALATION OF FORCE

Escalation of force is a process that ensures minimal force is being used to control a *life-threatening* situation. This process must be followed when the need arises to stop an individual from approaching you in a life-threatening manner. If you are ever accused of using excessive force, you should be able to testify that you used the following procedure.

An individual(s) is approaching you or others, and you fear for your life or the lives of others, your actions will be as follows:

1. Raise your nonfiring hand in the air, palm facing forward toward the individual and loudly say, "*Stop!*"

2. Position your body in an aggressive stance by squarely facing the individual with your legs spread shoulder-width apart, and loudly repeat "*Stop!*"

3. Place your hand on your weapon and loudly repeat, "*Stop!*"

4. Draw your weapon from your holster, point the weapon at the ground, and loudly repeat, "*Stop!*"

5. Point your weapon at the individual and loudly repeat, "*Stop!*"

6. If the individual continues to not comply with your directives and you perceive that individual to be life-threatening to you or others, fire your weapon in a controlled manner to stop the threat. You must account for every bullet leaving your weapon and clearly explain where each bullet was intended to go.

Note: Every bullet has a lawyer's name inscribed on it. Be able to explain your escalation of force and your intended shot placement.

DEADLY FORCE

Learning Objective: Security agent will be able to understand the meaning of deadly force and the appropriate times to use it.

Definition of *deadly force*—any force that is likely to cause death or serious injury.

Permissible use of deadly force—to prevent imminent or grave danger to yourself, other guards, or any innocent person in the area

Determining factors for the use of deadly force—the likelihood that the subject will cause serious bodily injury or death to the agent or other innocent persons, the capabilities of the subject, the nature of the danger posed. Would other agents in your same situation use the same force?

The Bottom Line

You are here to protect lives. Your decision to use deadly force is one that you will have to answer for. As a security agent, the likelihood of you being engaged in a deadly force situation is greatly improved. There are many situations that can occur that will require the use of deadly force (suicide bombers, car bombers, and so on). Just remember that you will have to use your best judgment. Always remember that warning shots are not authorized, and we shoot at the threat until the threat has stopped the action that caused the use of deadly force.

STANDARD OPERATING PROCEDURE FOR THE USE OF DEADLY FORCE

The Use of Force

The use of force is defined as the physical application of violence upon or against a person in any way, including the use of the baton. The baton (nightstick) serves as a defensive weapon for the security agent. Its use by the security agent is defined as follows:

a. The baton will only be used after all nonviolent efforts are exhausted to quell a disturbance at any post manned by a security agent.

b. It will only be used to protect the security agent or persons on the post from actual bodily harm by another person or persons. The oral threat of bodily harm is insufficient justification for the use of the baton.

c. Abusive and/or obscene language directed at the security agent or a third party is insufficient justification for the use of the baton.

d. Any person attempting to strike the security agent in the performance of duty or to forcibly detain him or her, causing a serious disturbance on the post by striking or assaulting the security agent or another party, or in any way causing injury constitutes sufficient justification to use the baton.

e. Only the minimum use of force necessary for the restoration of order is authorized.

The Use of Deadly Force

The use of deadly force is defined as the application of lethal force by use of a firearm upon a person attempting to inflict bodily harm to or threatening the life of the agent or another person. The use of a firearm by local security agents serves as a defensive weapon. The security agent's use of a firearm to apply deadly force is justified as follows:

f. Deadly Force will only be used after all nonviolent efforts are exhausted to stop a life-threatening disturbance at any post manned by a security agent.

g. Deadly force will only be used to protect the life of the security agent or another person on the post from lethal bodily harm by another individual or individuals. The oral threat of bodily harm is insufficient justification for the use of deadly force.

h. Abusive and/or obscene language directed at the security agent or another individual is insufficient justification for the use of deadly force.

i. Any person attempting to use lethal force on a security agent, lethally assaulting the agent or another individual, or in any way causing the death of another individual constitutes sufficient justification for the use of deadly force.

j. The use of deadly force represents the last resort by a security agent for the restoration of order.

Example of a Policy Regarding the Use of Deadly Force

1. Definition of *Deadly Force*

   "Deadly force" is the use of any force that is likely to cause death or serious physical injury. When an armed agent uses such force, it may only be done consistent with this policy. Force that is not likely to cause death or serious physical injury but unexpectedly results in such harm or death is not governed by this policy.

2. Probable Cause for the Use of Deadly Force

   Probable cause, reason to believe, or a reasonable belief, for the purposes of this policy, means facts and circumstances, including the reasonable inferences drawn therefrom, known to the armed security agent at the time of the use of deadly force would cause a reasonable armed security agent to conclude that the point at issue is probably true. The reasonableness of a belief or decision must be viewed from the perspective of the armed security agent on the scene, who may often be forced to make split-second decisions in circumstances that are tense, unpredictable, and rapidly evolving. Reasonableness is not to be viewed from the calm vantage point of hindsight.

3. Principles on Use of Deadly Force

   The professional security agent recognizes and respects the integrity and paramount value of all human life. Consistent with that primary value, but beyond the scope of the principles articulated here, is the full commitment by the professional security agent to take all reasonable steps to prevent the need to use deadly force. Yet even the best prevention policies are on occasion insufficient, as when an armed security agent is confronted with a threat to his or her life or the life of a protectee or other individual. With respect to these situations and in keeping with the value of protecting all human life, the touchstone of this policy regarding use of deadly force is necessity. Use of deadly force must be objectively reasonable under all the circumstances known to the armed security agent at the time.

4. Permissible Uses of Deadly Force

    a. The necessity to use deadly force arises when all other available means of preventing imminent and grave danger to the armed security agent or other persons have failed or would be likely to fail. Thus, employing deadly force is permissible when there is no safe alternative to using such force, and without it, the armed security agent or others would face imminent and grave danger. An armed security agent is not required to place himself or herself, another armed security agent, or the public in unreasonable danger of death or serious physical injury before using deadly force. An armed security agent will fire at a person only in response to an imminent threat of deadly force or serious physical injury against the security agent, protectees, or other individuals.

    b. Determining whether deadly force is necessary may involve instantaneous decisions that encompass many factors, such as the following:

        -   the likelihood that the subject will use deadly force on the armed security agent or others if such force is not used by the armed security agent

        -   the armed security agent's knowledge that the subject will likely continue to be a life threat if the armed agent uses lesser force or no force at all

-   the capabilities of the subject

-   the presence of other persons who may be at risk if force is or is not used

-   the nature and the severity of the danger posed

c. Deadly force should never be used upon mere suspicion that the actions of an individual or group of individuals will result in the serious injury or death of an armed security agent, protectees, or others.

5. Use of Lesser Means than Deadly Force

a. Intermediate Force

If force less than deadly force could reasonably be expected to accomplish the same end, such as restraining a dangerous subject, without unreasonably increasing the danger to the armed security agent or to others, then it must be used. Deadly force is not permissible in such circumstances, although the reasonableness of the armed security agent's understanding at the time deadly force was used will be the benchmark for assessing applications of this policy.

b. Verbal Warnings

Prior to using deadly force, if feasible, the armed security agent will audibly command the subject to submit to his or her authority. If, however, giving such a command would itself pose a risk of death or serious physical injury to the armed security agent or others, it need not be given.

6. Warning Shots and Shooting to Disable

   a. Warning shots are not authorized. Discharge of a firearm is usually considered to be permissible only under the same circumstances when deadly force may be used—that is, only when necessary to prevent loss of life or serious physical injury. Warning shots themselves may pose dangers to the armed security agent or others.

   b. Attempts to shoot to wound or to injure are unrealistic and, because of high miss rates and poor stopping effectiveness, can prove dangerous for the armed agent and others. Therefore, shooting merely to disable is strongly discouraged.

7. Motor Vehicles and Their Occupants

   Shooting to disable a moving motor vehicle is forbidden. An armed security agent who has reason to believe that a driver or occupant poses an imminent danger of death or serious physical injury to the armed security agent or others may fire at the driver or an occupant only when such shots are necessary to avoid death or serious physical injury to the armed security agent or another and only if the public safety benefits of using such force reasonably appear to outweigh any risks to the armed guard or the public, such as from a crash, ricocheting bullets, or return fire from the subject or another person in the vehicle.

8. Vicious Animals

   Deadly force may be directed against vicious animals when necessary in self-defense or the defense of others.

9. Investigation of Incidents of Deadly Force

Administrative Leave/Duty

An armed security agent who makes use of deadly force will be placed, as circumstances dictate, on administrative leave or assigned to duties not requiring the carrying of a firearm until the internal review and investigation are completed and the armed security agent is authorized to return to duty.

10. Firearms

No security agent shall carry a firearm unless

- The armed security agent has qualified with assigned weapon(s) in accordance with contract terms and conditions.

- The armed security guard is not disqualified by any law relating to convictions for misdemeanor crimes of violence.

- The armed security agent has been authorized to carry and use firearms in the performance of his or her duties with respect to maintaining the security and safety of persons designated in the contract.

11. Responsibility

An armed security agent is responsible for having a complete understanding of his or her authority and its limitations, as well as applicable guidelines and procedures.

12. Issues Requiring Clarification

All issues relating to this policy that require clarification shall be directed to the senior security agent on duty.

13. Authorized Firearms and Related Equipment

An armed security agent may carry only handguns, holsters, support weapons, and ammunition that has been issued or approved. Under no circumstances is an armed security agent to modify any support weapon or ammunition that has not been approved by the client.

14. Qualification

To be authorized to carry a company-issued or approved firearm, an armed security agent shall qualify by meeting or exceeding a specified score with an approved firearm in accordance with the contract. Under no circumstance shall an armed security agent carry a firearm if he or she has not successfully completed the required firearms qualification procedures.

15. Firing Range Procedures

The firing range instructor shall ensure that all training is conducted safely in accordance with approved guidelines, lesson plans, and manuals.

16. Prescription Medication

An armed security agent who is taking prescription medication, except for short-term antibiotics and oral contraceptives, which are not already a matter of record, shall notify his or her supervisor and submit a medical certificate or other administratively acceptable documentation of the prescription and its effect(s) to the human resources representative of the client. The human resources representative shall determine whether such armed security agent shall be allowed to continue to carry a firearm while taking the medication. Pending written approval, the armed security agent shall not perform armed guard duties.

17. Standards of Conduct for Professional Armed Security Agents

a. Armed security agents shall remember at all times the serious responsibility and potential dangers attendant to their authority to carry firearms and conduct themselves accordingly.

b. Armed security agents are accountable for their actions and shall conduct themselves in a manner that shall not bring discredit to themselves or the professional security profession.

c. An armed security agent shall treat a firearm at all times as if it were loaded.

d. All incidents involving misconduct with a firearm shall be reported immediately to the human resources representative. Any such incidents shall be considered serious, and the armed security agent involved may be subject to criminal and civil penalties and disciplinary action.

18. Activities Specifically Prohibited

The following activities are specifically prohibited for armed security agents while armed:

a. careless or irresponsible behavior

b. careless or unnecessary display of a firearm in public

c. dry-firing or practicing quick draws other than during training or qualification practice

d. threatening a person or making an unwarranted allusion to being armed in any situation not directly related to an official purpose

e. consumption of any alcoholic beverage while armed, six hours prior to being armed, or at any time prior to being armed sufficient to impair the armed guard's judgment or ability to perform his or her duties

f. use of medications or drugs that may impair judgment or ability while on duty

g. carrying or using any firearm, ammunition, or related equipment not specifically issued or approved by the client.

h. carrying or using a modified firearm not previously approved by the client

19. Securing Firearms

a. An armed security agent is responsible for maintaining the safety and security of his or her firearm. An armed security agent shall secure his or her firearm in accordance with established policies.

b. If an armed security agent loses his or her firearm or if the firearm is stolen, the armed security agent shall immediately notify the client.

20. Drawing Firearms

An armed security agent will not draw his or her firearm unless confronted with the threat of deadly force or serious physical injury.

21. Discharges

a. Reporting—an armed security agent who has discharged a firearm shall orally report such discharge immediately to his or her direct supervisor and shall prepare a written report delineating the circumstances of the discharge within twenty-four hours.

b. Investigation—internal investigations of all discharges of firearms shall be under the direction of the human resources representative. Pending the results of the investigation, the armed security agent who has discharged his or her firearm may be placed on administrative leave or may be assigned duties that do not require the carrying of a firearm.

c. Media inquiries—armed security agents shall make no comment to the media regarding a discharge. Armed security agents shall refer inquiries from the press regarding a discharge to the human resources representative.

d. Discharge involving injury or death—after meeting the requirements of a shooting situation and securing the area as required, the first concern of armed security agents shall be the physical and mental well-being of all armed security agents.

e. Notification of appropriate law enforcement authorities—the responsible supervisor of the armed security agents shall notify local law enforcement immediately of the discharge.

f. Investigation—armed security agents on the scene at the time of the discharge shall not investigate the discharge. The firearm that was discharged shall be secured, preserved as evidence, and relinquished to local law enforcement.

22. Disciplinary and Other Actions

a. The human resources representative shall be kept fully informed of any discharge of a firearm by an armed security agent or of any incident that results in an allegation of misconduct with a firearm by an armed guard.

b. The human resources representative may ask the immediate supervisor to reassign an armed security agent to duties that do not require the carrying of a firearm, require the armed security agent to undergo remedial training, or ask the supervisor to reassign the armed security agent to another contract.

c. The human resources representative may refer matters to relevant law enforcement authorities, when appropriate.

23. Applicability of Policy and Regulation

Nothing contained in this policy shall be construed to limit or impair the authority or responsibility of any local or federal law enforcement agency.

This policy will be used in conjunction with a client's firearm policy. If any provision of this policy conflicts with the client's firearm policy, the client's firearm policy is controlling.

WEAPONS SAFETY REGULATIONS

Weapons Safety Measures

To maintain weapons safety, we must adopt certain measures of security in order to reduce the risk of having an accident. The following are the main measures we must adhere to.

1. Shoot at your target with precision, not blindly.

2. Consider every weapon loaded until you have checked it yourself.

3. Never use the weapon to intimidate. The weapon is for defensive purposes only.

4. Never hand the weapon to anyone without first verifying that the weapon is unloaded.

5. Never point a weapon at anyone you do not intend to shoot even if the weapon is unloaded.

6. Never put your finger in the trigger well until you are ready to shoot.

7. Make sure that your weapon is operative and clean from dust or any other element that could cause your weapon to malfunction.

8. Always load your weapon in a safe place.

COMPONENTS OF AN IMPROVISED EXPLOSIVE DEVICE (IED)

Objective: Security agents will know the necessary components to make an improvised explosive device (IED).

There are five necessary components to make an IED.

1. Power source
2. Detonator/primer (electrical, nonelectrical)
3. Switches (electrical, nonelectrical)
4. Wires
5. Explosive

The items listed above always have to be present to start an explosion.

1. Power source—power sources are batteries, cell phones, or any other source that could generate more than one volt of energy.

2. Detonators—these are activated with electricity or without it (primers).

3. Switches (electrical or nonelectrical)—there are many kinds of switches that could be used to finish/close the circuit.

4. Wires—wires will always be present in an IED.

5. Explosives—the bigger the damage terrorists want to cause, the bigger the charge of explosive they will use.

Task: Talk about the different power sources and switches that could be used in an IED.

TERRORIST ATTACK CYCLE

Learning Objective: Security agent will understand the terrorist attack cycle for the purpose of surveillance detection on the various sites.

Terrorist Attack Cycle

There are common steps that terrorists will use when deciding what, when, where, and how to attack a target. These steps are known as the *terrorist attack cycle*. The terrorist attack cycle is a full circle of events the terrorists will use to plan and carry out an attack and escape. The terrorist attack cycle is composed of several elements and flows as follows:

1. Identify potential targets—terrorists develop a list of potential targets.

2. Surveillance / information gathering—terrorists use surveillance to gather information to determine whether potential targets can be successfully attacked.

3. Target selection—based on the initial surveillance, terrorists identify their intended targets. Terrorists will normally seek the highest profile *soft* target available to maximize the odds of a successful attack.

4. Attack planning—surveillance continues as the terrorists develop a detailed plan identifying the time, location, and method of attack that will yield the highest probability of success.

5. Deployment and attack—prior to a terrorist attack, the perpetrators of the attack will preposition at the attack site. Surveillance will continue up until the moment of attack.

6. Escape and exploit—after the attack, the attackers will depart the attack site to avoid apprehension and exploit the attack.

We have seen how terrorists use surveillance to choose targets and to plan their attacks. Only by being aware of what is going on around us, looking at everything around us, and having a security mind-set can we be successful in making it harder for terrorists or criminals to gain operational information.

Practical Exercise
List the different ways that knowledge of the terrorist attack cycle will help you to better conduct surveillance detection in your area of responsibility.

SURVEILLANCE DETECTION

Learning Objective: Security agent will understand the meaning of surveillance and surveillance detection as applies to his or her assigned post.

Surveillance is the surreptitious close watch or close observation kept over someone or something. *The purpose of surveillance is to gather pertinent information on an individual or site and formulate it into a plan that will enhance the likelihood of a successful operation.*

Surveillance Detection

Surveillance detection (SD) is an organized, systematic methodology designed to identify hostile surveillance by discovering the type of surveillance being used by their indicators. *The purpose of surveillance detection is to* identify hostile surveillance.

The priority of the work done by professional security agents should be surveillance detection. SD is one of the top priorities the security agent will have on a daily basis. SD is the precursor to interrupting the terrorist attack cycle. Good SD can be the best deterrence to an attack.

Practical Exercise: Look around and name the types and ways terrorists can conduct surveillance against your site.

Practical Exercise: Think about the ways and areas in which you can perform good surveillance detection.

ASPECTS OF SURVEILLANCE DETECTION

Learning Objective: Security agent will understand the aspects of generalized surveillance detection.

Surveillance detection is an organized, systematic methodology designed to identify hostile surveillance by discovering the type of surveillance being used by their indicators.

The purpose of surveillance detection is to *identify hostile surveillance.* Static, mobile, technical, progressive, and combination are all examples of the different types of surveillance. We must know what to look for in order to conduct good surveillance detection. During surveillance detection operations, the agent will be looking for specific indicators that will aid him or her in determining the knowledge, sophistication, and ability of the hostile surveillance. Once you have discovered those indicators and identified surveillance against a potential target or facility, you may also be able to determine their capability according to the level of sophistication in their operational techniques. Surveillance phases have indicators that are common among terrorist operations and should be visible to the trained observer. Some of these may include the following:

- the same person at the same location for no apparent reason

- suspicious activity in or around the facility (e.g., persons taking photographs or videotaping the facility or area)

- the same vehicle passing repeatedly

- repeated suspicious activity in the vicinity of the facility (e.g., mechanical failure of a vehicle in the same area or at the same time of day)

Once surveillance is confirmed, countermeasures should be taken to identify the actual participants, and a supervisor should be informed immediately.

To be truly observant means that a level of awareness must be trained and maintained. The casual observer has no place in security work! However, the trained or professional observer has the potential to thwart a terrorist attack merely by being observant and a *part* of the surroundings, not just surrounded by people or structures.

RESPONDING TO A TELEPHONE BOMB THREAT

Record the following:
- number at which call is received
- length of call
- time of call
- date of call
- *exact wording of the threat*

Remain calm, and keep the caller on the line.
Follow the instructions on this card.
Determine if the call is real world or exercise
Call or have a coworker call 911.
Follow security forces' instructions.

Questions to Ask
- When is the bomb going to explode?
- Where is it right now?
- What does it look like?
- What kind of bomb is it?
- What will cause it to explode?
- Why?
- Where are you?
- What is your name?

Make note of caller's
- sex
- age
- accent

Make Note of Caller's Voice and Mannerisms
- calm, loud, nasal, raspy
- angry, laughing, stuttering, deep

- excited, crying, ragged, clearing throat
- slow, normal, lisp, deep breathing
- rapid, distinct, disguised, foreign
- soft, slurred, cracking, familiar

If the voice sounded familiar, whose voice did it sound like?

Background Noises
- street (cars, buses, etc.), PA system, motor (fan, air conditioner, etc.)
- airplanes, music, office machinery
- voices, houses (dishes, TV, etc.), factory machinery
- animal noises, clear, static
- local call, long distance call, phone booth
- other (specify) *language*
- well spoken (educated), incoherent
- foul, taped message
- irrational message read by threat maker

Date: **Phone Number:**

Name: **Position:**

Remarks:

LABOR DISPUTE SECURITY

Throughout your career as a *professional security agent*, you may be called upon to perform many different types of security functions. Many of your assignments may be similar, and you can transfer your skills from one job to the next. However, there is one assignment that you need to pay particular attention to. That is *labor dispute security.*

Labor dispute security is a very technical type of security. You must know what you legally can and cannot do, and *stay within the parameters of your authority.* Your duty performance will be closely observed by union members on strike. If you commit actions that are against the legal rights of the union members on strike, their union representatives may file a grievance against you, which could result in legal ramifications (monetary fines) against you, your security company, and the company that you are protecting. It is imperative that you know how to preserve *your* legal rights under the law to perform your duties, the legal rights of the union members on strike, and the rights of the client you're protecting.

Statutes for labor dispute security may vary from state to state. It is your responsibility to know the legal requirements for your particular venue. Google *"Labor dispute security laws for (state in which you're assigned),"* or ask your immediate supervisor for guidance. Remember—it is *your* responsibility to know the requirements for labor dispute security.

The following are guidelines that you should know intimately:

APPLICABLE LAWS

Federal Law

The National Labor Relations Act (NLRA), also known as the Wagner Act of 1935, states and defines the rights of employees to organize and to bargain collectively with their employers through representatives of their own choosing—or not to do so.

Section 8 of the NLRA prohibits surveillance and photographing of employees engaged in protected activities. The theory is that such surveillance has a chilling effect on the rights of employees to picket. The NLRA does not prohibit observation of employee activity or misconduct, where this observation is required for *security*, product integrity, quality control, *good order*, and productivity. The issue is whether videoing is necessary or justified.

The following have been routinely regarded as unprotected/illegal union activities:

1. Violent, abusive, or malicious conduct

2. Insubordination

3. Disparagement of employer's business or product (disloyalty)

4. Sharing or disclosing information during business hours if prohibited by contract or company policy

5. Work stoppage (partial strikes, slowdown, or sit-in strikes)

It is the right of the employer to protect his or her interest during a work stoppage or strike and for the business to continue to operate during stoppage!
It is the legal right of employees and their representing union to engage in a strike and picket. However, the law requires the picketing is peaceful.

No one desiring to enter the property will be prevented from doing so by force, threats, mass picketing, or any other means. Picketers are legally entitled to do no more than ask an individual to honor the picket line. Each individual must be allowed to make that decision of his or her own accord.

The NLRA sets out general rights and obligations. Enforcing the act in particular situations is the job of the NLRB.

State Law

Rules of evidence are the set of governing guidelines by which the courts evaluate the admissibility of a type of evidence and usually vary from state to state. The importance of knowing the rules of evidence for the state you are documenting and collecting evidence in is of the utmost importance. Ask your supervisor about any unique rules before you man your post.

The *best evidence rule* is common in the United States and may have a direct impact on you at your post. It means that the responding officers or the courts have the right to take custody of the best form of evidence gathered.

This means the responding officers may ask you for any evidence you have. You are required to release the evidence; however, fill out an evidence chain-of-custody form, and give your evidence to the officer. If your evidence is a video or photo, ask the officer to allow you to make a copy.

UNIQUE LAWS BY STATE

~California~

A. Children can be given an excused absence from school to be on a picket line.

B. There are statutes prohibiting the photographing or videoing of a child.

C. Courts will award unfair labor practice charges against the client if any video or photographs are deemed to be of peaceful picketing activity.

D. Each local jurisdiction has a "strike liaison" to ensure all sides are following the rules.

E. Most jurisdictions require a parade permit to be issued well in advance for any rally that may be held.

~Illinois~

A. Picketers can be asked to move or remove any shelter that obstructs views of oncoming traffic near a picket line.

B. It is illegal to manufacture or possess jackrocks. Jackrocks are large items that resemble toy jacks. They are designed to be thrown in the streets to puncture tires.

~Pennsylvania~

A. Depending on the circumstances, spitting can be considered an assault. If someone spits on an employee during a strike, that will be considered an assault. If someone spits and it lands on someone else, there will probably be no charges.

~Washington~

A. Any sworn officer of the law can witness a murder or other violent crime taking place in front of him or her and does not have a duty to respond.

B. Two-party consent is required before you can record audio of a person. You must disable your video camera's audio before you go on duty.

C. Anyone can call the Department of Motor Vehicles and have a license plate run if he or she is trying to get in touch with next of kin or reporting an abandoned vehicle.

D. Using large dogs as a means to intimidate or threaten people is prohibited.

TYPES OF LEGAL PROCEEDINGS ARISING OUT OF A STRIKE

The only effective means for ending strike misconduct or violence on the picket line is to secure a court order requiring the union and its members to stop unlawful conduct. These court orders come in various forms.

Temporary Restraining Order

These are usually valid for fourteen to twenty-eight days. It is temporary in nature because both parties are usually required to come back to court at a later date to prove whether there is a need to lift the temporary restraining order or to issue an outright restraining order. It is very important that the following statement is written into the text of any order: "This temporary restraining order will be enforced by all applicable law enforcement agencies."

Injunctions

Obtaining an injunction not only prohibits picket line misconduct but also has significant emotional and psychological impact on picketers during the early days of the strike. They are usually filed in the state court and seek an order limiting the number of picketers and preventing misconduct. Injunctive relief should not be sought until major incidents have occurred. Attempts to secure an injunction prematurely can place the client's litigation strategy unnecessarily at risk. It could also lead the union to escalate tensions to more serious forms of misconduct or violence.

Security agents are critical to providing the evidence necessary to obtain injunctions and allow the company to continue operations. The union will be represented by legal counsel and can use video and documentation to attempt to disprove our position.

CONTEMPT HEARINGS

Contempt proceedings are available if union member / picketers do not comply with the court order. The courts can invoke economic and criminal penalties when a judge makes a ruling that is set forth in the temporary restraining order (TRO). The violation can occur when a person returns to the picket line after having been barred or commits an act that the judge had deemed criminal or unsafe.

Once you receive a copy of the TRO, copies should be made for each post as well as discussed in the shift briefing. When involving the removal of an individual from the picket line, his or her color photo should be at each of the posts. Once the person has returned or the prohibited act been committed, your supervisor should be notified immediately. The director of security will then notify the client and/or the attorney. The only time you should notify local law enforcement is if the person or act represents immediate harm to personnel or damage to property.

CRIMINAL PROSECUTIONS

Picketers can be arrested and prosecuted for criminal acts. The burden of proof is on the professional security agent to show that an act actually took place.

Fines

The primary method of punishment for violations of the NLRA is in the form of fines. These can be levied against the union, the union member, the company, or the security company.

CONSTITUTIONAL AMENDMENTS

First Amendment

Freedom of Religion, Speech, Press, Petition, Assembly (Picketing)

Congress shall make no law respecting an establishment of religion, or prohibiting the free exercise thereof, or abridging the freedom of speech, or of the press; or the right of people to peaceably assemble and to petition the Government for a redress of grievance.

Fourth Amendment

Right against Unreasonable Search and Seizure

Police officers have to have either probable cause or a warrant to conduct a search. Professional security agents have to have reasonable suspicion to conduct a search. *You will not conduct a search without the approval of the person who will be or have his or her property searched.* Video the permission to search and the actual search. If a client wants the professional security agent to search one of their employees, the client management personnel must be a witness.

Local Laws and Helpful Ordinances

Local laws and ordinances vary by location. Research local ordinances online, but take direction from your supervisor.

RACIAL MISCONDUCT AND HATE CRIMES

Any time you are faced with this situation, you must focus immediate attention on all the mandatory requirements and obtaining positive identification of all personnel involved. Your intent is to remove this dangerous element from an already volatile situation that is most likely to provoke retaliatory crimes. These crimes may create severe emotional harm and incite community unrest, resulting in a negative image of you or the client.

Once union members/picketers engage in racial misconduct and the client and/or attorney are notified, the professional security agent will begin the process of positively identifying those involved. Once you have completed this assignment, give the information to your immediate supervisor.

CHILD WELFARE

Notify your supervisor immediately when a child or children are observed on the picket line. Begin video documentation, and use a wide-angle shot to show the child/children with the parent/guardian, emphasizing the activity, conditions, and mood on the picket line.

Zoom in smoothly for the close-up shot to show how the child/children and the parent/guardian are dressed. Pay attention to identify the adult in charge of the child's/children's safety and welfare. Observe and document anything that places the child/children in harm's way.

Important Note: At this point some member of the client's management team should be deployed to this location. Keep in mind that your video and written report could save the life of a child. Include the picketers' mood, traffic in respect to the location of the child/children, violence, and weather conditions. Be aware that there are three avenues or agencies where you can file concerns for children on the picket line.

1. the National Labor Relations Board
2. local law enforcement agency
3. child welfare and protective offices

The Professional Security Agent's Responsibilities

Improper behavior by a professional security agent can greatly complicate the bargaining process, lead to a charge of an unfair labor practice, and result in costly and disruptive litigation against the security company and the client.

As a professional security agent, you will be required to document strike activity for the purpose of obtaining a temporary restraining order (TRO), injunction, and further legal relief. If peaceful picketing proves to be totally ineffective, some union members may begin to engage in some sort of prohibitive conduct, which is often coercive, intimidating, or violent.

What to Look for and Report to Your Supervisor

1. *Abusive or threatening language*—this was tolerated in the past if done by strikers who became momentarily carried away in the heat of their emotions by the labor board. However, there is now a stricter code that includes non-striking employees, contractors, or vendors.

2. *Mass picketing* refers to picketers in large numbers blocking gate entrances or intimidating anyone wanting to enter or leave the client's property.

3. *Physical violence*—violence of any type against any non-striking employee, contractor, vendor, or any other agent of the client wanting to enter or leave the client's property. This also includes spitting (which may be a misdemeanor or felony charge, depending on the state).

4. *Property damage*—the direct or indirect intentional act of damaging client property, the property of non-striking employees, contractors, vendors, client vehicles, or other real property owned or operated by any of the above.

5. *Alcohol*—any type or form is not permitted on the picket line at any time.

6. *Impeding or blocking* is deliberate impeding or blocking of ingress or egress entering or exiting the client's property by use of picketers, vehicles, or foreign objects, such as chairs, buckets, burn barrels, signs, and so on. This includes the tactic of lockstep picketing. Lockstep picketing is a movement of picketers that prevents anyone or anything from coming between individual picketers.

7. *Minor children*—any age under sixteen are usually not allowed on the picket line (except in California). Check with your supervisor for laws for the state that you're operating.

8. *Harassment and intimidation*—picketers are prohibited from committing verbal harassment and photographing or writing down employees', contractors', vendors', and so on license numbers or vehicle descriptions while they are entering or leaving the client's property. *Important note*: it is important that people actually feel intimidated or that a court would rule that a reasonable person would feel intimidated.

9. *Masks or disguises*—the wearing of any type of mask in cold or warm weather is a violation for the professional security agent and the picketers.

10. *Stalking*—the following of vehicles, employees, contractors, or vendors is a misdemeanor in most states. It may be a felony in the *state* where you're working. Check with your supervisor.

11. *Weapons*—most often, you will be required to have an armed guard card / license. This does not mean you are authorized to carry a weapon. Most labor dispute contracts are "unarmed" contracts. If you have a concealed carry permit/license, you still cannot carry a weapon concealed if the contract is an unarmed contract. Picketers cannot carry or use a device or objects such as rocks, bricks, baseball bats, clubs, boards, knives, hatchets, axes, firearms, and other objects that can in any way be reasonably construed as being a weapon. This includes saliva and other bodily fluids. The use of reflectors or mirrors to potentially blind or render video documentation useless is prohibited. *Any evidence of a weapon on the picket line must immediately be reported to your immediate supervisor.*

12. *Abandoned picket line*—this is in violation of the NLRB law. Once a union establishes a strike and picket line, they must man the picket line until they either accept a tentative agreement, vote to end the strike, or get disbanded by the NLRB.

13. *Performance by local police*—document the actions of the local police. This will act as a record to protect the client from liability. Try to establish a good relationship with the police. If that is not possible, keep the police neutral toward both parties. Make note of the following:
    a. number of police officers present
    b. what equipment they are using
    c. the police officers' attitude toward company activity
    d. the police officers' attitude toward picketers
    e. identify individual police officers

14. *Trespassers on company property*—all visitors must be escorted when on company property. Picketers are not allowed on the client's property unless previously authorized. In the event a picketer does trespass, document the activity, warn the trespasser three times that he or she is trespassing, and ask him or her to leave. If he or she does not confirm, notify your supervisor and keep him or her in sight.

DO NOT

A. Make any type of gesture or motion toward the picketers.

B. Converse with the picketers while entering or leaving the property or while they are on line.

C. Use excessive speed or force to cross the picket line.

D. Exit your vehicle while crossing the picket line.

E. Flash your paycheck or cash.

NOTES

PHYSICAL FITNESS PROGRAM

	Day 1	Day 2	Day 3	Rest
Biceps				
One-Arm Dumbbell Rows	3 x 8			
Barbell Curls	3 x 8			
Preacher Curls	3 x 8			
Undergrip Chin-Ups	3 x 8			
Dumbbell Curls	3 x 8			
Concentration Curls	3 x 8			
Triceps				
Triceps Dips	3 x 8			
Triceps Extensions	3 x 8			
Overhead Extensions	3 x 8			
Kickbacks	3 x 8			

	Day 1	Day 2	Day 3	Rest
Chest				
Seated Row		3 x 8		
Seated Chest		3 x 8		
Bench Press		3 x 8		
Incline Press		3 x 8		
Decline Press		3 x 8		
Shoulders				
Shrugs		3 x 8		
Military Press		3 x 8		
French Press		3 x 8		

	Day 1	Day 2	Day 3	Rest
Back				
Overgrip Chin-Ups			3 x 8	
Dead Lifts			3 x 8	
T-Bar			3 x 8	
Hyperextensions			3 x 8	
Legs				
Leg Extensions			3 x 8	
Calves			3 x 8	
Horizontal Leg Curls			3 x 8	
Leg Press			3 x 8	
Squats			3 x 8	

Choose any three exercises for each muscle group.
Don't always choose the same exercise.
Increase repetitions as your muscles allow.

This physical fitness program is written for minimal physical exertion. It is designed to maintain a body fitness regimen. It is not written for bodybuilding or to get your body in shape.

FIRST AID

On October 19, 1998, President Clinton signed the Good Samaritan Law. The Good Samaritan law offers legal protection to people who give reasonable assistance to those who are, or whom they believe to be, injured, ill, in peril, or otherwise incapacitated. By contrast, a Duty to Rescue law requires people to offer assistance and holds those who fail to do so liable.

A Good Samaritan is somebody who offers help to a person in need. Why is checking the scene so important? Before administering help in an emergency situation, it is important to check the scene to ensure the safety of the injured or ill person, bystanders, and yourself. Without checking the scene, one may overlook potential danger that can create more harm.

EVALUATE A CASUALTY

Conditions: You have a casualty who has signs/symptoms of an injury.

Standards: Evaluate the casualty following the correct sequence. Identify all life-threatening conditions and other serious wounds.

Warning: If a broken neck or back is suspected, do not move the casualty unless to save his or her life.

1. Reassure the casualty.

2. Administer life-saving hemorrhage control.

3. If the casualty has severe bleeding from a limb or has suffered amputation of a limb, administer life-saving hemorrhage control by applying a tourniquet.

4. Recheck bleeding control measures as needed.

   Note: When evaluating and/or treating a casualty, seek medical aid as soon as possible. Do not *stop treatment. Send another person to find medical aid.*

5. Form a general impression of the casualty as you approach (extent of injuries, chance of survival).

   Note: If a casualty is being burned, take steps to remove the casualty from the source of the burns before continuing evaluation and treatment.

6. Check for responsiveness.

7. Ask in a loud but calm voice, "Are you okay?" Gently shake or tap the casualty on the shoulder.

8. Determine the level of consciousness by using AVPU: A = alert; V = responds to voice; P = responds to pain; U = unresponsive.

   Note: To check a casualty's response to pain, rub the breastbone briskly with a knuckle, or squeeze the first or second toe over the toenail.

9. If the casualty is conscious, ask where his or her body feels different than usual or where it hurts.

   Note: If the casualty is conscious but is choking and cannot talk, stop the evaluation and begin treatment.

10. Position the casualty, and open the airway.

11. Assess for breathing and chest injuries.

12. Look, listen, and feel for respiration.

13. If the casualty has a penetrating chest wound and is breathing or making an effort to breathe, stop the evaluation to apply a dressing.

14. Monitor for increasing respiratory distress. If this occurs, decompress the chest on the same side as the injury.

15. Position or transport with the affected side down, if possible.

16. Identify and control bleeding.

17. Check for bleeding.

18. Remove only the minimum amount of clothing to expose and treat injuries. Protect the casualty from the environment (heat and cold).

19. Look for blood-soaked clothes.

20. Look for entry and exit wounds.

21. Place your hands behind the casualty's neck, and pass them upward toward the top of the head. Note whether there is blood or brain tissue on your hands from the casualty's wounds.

22. Place your hands behind the casualty's shoulders, and pass them downward behind the back, the thighs, and the legs. Note whether there is blood on your hands from the casualty's wounds.

23. If life-threatening bleeding is present, stop the evaluation and control the bleeding. Apply a tourniquet, chitosan dressing, emergency bandage, or field dressing, as appropriate. Treat for shock

24. Dress all wounds, including exit wounds.

25. Check for fractures.

26. Check for open fractures by looking for bleeding or a bone sticking through the skin.

27. Check for closed fractures by looking for swelling, discoloration, deformity, or unusual body position.

28. If a suspected fracture is present, stop the evaluation and apply a splint.

29. Check for burns.

30. Look carefully for reddened, blistered, or charred skin. Also check for singed clothes.

31. If burns are found, stop the evaluation and begin treatment.

32. Document the casualty's injuries and the treatment given.

CLEAR AN OBJECT STUCK IN THE THROAT OF A CONSCIOUS CASUALTY

Conditions: You see a conscious casualty who is having a hard time breathing because something is stuck in his or her throat.

Standards: Clear the object from the casualty's throat. Give abdominal or chest thrusts until the casualty can talk and breathe normally, you are relieved by a qualified person, or the casualty becomes unconscious, requiring mouth-to-mouth resuscitation.

Performance Steps

1. Determine if the casualty needs help.

   a. If the casualty has a mild airway obstruction (able to speak or cough forcefully, may be wheezing between coughs), do not interfere except to encourage the casualty.

   b. If the casualty has a severe airway obstruction (poor air exchange and increased breathing difficulty, a silent cough, or inability to speak or breathe, move to step 2.

   Note: You can ask the casualty one question, "Are you choking?" If the casualty nods yes, help is needed.

   Caution: Do not slap a choking casualty on the back. This may cause the object to go down the airway instead of out.

2. Perform abdominal or chest thrusts.

Note: Abdominal thrusts should be used unless the victim is in the advanced stages of pregnancy, is very obese, or has a significant abdominal wound.

Note: Clearing a conscious casualty's airway obstruction can be performed with the casualty either standing or sitting.

a. Abdominal thrusts

   (1)   Stand behind the casualty.

   (2)   Wrap your arms around the casualty's waist.

   (3)   Make a fist with one hand.

   (4)   Place the thumb side of the fist against the abdomen slightly above the navel and well below the tip of the breastbone.

   (5)   Grasp the fist with the other hand.

   (6)   Give quick backward and upward thrusts.

Note: Each thrust should be a separate, distinct movement. Thrusts should be continued until the obstruction is expelled or the casualty becomes unconscious.

b. Chest thrusts

   (1)   Stand behind the casualty.

   (2)   Wrap your arms under the casualty's armpits and around the chest.

(3)   Make a fist with one hand.

(4)   Place the thumb side of the fist on the middle of the breastbone.

(5)   Grasp the fist with the other hand.

(6)   Give backward thrusts.

Note: Each thrust should be performed slowly and distinctly with the intent of relieving the obstruction.

3.   Continue to give abdominal or chest thrusts, as required. Give abdominal or chest thrusts until the obstruction is clear, you are relieved by a qualified person, or the casualty becomes unconscious.

Note: If the casualty becomes unconscious, lay him or her down, and then start mouth-to-mouth resuscitation procedures.

4.   If the obstruction is cleared, watch the casualty closely and check for other injuries, if necessary.

PREVENT OR CONTROL SHOCK

Conditions: You see a casualty who is breathing. There is no uncontrolled bleeding. The casualty has one or more of the symptoms of shock.

Standards: Attempt to prevent a casualty from going into shock by correctly positioning the casualty, loosening binding clothes, calming and reassuring the casualty, and providing shade from direct sunlight during hot weather or covering to prevent body heat loss during cold weather. Do not cause further injury to the casualty.

Performance Steps

1. Check the casualty for signs and symptoms of shock.
   a. sweaty but cool skin
   b. pale skin
   c. restlessness or nervousness
   d. thirst
   e. severe bleeding
   f. confusion
   g. rapid breathing
   h. blotchy blue skin
   i. nausea and/or vomiting

2. Position the casualty.
   a. Move the casualty to shade.
   b. Lay the casualty on his or her back unless a sitting position will allow the casualty to breathe easier.
   c. Elevate the casualty's feet higher than the heart using a stable object so the feet will not fall.

Warning: If the casualty has an unsplinted fractured leg, an abdominal wound, or a head or spinal injury, do not elevate the casualty's legs.

3. Loosen clothing at the neck, waist, or anywhere it is binding.

4. Splint the limb, if appropriate.
   a. Apply a splint to the injured limb if one or more bones in the limb have been fractured.

   Note: If a splint is not applied to the extremity, broken bone fragments may grate on blood vessels and nerves and cause additional damage.

   b. Splint the arm, forearm, thigh, or leg when a severe wound is present even if the limb is not fractured.

   Note: Immobilizing the limb reduces muscular activity, helping to stop bleeding and reduce pain.

5. Prevent the casualty from getting chilled or overheated.
   a. Cover the casualty to avoid loss of body heat, and, in cold weather, place cover under as well as over the casualty. Use a blanket or clothing, or improvise a cover.

   b. Place the casualty under a permanent or improvised shelter in hot weather to shade him or her from direct sunlight.

   Warning: Do not give the casualty anything to eat or drink.

6. Calm and reassure the casualty.
   a. Take charge, and show self-confidence.

   b. Assure the casualty that he or she is being taken care of.

Warning: If you must leave the casualty, turn his or her head to the side to prevent choking if vomiting occurs.

7. Watch the casualty closely for life-threatening conditions and check for other injuries, if necessary. Seek medical aid.

FIRST AID FOR BURNS

Conditions: You see a casualty who is suffering from a burn.

Standards: Give first aid for a burn without causing further injury to the casualty. Eliminate the source of the burn, if necessary. Apply a dressing lightly over the burn. Ensure that the sides of the dressing are sealed and the dressing does not slip.

Performance Steps

1. Eliminate the source of the burn.

   a. Thermal burns—remove the casualty from the source of the burn. If the casualty's clothing is on fire, cover the casualty with a jacket or any large piece of nonsynthetic material and roll him or her on the ground to put out the flames.

   Caution: Synthetic materials, such as nylon, may melt and cause further injury.

   b. Electrical burns—if the casualty is in contact with an electrical source, turn the electricity off, if the switch is nearby. If the electricity cannot be turned off, use any nonconductive material (rope, clothing, or dry wood) to drag the casualty away from the source.

   Warning: Do not touch the casualty or the electrical source with your bare hands. You will be injured too!

Warning: High-voltage electrical burns from an electrical source or lightning may cause temporary unconsciousness, difficulties in breathing, or difficulties with the heart (irregular heartbeat).

c. Chemical burns

Warning: Blisters caused by a blister agent are actually burns. Do not try to decontaminate skin where blisters have already formed. If blisters have not formed, decontaminate the skin.

(1) Remove liquid chemicals from the burned casualty by flushing with as much water or other nonflammable fluid as possible.

(2) Remove dry chemicals by carefully brushing them off with a clean, dry cloth. If large amounts of water are available, flush the area. Otherwise, do not apply water.

(3) Laser burns. Move the casualty away from the source while avoiding eye contact with the beam source. If possible, wear appropriate laser eye protection.

Note: After the casualty has been removed from the source of the burn, continually monitor the casualty for conditions that may require basic lifesaving measures.

Warning: Do not uncover the wound in a chemical environment. Exposure could cause additional harm.

a. Cut clothing covering the burned area.

Warning: Do not attempt to remove clothing that is stuck to the wound. Additional harm could result.

b.   Gently lift away clothing covering the burned area.

Caution: Do not pull clothing over the burns.

c.   If the casualty's hand(s) or wrist(s) have been burned, remove jewelry (rings, watches) and place them in his or her pockets.

Caution: Do not place the dressing over the face or genital area. Do not break the blisters. Do not apply grease or ointments to the burns.

d.   Apply the dressing/pad, white side down, directly over the wound.

e.   Wrap the tails (or the elastic bandage) so that the dressing/pad is covered and both sides are sealed.

f.   For a field dressing, tie the tails into a nonslip knot over the outer edge of the dressing, not over the wound.

g.   Check to ensure that the dressing is applied lightly over the burn but firmly enough to prevent slipping.

Note: Electricity often leaves entry and exit burns. Both burns should be treated.

Note: If the casualty is conscious and not nauseated, give him or her small amounts of water to drink.

(1)   Watch the casualty closely for life-threatening conditions, check for other injuries (if necessary), and treat for shock. Seek medical aid.

FIRST AID FOR HEAT INJURIES

Conditions: You see a casualty who has signs and symptoms of a heat injury.

Standards: Recognize the type of heat injury, and give appropriate first aid.

Performance Steps

1. Identify the type of heat injury.
   a. a. heat cramps symptoms
      (1) cramping in the extremities (arms and legs)
      (2) abdominal (stomach) cramps
      (3) excessive sweating

   Note: Thirst may or may not occur. Cramping can occur without being thirsty.

   b. heat exhaustion symptoms
      (1) profuse sweating with pale, moist, cool skin
      (2) headache
      (3) weakness
      (4) dizziness
      (5) loss of appetite
      (6) cramping
      (7) nausea (with or without vomiting)
      (8) urge to defecate
      (9) chills (gooseflesh)
      (10) rapid breathing
      (11) tingling of the hands and/or feet
      (12) confusion (not answering easy questions correctly)

c. heatstroke symptoms
    (1)   red (flushed), hot, dry skin
    (2)   weakness
    (3)   dizziness
    (4)   confusion
    (5)   headache
    (6)   seizures
    (7)   nausea
    (8)   stomach pains or cramps
    (9)   respiration and pulse may be rapid and weak
    (10) unconsciousness and collapse may occur suddenly

2. Provide the proper first aid for the heat injury.
    a. a. heat cramps
        (1)   Monitor the mental status by asking simple questions, such as the date or the president's name.
        (2)   Move the casualty to a cool, shady area or improvise shade if none is available.
        (3)   Loosen the casualty's clothing.
        (4)   Have the casualty slowly drink cool water.
        (5)   Seek medical aid if the cramps continue.
        (6)   Monitor the casualty for signs and symptoms of heat exhaustion.

    b. heat exhaustion
        (1)   Monitor mental status by asking simple questions.
        (2)   Move the casualty to a cool, shady area or improvise shade if none is available.
        (3)   Loosen or remove the casualty's clothing and boots.
        (4)   Pour water on the casualty and fan him or her.

Note: Apply iced sheets, if available. (Sheets soaked in cold/icy water and placed directly onto the skin of the casualty will lower body temperature rapidly.)

    (5)   Have the casualty slowly drink cool water.

    (6)   Elevate the casualty's legs.

Warning: Heatstroke is a medical emergency that may result in death if treatment is delayed. Start cooling measures immediately and continue while waiting for transportation.

    (1)   Monitor the casualty's mental status by asking simple questions.

    (2)   Move the casualty to a cool, shady area or improvise shade if none is available.

    (3)   Loosen or remove the casualty's clothing and boots.

    (4)   Spray or pour water on the casualty and fan him or her. (Apply iced sheets if available.)

    (5)   Massage the casualty's arms and legs.

    (6)   Elevate the casualty's legs.

    (7)   If the casualty is conscious, have him or her slowly drink cool water.

3.   Watch the casualty closely for life-threatening conditions, check for other injuries, and seek medical aid.

DEHYDRATION

Learning Objective: Agent will understand the necessity and proper way for rehydration.

Dehydration is the loss of water and important blood salts, like potassium (K+) and sodium (Na+). Vital organs, like the kidneys, brain, and heart, can't function without a certain minimum of water and salt. In Iraq, dehydration from diseases like cholera and dysentery kills many people every year. In the Egypt-Israel war, twenty thousand men died from dehydration. Still, with excessive sweating, you can become dangerously dehydrated. The following are some warning signs for dehydration.

Signs of Dehydration
Mild
Thirst

Dry lips

Slightly dry mouth membranes

Moderate
Very dry mouth membranes

Sunken eyes

Skin doesn't bounce back quickly when lightly pinched and released

Moodiness

Severe
All signs of moderate dehydration

Rapid, weak pulse (more than 100 at rest)

Cold hands and feet

Rapid breathing

Blue lips

Confusion, lethargy, difficult to arouse

If you're severely dehydrated, you must get to the medical office right away. Intravenous fluids (IVs) will quickly reverse dehydration and are often life-saving.

In adults with moderate dehydration, careful self-treatment can be safe, but contact with a doctor is advisable.

Mild dehydration is safe to self-treat as long as it doesn't worsen.

The best way to prevent dehydration is to drink plenty of water each day. Soda, coffee, tea, energy drinks, and even Gatorade can aggravate and worsen dehydration.

Security agents must monitor how much fluid they are taking in each day to prevent dehydration. It is recommended that each guard drink at least five bottles of water each day. One way to keep track of how many bottles one drinks is to save the caps of the water bottles. This can help the security agent remember how much he has drunk throughout the day.

RESTORE BREATHING AND/OR PULSE

Conditions: You see an adult casualty who is unconscious and does not appear to be breathing.

Standards: Take appropriate action, in the correct sequence, to restore breathing and, if necessary, restore the pulse. Continue until the casualty's breathing/pulse returns, a qualified person relieves you, a physician stops you, or you are too tired to continue.

Performance Steps

1. Roll the casualty onto his or her back, if necessary, and place him or her on a hard, flat surface.

   Warning: The casualty should be carefully rolled as a whole, so the body does not twist.

   a. Kneel beside the casualty.

   b. Raise the near arm, and straighten it out above the head.

   c. Adjust the legs so they are together and straight or nearly straight.

   d. Place one hand on the back of the casualty's head and neck.

   e. Grasp the casualty under the arm with the free hand.

   f. Pull steadily and evenly toward yourself, keeping the head and neck in line with the torso.

   g. Roll the casualty as a single unit.

h. Place the casualty's arms at his or her sides.

2. Open the airway.

   Note: If foreign material or vomit is in the mouth, remove it as quickly as possible.

   a. Head-tilt/chin-lift method.

   Caution

   Do not use this method if a spinal or neck injury is suspected.

   (1) Kneel at the level of the casualty's shoulders.

   (2) Place one hand on the casualty's forehead, and apply firm backward pressure with the palm to tilt the head back.

   (3) Place the fingertips of the other hand under the bony part of the lower jaw and lift, bringing the chin forward.

   Note: Do not use the thumb to lift.

   Note: Do not completely close the casualty's mouth.

   Caution: Do not press deeply into the soft tissue under the chin with the fingers.

   b. Jaw-thrust method.

   Caution: Use this method if a spinal or neck injury is suspected.

Note: If you are unable to maintain an airway after the second attempt, use the head-tilt/chin-lift method.

    (1)   Kneel above the casualty's head (looking toward the casualty's feet).

    (2)   Rest your elbows on the ground or floor.

    (3)   Place one hand on each side of the casualty's lower jaw at the angle of the jaw, below the ears.

    (4)   Stabilize the casualty's head with your forearms.

    (5)   Use the index fingers to push the angles of the casualty's lower jaw forward.

Note: If the casualty's lips are still closed after the jaw has been moved forward, use your thumbs to retract the lower lip and allow air to enter the casualty's mouth.

Caution: Do not tilt or rotate the casualty's head.

3. Check for breathing.

    a. While maintaining the open airway position, place an ear over the casualty's mouth and nose, looking toward the chest and stomach.

    b. Look for the chest to rise and fall.

    c. Listen for air escaping during exhalation.

    d. Feel for the flow of air on the side of your face.

e. Place the casualty in the recovery position by rolling him or her as a single unit onto his or her side, placing the hand of his or her upper arm under his or her chin and flexing his or her upper leg.

f. Watch the casualty closely for life-threatening conditions and check for other injuries, if necessary. Seek medical aid.

If the casualty is not breathing, move to step 4.

Note: If the casualty resumes breathing at any time during this procedure, the airway should be kept open, and the casualty should be monitored. If the casualty continues to breathe, he or she should be transported to medical aid. Otherwise, the procedure should be continued.

4. Give breaths to ensure an open airway.

Note: When mouth-to-mouth resuscitation breathing cannot be performed because the casualty has jaw injuries or spasms, the mouth-to-nose method may be more effective. Perform the mouth-to-nose method as follows:

-   Blow into the nose while holding the lips closed.

-   Let air escape by removing your mouth and, in some cases, separating the casualty's lips.

a. Insert a face shield, if available, into the casualty's mouth, with the short airway portion over the top of the tongue, and flatten the plastic sheet around the mouth.

b. Maintain the airway, and gently pinch the nose closed, using the hand on the casualty's forehead.

c. Take a normal breath, and place your mouth, in an airtight seal, around the casualty's mouth.

d. Give two breaths (one second each), taking a breath between them, while watching for the chest to rise and fall and listening and/or feeling for air to escape during exhalation.

Note: If the chest rises, go to step 7.

Note: If the chest does not rise after the first breath, continue with step 5.

5. Reposition the casualty's head slightly farther backward, and repeat the breaths.

Note: If the chest rises, go to step 7.

Note: If the chest does not rise, continue with step 6.

6. Perform chest compressions to clear the airway.

a. Perform chest compressions.

(1) Kneel close to the side of the casualty's body.

(2) Locate the nipple line, and place the heel of one hand on the lower half of the sternum (breastbone).

(3) Place the heel of the other hand on top of the first hand on the lower half of the breastbone, extending or interlacing the fingers.

(4) Straighten and lock the elbows with the shoulders directly above the hands.

(5) Without bending the elbows, rocking, or allowing the shoulders to sag, apply enough pressure to depress the breastbone one and a half to two inches.

Note: Give compressions at a rate of one hundred per minute (hard and fast at a ratio of thirty compressions to two breaths) with the intent of relieving the obstruction.

b. Look in the mouth for the object between compressions and breaths and

if you can see it, remove it.

Warning: Only attempt to remove the object if you can see it. Do not force the object deeper into the airway.

c. Reopen the airway and repeat the breaths.

Note: If the chest rises, go to step 7.

Note: If the chest does not rise, repeat step 6 until the airway is clear.

7. Check for a pulse for five to ten seconds.

Note: Use the first two fingers in the groove in the casualty's throat beside the Adam's apple on the side closest to you. Do not use the thumb.

a. If a pulse is found but the casualty is not breathing, continue mouth-to-mouth resuscitation.

(1) Give breaths at the rate of one every five to six seconds (ten to twelve breaths per minute).

(2)   Recheck for a pulse and breathing every two minutes. If the pulse stops, go to step 8.

(3)   Continue until the casualty's breathing returns, a qualified person relieves you, a physician stops you, or you are too tired to continue. If the breathing returns, go to step 9.

b. If no pulse is found, you must perform cardiopulmonary resuscitation (CPR). Continue with step 8.

8. 8. Perform CPR.

a. Position your hands and body for chest compressions as in step 6a.

b. Give thirty compressions.

(1)   Press straight down to depress the breastbone one and a half to two inches.

(2)   Come straight up and completely release the pressure on the breastbone to allow the chest to return to its normal position. The time allowed for release should equal the time required for compression.

(3)   Give thirty compressions in about twenty-three seconds (at a rate of one hundred per minute).

Note: Do not *remove the heel of your hand from the casualty's chest or reposition your hand between compressions. However, all pressure must be released from the chest cavity to allow for full chest wall expansion.*

c. Give two breaths.

(1)   Open the casualty's airway.

(2)   Give two breaths (one second each).

d.   Repeat steps 8b through 8c for five cycles or two minutes.

e.   Reassess the casualty.

(1)   Check for the return of the pulse for three to five seconds.

(a) If the pulse is present, continue with step 8e(2).
(b) If the pulse is absent, continue with step 8f.

(2)   Check breathing for three to five seconds.

(a) If the casualty is breathing, continue with step 9.
(b) If the casualty is not breathing, continue mouth-to-mouth resuscitation.

f.   Resume CPR with compressions.

g.   Recheck for pulse every two minutes.

h.   Continue CPR until the casualty's pulse returns, you are relieved by a qualified person, you are stopped by a physician, or you are too tired to continue.

9.   Once the casualty is breathing and has a pulse, place the casualty in the recovery position until help arrives. Watch the casualty closely for life-threatening conditions, maintain an open airway, and check for other injuries, if necessary.

OPEN ABDOMINAL WOUND

Conditions: You see a casualty who has an open abdominal wound. The casualty is breathing. You will need material for an improvised dressing (clothing or blankets).

Standards: Apply a dressing to the wound following the correct sequence, without causing further injury to the casualty. Ensure that the dressing is secure and protects the wound without putting pressure on the bowel.

Performance Steps
Note: Always check for both entry and exit wounds. If there are two wounds (entry and exit), treat the wound that appears more serious first (for example, the heavier bleeding, protruding organs, larger wound, and so forth). It may be necessary to improvise dressings for the second wound by using strips of cloth, a T-shirt, or the cleanest material available.

1. Position the casualty on his or her back with the knees up (flexed).

2. Uncover the wound unless clothing is stuck to the wound or you are in a chemical environment.

   Caution: Removing stuck clothing or uncovering the wound in a chemical environment could cause additional harm.

3. Pick up any organs that are on the ground.

   a. Use a clean, dry dressing or the cleanest material available, and gently pick up the organs without touching them with your bare hands.

   b. Place the organs on top of the casualty's abdomen.

Caution: Do not *probe, clean, or try to remove any foreign object from the abdomen. Do* not *push organs back inside the body.*

4. Apply the casualty's dressing.

   Note: If the dressing is not *large enough to cover the entire wound, the inner surface of the plastic wrapper from the dressing may be used to cover the bowel before the dressing is applied. Other improvised dressings can be made from clothing, blankets, or the cleanest material available.*

   Warning: If an object is extending from the wound, do not *remove it. Place as much of the wrapper over the wound as possible without dislodging or moving the object. Do* not *place the wrapper over the object.*

   a. Apply the dressing/pad, white side down, directly over the wound.

   Warning: Do not *apply pressure to the wound or other exposed internal parts.*

   Caution: Do not *touch the white (sterile) side of the dressing. Do* not *allow it to come into contact with any surface other than the wound.*

   b. Wrap the tails (or the elastic bandage) around the casualty's body, completely covering the dressing/pad if possible.

   c. For a field dressing, loosely tie the tails into a nonslip knot at the casualty's side. For an emergency bandage, secure the hooking ends of the closure bar into the elastic bandage.

   d. Ensure that the dressing is secured firmly enough to prevent slipping, without applying pressure to the bowel.

Note: Dressings can be covered with improvised reinforcement materials (cravats, strips of torn cloth) for additional support and protection. The improvised bandages should be tied on the casualty's side—the side opposite to where the dressing is tied.

Warning: Do *not* give food or water to the casualty. (Moistening the casualty's lips is allowed.)

5. Watch the casualty closely for life-threatening conditions. Check for other injuries (if necessary), and treat for shock. Seek medical aid.

OPEN CHEST WOUND

Conditions: You see a casualty who has an open chest wound. The casualty is breathing. You will need an emergency bandage or field dressing, tape, and material to improvise a dressing (clothing or blankets).

Standards: Apply a dressing to the wound following the correct sequence, without causing further injury to the casualty. Ensure that the wound is properly sealed and the dressing is firmly secured without interfering with breathing.

Performance Steps

Note: Always check for both entry and exit wounds. If there are two wounds (entry and exit), treat the wound that appears more serious first (for example, the heavier bleeding, larger wound, and so forth). It may be necessary to improvise dressings for the second wound by using strips of cloth, a T-shirt, or the cleanest material available.

1. Uncover the wound unless clothing is stuck to the wound or you are in a chemical environment.

    Caution: Removing stuck clothing or uncovering the wound in a chemical environment could cause additional harm.

    Warning: Do not attempt to clean the wound.

2. Apply airtight material over the wound.

    a. Fully open the outer wrapper of the casualty's dressing or other airtight material.

b. Place the inner surface of the outer wrapper or other airtight material directly over the wound after the casualty exhales completely. The edges of the airtight material should extend two inches beyond the edges of the wound.

Note: When applying the airtight material, do not touch the inner surface.

c. Hold the material in place by taping on three sides, and then monitor the casualty for development of a tension pneumothorax, (an abnormal collection of air in the space between the lung and the chest wall).

Note: If the casualty has an open chest wound on his or her front and another open wound on his or her back on the same side, apply airtight material over each wound, taping down three sides of the material for the wound on the front and all four sides of the material for the wound on the back.

3. Apply the casualty's dressing.

a. Apply the dressing/pad, white side down, directly over the airtight material.

b. Have the casualty breathe normally.

c. Maintain pressure on the dressing while you wrap the tails (or elastic bandage) around the body and back to the starting point.

d. For a field dressing, tie the tails into a nonslip knot over the center of the dressing after the casualty has exhaled completely. For an emergency bandage, pass the tail through the plastic pressure device, reverse the tail while applying pressure, continue to wrap the tail around the body, and secure the plastic fastening clip to the last turn of the wrap.

e.   Ensure that the dressing is secured without interfering with breathing.

Note: When practical, apply direct manual pressure over the dressing for five to ten minutes to help control the bleeding.

4.   Position the casualty on the injured side or in a sitting position, whichever makes breathing easier.

BLEEDING AND/OR SEVERED EXTREMITY

Conditions: You have a casualty who has a bleeding wound of the arm or leg. The casualty is breathing. You will need materials to improvise a pressure dressing (wadding and cravat or strip of cloth), materials to elevate the extremity (blanket, poncho, log, or any available material), and materials to improvise a tourniquet—rigid object (stick or similar object) and a strip of cloth.

Standards: Control bleeding from the wound following the correct sequence. Place a dressing over the wound with the sides of the dressing sealed so it does not slip. Ensure that the dressings do not have a tourniquet-like effect. Apply a tourniquet to stop profuse bleeding not stopped by the dressings, for severed arms and legs, or to control life-threatening bleeding.

Performance Steps
Note: If the wound is a partial or complete amputation of the arm or leg, you will need to apply a tourniquet on the injured extremity. Also, if you need to control bleeding quickly, apply a tourniquet first. When the situation allows, you can loosen the tourniquet after applying other measures to control the bleeding, such as a pressure dressing. Go to step 5.

1. Uncover the wound unless clothing is stuck to the wound or you are in a chemical environment.

    Caution: Clothing or anything stuck to the wound should be left alone to avoid injury. Do not attempt to clean the wound.

    Caution: Do not remove protective clothing in a chemical environment. Apply dressings over the protective clothing.

2. Apply dressing on the casualty.

Warning: Field dressings and pressure dressings should not *have a tourniquet-like effect. The dressing must be loosened if the skin beyond the injury becomes cool, blue, or numb.*

a. Field dressing

    (1)   Apply the dressing, white side down, directly over the wound.

Caution: Do not *touch the white (sterile) side of the dressing. Do* not *allow it to come into contact with any surface other than the wound.*

    (2)   Wrap each tail, one at a time, in opposite directions around the wound so the dressing is covered, and both sides are sealed.

    (3)   Tie the tails into a nonslip knot over the outer edge of the dressing—*not* over the wound.

    (4)   Check the dressing to make sure that it is tied firmly enough to prevent slipping without causing a tourniquet-like effect.

    (5)   Check to see if you can detect a pulse below the bandage.

    (6)   If blood circulation is impaired, loosen and retie the tails, and then check the circulation again. If circulation is not restored, evacuate the casualty as soon as possible. Medical treatment may be needed to save the limb.

3. Apply manual pressure, and elevate the arm or leg to reduce bleeding, if necessary.

a. Apply firm manual pressure over the dressing for five to ten minutes, when practical.

b. Elevate the injured part above the level of the heart, unless a fracture is suspected and has not been splinted.

4. If a field dressing was applied and bleeding continues, apply a pressure dressing.

a. Keep the arm or leg elevated.

b. Place a wad of padding directly over the wound.

c. Place an improvised dressing over the wad of padding, and wrap it tightly around the limb.

d. Tie the ends in a nonslip knot directly over the wound.

e. Check the dressing to make sure that it does not have a tourniquet-like effect.

Note: If the bleeding stops, watch the casualty closely, and check for other injuries.

Note: If the bleeding continues despite proper application of a field dressing and a pressure dressing, an emergency bandage, or a chitosan dressing, or if the wound is a partial or complete amputation of the arm or leg, apply a tourniquet on the injured extremity. If only part of a hand or foot has been severed, the bleeding should be stopped using a pressure dressing.

5. Apply a tourniquet.

Caution: Never place a tourniquet directly over a wound, fracture, or joint.

a. Improvised tourniquet

    (1)   Make a tourniquet at least two inches wide.

    (2)   Position the tourniquet.

b. Place the tourniquet over the smoothed sleeve or trouser leg if possible.

c. If the wound is above the knee or elbow, place the tourniquet around the limb two to four inches above the wound between the wound and the heart but not on a joint or directly over a wound or a fracture.

d. If the wound is below the knee or elbow, initially position the tourniquet band two inches above the wound. If a tourniquet applied below the knee or elbow is not successful at stopping the bleeding, apply a second tourniquet two to four inches above the joint (knee or elbow). Do not remove the first tourniquet until the second tourniquet has been applied.

    (3)   Put on the tourniquet.

       (a) Tie a half knot.
       (b) Place a stick (or similar object) on top of the half knot.
       (c) Tie a full knot over the stick.
       (d) Twist the stick until the tourniquet is tight around the limb and bright-red bleeding has stopped.

Note: In the case of an amputation, dark, oozing blood may continue for a short time.

6. Secure the tourniquet. The tourniquet can be secured using the ends of the tourniquet band or with another piece of cloth, as long as the stick does not unwind.

   Note: If a limb is completely amputated, the stump should be padded and bandaged (do not cover the tourniquet). If the casualty has suffered an incomplete amputation, splint the limb.

   Note: If a tourniquet was applied to quickly control bleeding, once the situation allows, you can loosen the tourniquet after other measures have been applied to control the bleeding if it has been in place for less than six hours. However, do not remove it. Use direct pressure or a pressure dressing to control the bleeding prior to loosening the tourniquet. If unable to control bleeding by these methods, retighten the tourniquet until the bleeding stops.

7. If a tourniquet was applied, mark the time.

8. If applicable and the situation allows, save severed limbs or body parts and transport them with, but out of sight of, the casualty.

   a. Rinse the amputated part free of debris.

   b. Wrap the amputated part loosely in saline-moistened sterile gauze.

   c. Seal the amputated part in a plastic bag or cravat.

   d. Place the amputated part in a cool container.

Note: *If your location does not allow for the correct preserving of parts, do what you can.*

Caution: Do not freeze the amputated part, place it directly on ice, or use dry ice to cool it. Do not place amputated part in water. Do not place the amputated part so that it is in view of the casualty.

9. Watch the casualty closely for life-threatening conditions, check for other injuries (if necessary), and treat for shock. Seek medical aid.

OPEN HEAD WOUND

Conditions: You see a casualty who has an open head wound. The casualty is breathing. You will need a dressing and water.

Standards: Apply a dressing to the wound following the correct sequence, without causing further injury to the casualty. Properly position the casualty, and secure the dressing without applying unnecessary pressure.

Performance Steps

1. Check the casualty's level of consciousness.

   a. Question the casualty.

      (1) "What is your name?"

      (2) "Where are you?"

      (3) "What is today's date (day, month, and year)?"

   b. Report incorrect answers, inability to answer, or changes in answers to medical personnel.

2. Position the casualty.

   Warning: Do not *move the casualty if the casualty exhibits signs or symptoms—other than minor bleeding—of a neck, spine, or severe head injury.*

   a. The casualty is conscious or has a minor scalp wound.

(1) Have the casualty sit up unless other injuries prohibit sitting up.

(2) Raise the head slightly if the casualty is lying down and is not accumulating fluids in his or her throat.

(3) Turn his or her head to the side or position the casualty on his or her side (opposite the wound) if the wound is bleeding into the mouth or throat.

b. The casualty is unconscious or has a severe head injury.

(1) Treat the casualty as having a potential neck or spinal injury. Immobilize, and do not move the casualty unless absolutely necessary.

(2) Turn the casualty if he or she is choking, vomiting, or bleeding into the mouth. Position the casualty on his or her side opposite the wound.

Warning: If it is necessary to turn a casualty with a suspected neck or spinal injury, you will need assistance. Keeping the head, neck, and body aligned while providing support for the head and neck, roll the casualty gently onto his or her side.

3. Expose the wound.

4. Apply the dressing to the wound.

Warning: Do not *attempt to clean the wound or remove a protruding object. Do* not *put unnecessary pressure on the wound or attempt to push any brain matter back into the head (skull). Do* not *apply a pressure dressing. Do not give the casualty any food or drink. Keep the dressing moist.*

Caution: Do not touch the white (sterile) side of the dressing. Do not allow it to come into contact with any surface other than the wound.

Note: The following procedures are for applying a field dressing.

a. Forehead or back of the head

    (1)   Apply the dressing, white side down, directly over the wound with the tails extending toward the sides of the head.

    (2)   Wrap the tails, one at a time, around the head in opposite directions, making sure the tails cover the dressing but not the eyes and ears.

    (3)   Tie the tails at the side of the head using a nonslip knot.

b. Top of the head

    (1)   Apply the dressing, white side down, directly over the wound.

    (2)   Wrap one tail down under the chin, and bring it up in front of the ear over the dressing to a point just above, and in front of, the opposite ear.

Warning: Ensure the tails remain wide and close to the front of the chin to avoid choking the casualty.

(3)   Wrap the other tail down under the chin in the opposite direction and up the side of the head to meet the first tail.

(4)   Cross the tails.

(5)   Wrap one tail across the forehead above the eyebrows to a point just above and in front of the opposite ear.

(6)   Wrap the other tail above the ear, low over the back of the head, and above the opposite ear to meet the other tail.

(7)   Tie the tails using a nonslip knot.

c. Side of the head or cheek

(1)   Apply the dressing, white side down, directly over the wound with the tails extending up and down.

(2)   Wrap the top tail over the top of the head, down in front of the ear, under the chin, and up over the dressing to a point just above the ear.

(3)   Wrap the other tail in the opposite direction to meet the first tail.

(4)   Cross the tails, and complete the procedure as follows:

(a) Wrap one tail across the forehead above the eyebrows to a point just above, and in front of, the opposite ear.

(b) Wrap the other tail above the ear, low over the back of the head, and above the opposite ear to meet the other tail.

(c) Tie the tails using a nonslip knot.

5. Watch the casualty for life-threatening conditions, check for other injuries (if necessary), and treat for shock. Seek medical aid.

SUSPECTED FRACTURE

Conditions: You see a casualty who has an arm or leg that you think is broken. The casualty has no more serious wounds or conditions that have not been treated. You will need splint materials (boards, poles, tree branches), padding materials (clothing, blanket, dressing, leafy vegetation), and tie materials (strips of cloth, belts).

Standards: Splint the suspected broken arm or leg so that the arm or leg does not move and circulation is not impaired.

Performance Steps

1. Prepare the casualty for splinting.

   a. Reassure the casualty if he or she is conscious and able to understand. Tell the casualty that you will be taking care of him or her.

   b. Loosen any tight or binding clothing.

   Warning: Do not remove any protective clothing or boots in a chemical environment. Apply the splint over the clothing.

   Warning: Do not remove boots from the casualty unless they are needed to stabilize a neck injury, or there is actual bleeding from the foot.

   c. Remove all jewelry from the affected limb, and place it in the casualty's pocket. Tell the casualty that you are doing this to prevent further injury if swelling occurs later.

2. Get splinting materials.

a. Get splints (wooden boards, tree branches, poles) long enough to reach beyond the joints above and below the broken part.

b. Get materials to pad the splints, such as a jacket, blanket, poncho, or leafy vegetation.

c. Get tie materials, such as strips of cloth or belts, to tie the splints.

Note: If splinting materials are not available, use the chest wall to immobilize a suspected fracture of the arm and the uninjured leg to immobilize the fractured leg. Continue with steps 7 and 8.

3. Pad the splints. Apply padding between the splint and the bony areas of the body. Suggested sites for padding: wrist, elbow, ankle, knee, crotch, and armpit.

Note: You may have access to a universal or "SAM" splint. This splint is coated with a synthetic padding and does not require additional padding.

4. Check for signs of blood circulation problems below the injury.

a. Check light-skinned persons for color of skin (skin may be pale, white, or a bluish-gray color).

b. Check dark-skinned persons by depressing the toenail or fingernail beds and seeing how fast the color returns. A slower return of color to the injured side indicates a circulation problem.

c. Feel the injured arm or leg to see if it is colder than the uninjured one.

d. Ask the casualty about the presence of numbness, tightness, or a cold sensation.

Warning: If there is a blood circulation problem, evacuate the casualty as soon as possible.

5. Put on a splint.

Warning: If the fracture is open, do not attempt to push bones back under the skin. Apply a dressing to protect the area.

a. As a rule, splint the fracture in the position found.

Caution: Do not try to reposition or straighten the fracture unless there is no circulation below the fracture site or you cannot effectively splint it. Realigning the limb may restore circulation.

(1) If there is no circulation below the fracture site, or if the limb is grossly angulated and you cannot effectively splint it, you may need to gently realign the limb to effectively splint the fracture site.

(2) With one hand supporting the fracture site, use the other hand to grasp the part of the limb farthest from the fracture, and gently place traction on it (pull in the direction of the long axis of the bone, like extending a telescope).

b. Place one splint on each side of the arm or leg. Make sure the splints reach beyond the joints above and below the fracture.

c. Tie the splints with improvised (or actual) cravats.

      (1)   Gently place at least two cravats above and two cravats below the fracture if possible.

Warning: Do not *tie any cravats directly over the fracture.*

      (2)   Tie nonslip knots on the splint away from the injury.

6. Check the splint for tightness.

   a. Make sure the cravats are tight enough to hold the splinting materials securely in place.

   b. Recheck circulation below the injury to make sure that circulation is not impaired.

   c. Make any adjustments without allowing the splint to become ineffective.

7. Apply an arm sling if applicable.

Note: An arm sling can be used to further immobilize an arm and to provide support by the uninjured side.

   a. Make a sling from any nonstretching material (such as a strip of clothing or blanket, poncho, belt, or shirttail).

   b. Apply the sling so the supporting pressure is on the casualty's uninjured side.

   c. Make sure the hand of the supported arm is slightly higher than the elbow.

8. Apply swathes if applicable.

Note: Apply swathes when the casualty has a splinted, suspected fracture of the elbow or leg or when a suspected fracture cannot be splinted. (Improvise swathes from large pieces of cloth or belts.)

Warning: Place swathes above and/or below the fracture, not over it.

a. Apply swathes to an injured arm by wrapping the swathes over the injured arm, around the casualty's back, and under the arm on the uninjured side. Tie the ends on the uninjured side.

b. Apply swathes to an injured leg by wrapping the swathes around both legs and tying the swathes on the uninjured side.

9. Watch the casualty closely for life-threatening conditions, and check for other injuries. Seek medical aid.

NOTES

_____

_____

_____

_____

_____

_____

_____

_____

_____

_____

_____

_____

_____

A FINAL WORD TO THE PROFESSIONAL SECURITY AGENT

Today's society expects a great deal from private security agents. These expectations include placing faith that property and lives will be safe. The job of protecting life and property focuses much attention on the individual security agent. The *professional security agent* must not only protect the general public but be mindful of protecting himself or herself from civil liability as a *professional security agent.* The security professional must know the potential for civil liability and what measures are in place to mitigate organizational and institutional liability.

The professional security agent must constantly be aware of the need for professional conduct at all times. With strict adherence to each section of a code of ethics, it may be expected that the security agent fully knows and understands civil, organizational, and institutional liability. However, it is imperative for the ethical security agent to study the liabilities one faces as a *professional security agent* and not just rely on a code of ethics.

Professional Security Agent Code of Ethics

1. Respond to employer's professional needs.

2. Exhibit exemplary conduct.

3. Protect confidential information.

4. Maintain a safe and secure workplace.

5. Dress to create professionalism.

6. Enforce all lawful, rules, and regulations.

7. Encourage liaison with public officers.

8. Develop good rapport within the profession.

9. Strive to attain professional competence.

10. Encourage high standards of agent ethics

Looking at the code of ethics, one can see a need to be knowledgeable of civil, organizational, and institutional liabilities because the security professional is encouraged to exhibit exemplary conduct, enforce all lawful rules and regulations, and strive to attain professional competence. Just the fact of achieving these goals may place the security professional in a position of legal vulnerability if he or she is not aware of the liabilities.

The private *professional security agent* works within very complex legal standards. On a daily basis, the professional security agent must know and utilize laws governing the employment relationships present in the workplace, civil and criminal law, and standards of practice, as well as numerous government regulations.

Civil liability effects the actions and inactions of security professionals each and every day. The possibility of being sued includes the necessity to pay an attorney to represent oneself and spend an enormous amount of time on the case. Should a lawsuit go to court and the plaintiff prevail, the possibility of having to pay the plaintiff's legal fees, compensatory damages, and possible punitive damages raises the liability even further. A clear understanding of intentional torts can aid the security agent in the execution of his or her duties and allow him or her to present him- or herself professionally while protecting him- or herself from liabilities. It is imperative to know the following intentional torts:

Assault

*   an intentional act causing an apprehension of imminent physical contact

- no contact must be made

Battery

- unconsented, unlawful touching

- no apprehension or touching necessaryk

- any degree of physical contact can be battery

- may also include causing contact with the person by his or her clothing, such as knocking off someone's hat

False Arrest

- unlawful restraint of another

False Imprisonment

- an act that completely confines a plaintiff within fixed boundaries

- intent to confine

- defendant is responsible for or causes the confinement

- plaintiff was aware and knowledgeable of the confinement or was harmed by it

Defamation

- false accusations

- injury to another's reputation

- can be written (libel) or spoken (slander)

- accusation of commission of a crime is defamation per se

Invasion of Privacy

- unlawful, unreasonable intrusion upon another's privacy

- can be physical or mental privacy

- can include unconsented publication of a private fact to a third person

Malicious Prosecution

- bringing groundless criminal charges against another

- lack of probable cause is key

- criminal proceeding terminates in favor of the defendant

Negligent Infliction of Emotional Distress

- an act that is deemed extreme or outrageous

- the intent to cause another severe emotional distress

- actual suffering of severe emotional distress

- causation—defendant is the actual cause of the emotional distress

- may need to be caused by physical contact

- can be limited as a parasitic action in that it must follow another tort action, such as assault, defamation, and so on—Whether or not this is true in a particular state, infliction of emotional distress does give the plaintiff another avenue of recovery.

Conversion

- wrongful appropriation of the property of another, depriving the owner of the property for an indefinite time, altering something or exercising control over something so that the owner's rights are excluded—conversion is the civil aspect of theft.

Wrongful Discharge or Termination

- an action by an at-will employee alleging that the employer discharged the employee in violation of a law or a contractual agreement

Negligence

- failing to prevent loss, harm, or injury when there was a duty owed to the plaintiff and reasonable and due care would have prevented the injury from occurring.

In essence, negligence consists of five elements:

(1) The existence of a duty as established via law or contract
(2) A failure to perform that duty
(3) Harm or injury to a party to whom the duty was owed
(4) The harm was reasonably foreseeable
(5) The harm was caused by the failure to perform the duty

Unfortunately, traditional texts on legal aspects have focused too narrowly on criminal law and civil liability. Different states have different torts, and it is the responsibility of the professional security agent to investigate and know the torts applicable in the state(s) in which he or she is employed for his or her own protection and the protection of the client.

Measures that are in place to mitigate organizational and institutional liability are similar to torts in that they are many and vary depending upon the state in which they are requested. Organizational and institutional liabilities are obviously important to security professionals who generally deal with a limited set of crimes within their respective work environments. Professional security agents must be knowledgeable of these offenses. Gaining this knowledge can be very difficult and time-consuming. They may have to seek legal counsel or meet with prosecuting attorneys to understand the nuances behind the new legislation.

Mitigations of organizational and institutional liability that are most applicable to a security professional can be researched under the following headings:

- trespassing
- dealing with trespassers
- labor laws
- discipline
- dismissal
- employment at will
- Wagner Act of 1935 (National Labor Relations Act)
- court injunctions
- Fair Labor Standards Act of 1938
- Taft-Hartley Act of 1947
- Landrum-Griffin Act of 1959
- strike surveillance
- Polygraph Protection Act of 1988
- Federal False Claims Act of 1863
- Privacy Act
- Freedom of Information Act
- Fair Credit Reporting Act of 1970
- trade secrets

- administrative law
- Federal agencies such as OSHA, EEOC, NRC, EPA, NLRB, FCC, and FAA
- State agencies such as OSHA, Human Relations Commission, and Department of Environmental Resources
- Municipal agencies such as the zoning commission and board of health
- administrative language
- audits
- interrogation
- search and seizure
- regulations governing the security industry
- depositions
- testifying in legal and quasi-legal proceedings

This is *not* an all-inclusive list; the professional security agent is encouraged to expand this list. Laws, torts, and measures for protecting oneself are forever changing. One could literally be employed full-time researching and discovering legal measures to protect oneself from liability. Unfortunately, a security professional does not have the time or means to be articulate in all aspects of the law. Even though having this knowledge is beneficial to him or her; it is literally impossible to obtain all of this knowledge.

Therefore, the next best thing to not knowing all of the laws is to have a good code of ethics and *general* knowledge of the laws, liabilities, and means of relief in the area in which one works. However, perhaps more important would be to have the ability to research the laws pertinent to the environment in which one is working.

Despite the large amount of criminological work in a variety of different types of work environments by the security professional, there is still comparably very little research on relief for civil, organizational, and institutional liability. Our ever-changing world virtually requires a good foundation of resources for the professional security agent to access when needed. These resources are built through education, experience, and knowledge of whom to turn to for information in a critical situation.

Best wishes for a successful career as a professional security agent!

Robert Nile Nolan

PROFESSIONAL SECURITY AGENT

This is to certify that

JOHN DOE

Has successfully completed 28 hours of training as a

S A M P L E

Professional Security Agent

*Having passed the exam for Professional Security Agent Basic Training, First Edition
and in recognition thereof is awarded this certificate on 25 July 2021*

Robert N. Nolan

Director of Security
Shadow Security LLC.

To Receive a Certificate of Training

1. Send $25.00 via **PayPal** to ShadowSecEP@gmail.com Include your name how you want it on your certificate and your **email address.**

2. You will receive a one-hundred-question exam via email.

3. Email your answers and **mailing address** to: ShadowSecEP@gmail.com.

4. You must pass the examination with a 70 percent score.

5. You will be notified via email if you passed or failed within 7 to 10 business days.

6. Upon passing the exam, your certificate (in color) will arrive in the mail within 30 business days.

CONCEALED CARRY RECIPROCITY AND UNARMED AND ARMED LICENSE REQUIREMENTS BY STATE

ALABAMA

Concealed carry honored in all states except California, Connecticut, Delaware, District of Columbia, Hawaii, Illinois, Maryland, Minnesota, Massachusetts, Nebraska, Nevada, New Jersey, New Mexico, New York, Oregon, Rhode Island, South Carolina, and Washington and **with restrictions** (must be twenty-one years of age) in Alaska, Arizona, Colorado, Florida, Iowa, Kansas, Kentucky, Louisiana, Maine, Oklahoma, Texas, Virginia, West Virginia, and Wisconsin.

The Alabama Security Regulatory Board licenses the state's security officers and armed security officers. Prospective security guards must clear background checks and meet training requirements.

An individual must be at least eighteen to work as a security officer and at least twenty-one to work as an armed security officer. An armed security officer will hold a board-issued certification and a pistol permit issued by the county of residence (http://www.asrb.alabama.gov/Law.aspx). The latter will come from the sheriff.

The Alabama Security Regulatory Board also recognizes certified trainers and qualifying agents. Qualifying Agents are professionals who take responsibility for regulated activities carried out by their contract security company.

Security Officer Training Requirements
Security officers must meet training requirements described in Section 34-27C-8. An unarmed security officer will need eight hours of initial/basic training from a certified trainer unless exempted on the basis of other equivalent training or on the basis of employment within the field.

Training offered by a board-approved trainer will cover, at minimum, the following:
- fire prevention
- legal information
- handling of crisis situations
- detention procedures
- crowd control
- equipment usage

The individual can expect a test at course completion. An individual can be exempted from the standard initial training if he or she has completed security training through a military or governmental entity or through a security training institute within the prior three years. He or she may also be exempted on the basis of employment with a contract security company that provides training at the level required (or above) for licensure in Alabama.

Peace officers, whether sworn or retired, are exempted from the initial basic training requirement. This is also the case with security officers who meet requirements for continuous employment. Exemptions are summarized in application materials.

Armed Security Officer Training Requirements
An armed security officer will need fourteen hours of training. He or she will need to pass a qualifying course as part of his or her training. There are

several options. The course may be offered by the Alabama Peace Officers Standards and Training Commission or the National Rifle Association. If it is an NRA course, it must be approved by NRA Law Enforcement Activities Division as appropriate for private law enforcement. If the NRA course is offered by a contract security company, the company must be in an affiliate relationship with the NRA and in compliance with rules. The Alabama Security Regulatory Board offers an approved course. There are separate qualification standards for handgun, shotgun, and rifle; these are described in Alabama rules and regulations.

Background Check Requirements

An individual would be excluded from licensure based on registration as a sex offender or on conviction of certain criminal offenses. Felony offenses are disqualifying unless the individual has been granted a pardon. Some misdemeanor offenses are also disqualifying. Violent misdemeanor offenses, for example, are disqualifying for a period of ten years.

Fingerprints are to be made through a law enforcement agency. They are to be made on an FBI-approved fingerprint card or printout. The application packet includes instructions for officials who carry out fingerprinting. Those with questions may call (334) 353-4340.

The Application Process

Application forms can be downloaded from the board website (http://www. asrb.alabama.gov/Forms.aspx).

An individual must provide two passport-style color photos.

Citizenship status can be documented by a state-issued driver's license or ID. The licensing agency can also accept a passport, a military ID, or US Citizenship and Immigration Service documentation. Age must also be documented; a copy of a driver's license would also suffice for this purpose.

Applicants who are seeking a training exemption from the usual training must provide documentation.

Those who have been arrested or charged with violations (including traffic citations) must provide details.

An applicant who has served in the military will need to provide a copy of DD-214 or equivalent document.

The applicant must make several sworn statements, declaring, among other things, that he or she is neither addicted to narcotics nor habitually drunk and has not been declared incompetent by a court. The board reserves the right to require that an individual have alcohol or drug testing.

The application packet includes multiple forms that require notarization. In the case of the criminal history release form, the licensing agency can accept the names and addresses of two witnesses as an alternative to notarization.

The credentialing agency assesses a $50 license fee and $39.75 background check fee.

The Board may issue a temporary license to a security officer pending completion of training requirements.

Additional State-Recognized Credentials

In order to be designated as a qualifying agent, one must hold licensing as a security officer or armed security officer. A professional who will be serving as a qualifying agent must submit, in addition to the standard application materials, a cover letter from the contract security company that he or she will be providing services for.

Alabama law stipulates that, in order to be approved for licensing, a contract security company must have at least one qualifying agent who has at least three years of supervisory, management, or administrative experience in security or law enforcement.

Board certified trainers must be at least twenty-one years of age. They must have two years of supervisory experience; this may be in law enforcement or security. They must either 1) complete a two-week instructor course or 2) demonstrate a year of security-related instructional experience.

To be certified as a Certified Trainer 2, one must also be certified as a law enforcement firearms instructor by an approved organization. Approved organizations include the following:

- Alabama Peace Officers Standards and Training Commission
- Federal Bureau of Investigation
- Federal Law Enforcement Training Center
- National Rifle Association

Additional Information

Licensing information is available from the Alabama Security Regulatory Board (http://www.asrb.alabama.gov). The board can be reached by email at SecurityBoard at alstateboard.com or by telephone at (334) 269-9990.

Professional associations provide additional career resources. Alabama has several chapters of the American Society of Industrial Security; among them is ASIS North Alabama (http://www.asisnorthalabama.org).

ALASKA

Concealed carry honored in all states except California, Connecticut, District of Columbia, Hawaii, Illinois, Maine, Maryland, Massachusetts, New Jersey, New York, Oregon, Rhode Island, and Washington and **with restrictions** (must be twenty-one years of age) in Arizona, Maine, Oklahoma, Kansas, Kentucky, and West Virginia.

Alaska licenses security guards and armed security guards. Both must meet training and general eligibility requirements.

Requirements for Unarmed Security Guards

Security guards must be at least eighteen years of age (http://www.labor.state.ak.us/research/dlo/security.htm). They may be citizens or resident aliens of the United States. They must be mentally stable and free of addictions. An individual will be disqualified on the basis of a felony conviction.

The security guard must be covered under a bond or an insurance policy: either his or her own or that of an employer (http://www.legis.state.ak.us/basis/folioproxy.asp?url=http://wwwjnu01.legis.state.ak.us/cgi-bin/folioisa.dll/stattx08/query=[JUMP:%27AS1865400%27]/doc/{@1}/hits_only?firsthit).

The security guard is to receive eight hours of preassignment training, focused on job duties, and forty hours of in-service training (http://www.touchngo.com/lglcntr/akstats/aac/title13/chapter060/section110.htm). The latter must be completed within 180 days of employment. The following topics are to be covered:
* laws pertaining to arrest
* laws pertaining to search and seizure
* patrol techniques
* first aid
* fire prevention

The unarmed security guard will need eight hours of refresher training each year.

Requirements for Armed Security Guards

In order to be licensed as an armed security guard, an individual must have eight hours of preservice training. Training is to be provided by an approved instructor. It must cover the following:

- compliance with federal and state laws and regulations
- handling of firearms
- firearm safety and maintenance

Training can be provided by a security guard agency employee provided that the employee holds national certification as an instructor through a recognized national certifying body. Training may instead be obtained through an instructor who has been certified by a governmental law enforcement agency.

The prospective security guard must demonstrate competence with the particular type of firearm that he or she will be using on the job. Competency must be maintained. Alaska requires armed security guards to requalify on an annual basis.

An individual is disqualified from licensing as an armed security guard if he or she has ever been disqualified from firearm possession (for example, as a probation condition). The Department of Public Safety has provided a list of frequently asked questions about firearms prohibitions (https://dps. alaska.gov/statewide/r-i/permitslicensing/firearm-faq).

The Application Process

Alaska requires a fingerprint-based national criminal background check. This step should be carried out in advance. The fingerprint card is to be included in the application package. The Department of Public Safety has provided a list of organizations that provide fingerprinting services (https:// dps.alaska.gov/statewide/r-i/permitslicensing/securityguard); the list is not exhaustive.

License applications are also available from the website of the Department of Public Safety (https://dps.alaska.gov/statewide/r-i/permitslicensing/securityguard).

On the form, the applicant will provide five years of employment and residence history. He or she will list three references; at least one is to be an Alaska resident.

The licensing agency will require a recent photograph (taken within the previous thirty days). It is to show the applicant from the waist up.

Applicants will need to demonstrate evidence of insurance. Armed guard applicants will need to submit a copy of their firearms certification/qualification.

The applicant will attest to having read the applicable laws and regulations. These include 18.65.400–18.65.490 of Alaska Statutes and 13 AAC 60.010–60.900 of Alaska Administrative Code.

Both the security guard and the manager or qualified agent will sign the application form. The manager will attest that "reasonable" attempts have been made to determine the applicant's qualifications. The application requires notarization.

The licensing reserves the right to contact former employers. There are two associated fees: one for fingerprinting and one for the application/licensing. The application fee is $50. The background check is $49.75.

The security guard is employed on a temporary basis pending license approval. He or she will receive a state-issued identification card following approval.

The renewal period is two years. The renewal fee is currently $50. The Department of Public Safety requires notification of status changes. A security guard who has changed agencies will need to again provide evidence of insurance. A unarmed security guard who seeks armed status will provide a copy of the firearms qualification/certification.

Security Agent / Manager Requirements and Licensing Process

A security agency will need a manager or qualified agent who is a security guard. If the manager does not currently hold security guard status in Alaska, he or she will submit a license application and supporting documentation at the time of company application. The agency will demonstrate proof of insurance.

State Civil Service

Requirements for civil service may be different than those for private security services. The Division of Personnel and Labor Relations lists two levels of expertise: Security Guard I and Security Guard II (http://agency.governmentjobs.com/Alaska/default.cfm?action=agencyspecs). One difference between the two is that the latter exercises considerable independent judgment. Both require high school graduation or GED; many positions require the worker to obtain a security clearance. Security Guard II requires two years of work experience (with at least one in security or a related field, such as law enforcement).

Additional Information

Information about security guard licensing is available from the Department of Public Safety (https://dps.alaska.gov/statewide/r-i/permitslicensing/securityguard). The licensing agency can be reached by telephone at (907) 269-0393.

ARIZONA

Concealed carry honored in all states except California, Connecticut, District of Columbia, Hawaii, Illinois, Maryland, Massachusetts, Minnesota, New Jersey, New York, Oregon, Rhode Island, and Washington and **with restrictions** (must be twenty-one years of age) in Alaska, Colorado, Florida, Kansas, Kentucky, Maine, Michigan, Nebraska, Oklahoma, Pennsylvania, South Carolina, and West Virginia.

Arizona security guards are registered with the Department of Public Safety, or DPS. To be eligible, they must be at least eighteen years of age and authorized to work in the United States. The qualification process is based on background screening and preservice training.

The Department of Public Safety recognizes multiple security-related job roles. Armed security guards must complete additional training. Professionals employed as corporate officers hold associate registration. The minimum age is twenty-one for "agency associate" and related roles.

Security guards must hold registration unless they fall under exemption categories identified in Arizona Revised Statute found at: (http://www.azleg.state.az.us/FormatDocument.asp?inDoc=/ars/32/02606.htm&Title=32&DocType=ARS). Some employers who are exempt from registration requirements are still under DPS jurisdiction. Their security guards must go through a background check process. Armed guards must meet state-mandated training requirements.

Training Requirements

Training for Unarmed Guards

The security guard must complete eight hours of preservice training. The mandated training is completed after the individual has an offer of employment.

Training follows a curriculum prescribed by the department. It includes the following:

- orientation
- communications

- security guard procedures
- criminal law / arrest law
- use of force
- first response / crime scene preservation
- emergency response procedures
- ethics
- uniform/grooming

The security guard will need to complete eight hours of refresher training for renewal.

Training for Armed Guards
An armed security guard must complete sixteen hours of firearm training; this is in addition to the eight hours required for the unarmed credential. On the application form, the firearms instructor will note whether training was with a revolver or semiautomatic.

The agency will provide information about training. The firearm instructor must be certified by the department. He or she will have had firearm instructor training through one of the following:
- the Arizona Peace Officers Standards and Training Board
- the National Rifle Association
- a federal law enforcement agency

The department notes that concealed weapons training is not a substitute for DPS-mandated firearms safety training.

Firearms refresher training must be completed each year.

Background Screening Requirements
The prospective security guard must complete a fingerprint-based FBI criminal background check. In some cases, the instructor will do the fingerprinting. The Department of Public Safety notes that various other organizations

can perform the service (http://licensing.azdps.gov/Licensefingerprints.asp). The background check processing fee is paid at the time of application.

Security guards must meet background requirements described in Title 22 (http://www.azleg.state.az.us/FormatDocument.asp?inDoc=/ars/32/02622. htm&Title=32&DocType=ARS. Felony convictions are disqualifying. Some misdemeanor convictions are initially disqualifying, though the individual may regain eligibility after a period of time. In some cases, an exception may be granted for an individual who was convicted of a felony in the distant past or who was convicted of a disqualifying misdemeanor in the recent past (http://www.azleg.state.az.us/FormatDocument.asp?inDoc=/ars/32/02609. htm&Title=32&DocType=ARS). Individuals who seek "good cause exceptions" will need to provide evidence at a hearing. The board will consider evidence of rehabilitation as well as evidence related to the crime itself.

Noncriminal disqualifiers include having been adjudicated as mentally incompetent or having been found to be a danger to self or others. Dishonorable discharge from the armed services is a disqualifier for armed service. The Department of Public Safety has provided a fact sheet describing all disqualifiers (http://licensing.azdps.gov/Licensedisqualifiers.asp).

The Application Process

Application materials are available from the Department of Public Safety. They may be requested or downloaded from the website (http://licensing. azdps.gov/Licenseforms.asp).

The application form includes sections that are to be completed by different individuals at different stages of the hiring and training process. The employer fills out a portion of the registration application form. The unarmed trainer and (when applicable) the firearm safety trainer later sign to verify training.

The applicant will need a passport-style photograph; it is to be in color. DPS will also require a copy of an ID, such as a driver's license or passport.

Applicants with military experience are directed to include a copy of the DD214.

Applicants for the unarmed guard credential pay $72 ($22 for fingerprint processing and $50 for registration). Those applying for an armed guard credential pay $122. The fee may be paid by money order, cashier's check, or agency check. The department does not accept personal checks but can accept cash.

Applications may be mailed or hand-delivered. Mail is to be addressed to the Licensure Unit at the following address:

Arizona Department of Public Safety Licensing Unit
PO Box 6328, MD 1160
Phoenix, AZ 85005

Security guards wishing to upgrade to armed guard status will submit a new application verifying employment and completion of firearm safety training. The security guard will need to submit fingerprints again unless the previous submission was less than ninety days in the past. DPS will require a new photograph if the security guard's appearance has changed.

The armed security registration is agency-specific, though the licensing agency makes a distinction between the security guard card and the registration. DPS notes that an individual who has ended his or her employment is permitted to show his or her card to prospective employers (http://licensing.azdps.gov/Licensesecurityguard.asp).

Additional Information

Information about security guard registration is available from the Arizona Department of Public Safety Licensing Unit (http://licensing.azdps.gov/). The Licensing Unit can be reached by telephone at (602) 223-2361.

Requirements are described in statute and administrative code; interested individuals may consult Title 13, Chapter 26.

The Arizona Private Security Professionals Association is an additional professional resource (https://www.azapspa.com/).

ARKANSAS

Concealed carry honored in all states except California, Connecticut, District of Columbia, Hawaii, Illinois, Maryland, Massachusetts, Minnesota, New Jersey, Oregon, New York, Rhode Island, and Washington and **with restrictions** (must be twenty-one years of age) in Alaska, Arizona, Colorado, Florida, Kansas, Kentucky, Maine, Michigan, Nebraska, Oklahoma, Pennsylvania, South Carolina, and West Virginia.

Arkansas security guards are credentialed by the Arkansas Board of Private Investigators and Private Security Agencies, under the banner of the Arkansas State Police. They must hold credentials unless they fall under exemption categories described in the state statute.

The board recognizes different roles, including security officers, commissioned security officers, and professionals who own or manage security agencies. Training and education or experience requirements vary. All applicants will go through thorough background checks.

Credentials must be renewed periodically. A background check is carried out again upon renewal.

Security Officer Requirements

A registered security officer must be at least eighteen. He or she will need two hours of instruction in each of the following:
- legal authority of private security officers
- rules and regulations
- note taking / report writing

Each concept will be tested.

Commissioned Security Officer Requirements

A security guard must be commissioned in order to carry a firearm. Requirements are more stringent. A commissioned security officer must be at least twenty-one.

The prospective officer must be free of felony convictions (unless a pardon was granted). Additionally, the individual cannot have committed acts that would result in revocation or suspension of a license issued by the Arkansas board.

The prospective commissioned guard will need training in each of the following content areas: weapons and safety, legal limitations of firearm use, and marksmanship / range safety. The prospective armed guard can expect examination on each required topic. It will be necessary to qualify on the range.

Qualified employees of armored car businesses are commissioned as security officers.

The Security Officer Application Process

A prospective security officer will need to have fingerprints made. Criminal background checks are carried out by the Identification Bureau of the Department of the Arkansas State Police and by the FBI.

Application materials are available online (http://asp.arkansas.gov/services-and-programs/detail/private-investigators-and-alarm-installation-monitoring); the same application package is used for private security officers and commissioned security officers.

The trainer or training administrator will sign off on each required training content area.

Registration of a private security officer or commissioned security officer costs $40. There is an additional $37.75 fee for the state and federal background checks. The fingerprint cards are to be included in the application package.

The applicant will also need to provide two passport-style photographs. The application form requires notarization.

The applicant will list any pending charges as well as any potentially disqualifying criminal convictions. In the case of convictions, the licensing agency will require certified court documents.

Prospective security officers who were not born in the United States are directed to submit naturalization papers, permanent resident cards, or work permits.

The applicant will provide a notarized release of information form. He or she will authorize the Arkansas State Police to obtain information, as necessary, from various sources, including educational institutions, mental institutions, and credit reporting agencies.

Additional Requirements to Manage a Security Agency

Arkansas also has set requirements that must be met by managers of security agencies. Standards apply to individuals who go into the security business and also to managers of partnerships or corporations.

The responsible party must be at least twenty-one. He or she will meet one of the following experience requirements:

- two consecutive years of security-related supervisory experience
- two consecutive years of security-related law enforcement or armed services experience
- completion of an educational program approved by the Arkansas Board of Private Investigators and Private Security Agencies

The professional may not have been convicted of a felony, violent crime, Class A misdemeanor, or other comparable crime by any state, federal, or military court unless a pardon was granted. He or she cannot suffer from drug addiction or habitual drunkenness and cannot have been found mentally incompetent (unless competency has been restored). A professional would also be disqualified on the basis of dishonorable discharge from the military. According to state code, however, the Arkansas Board of Private Investigators and Private Security Agencies has the authority to waive some requirements.

The owner or manager must take a board examination. The examination covers the following:

- private security officer power and authority
- legal limits on firearm usage
- Arkansas rules and regulations
- report writing / taking notes from the field
- firearm safety, range firing, and procedure

A branch manager will also be tested. The minimum passing score is 70 percent.

An individual attempts the examination after making application. The applicant is allowed two examination attempts before the application is denied. Reexamination will entail a fifty-dollar fee.

Major shareholders must also go through a fingerprint-based process.

Additional Information

Licensing and registration information is available from the Arkansas State Police. Credentialing is governed by statute and rule. Individuals with questions may call 501-618-8600. Applicants may also email the Regulatory Services Division (http://asp.arkansas.gov/services-and-programs/detail/private-investigators-and-alarm-installation-monitoring).

Additional professional resources include the Arkansas Security Alarm Association (ASAA) and local chapters of ASIS International (https://www.asisonline.org/Membership/Member-Center/Chapters/Find/Pages/Chapter-Map.aspx). While not directly involved with the licensing process, the ASAA has provided links to licensing-related resources, including minutes from board meetings (http://arkansasalarm.org/licensing/).

CALIFORNIA

Concealed carry honored in all states except Colorado, Connecticut, Delaware, District of Columbia, Georgia, Hawaii, Illinois, Louisiana, Nevada, New Jersey, Maryland, Massachusetts, Minnesota, New Mexico, New York, North Dakota, Oregon, Pennsylvania, Rhode Island, South Carolina, Washington, and Wyoming and **with restrictions** (must be twenty-one years of age) in Alaska, Arizona, Kansas, Kentucky, Maine, Oklahoma, West Virginia, and Wisconsin.

The California Bureau of Security and Investigative Services registers the state's security guards and proprietary private security officers.

Proprietary private security officers (PPSO) provide security services directly to their employer and are not contracted by another entity; they are typically unarmed professionals who interact with the public while on the job (http://www.bsis.ca.gov/forms_pubs/ppso_fact.shtml). Security guards, in contrast, are authorized to work for companies that provide security services.

Both security guards and proprietary private security officers go through a background check process. The bureau requires that individuals employed in either role be at least eighteen years of age.

Security guards have state-mandated training requirements. Some security guards will also need a firearms permit or baton permit; this entails additional training.

Security guards have continuing education requirements.

Security Guard Training Requirements
A security guard must complete at least forty hours of education through a private patrol operator or certified training facility. Training must take place on a time line set by the bureau (http://www.bsis.ca.gov/industries/g_train.shtml). At least eight hours must be completed prior to assignment. Another sixteen hours are to be completed within thirty days of assignment and the remaining sixteen hours, within six months.

Preservice training must cover powers to arrest, terrorism awareness, and weapons of mass destruction. The candidate will take a test before credentialing.

The remaining thirty-two hours may include a combination of mandatory content and electives. Mandatory topics include the following:

- public relations
- observation and documentation
- communication
- legal aspects and liability

At least half of the mandatory coursework hours are to take place within the first thirty days.

Additional required hours may consist of electives. The bureau has provided a list and indicated the maximum number of hours that can be credited for each. The program may include any of the following:

- employer policies/ orientation
- post orders
- officer safety
- evacuation procedures
- access control
- trespass
- advanced arrests, search and seizure
- laws and regulations
- first aid and CPR
- workplace violence
- handling difficult people
- crowd control
- preserving incidence scenes
- driver safety
- chemical agents
- courtroom demeanor
- supervision
- radio procedures

- parking and traffic control
- school security guard training
- executive protection
- firearms training
- firearms requalification
- baton training
- fire safety
- Air Taser or Stun Gun

Half of the elective coursework is to be delivered within the first thirty days.

Peace officers (whether active duty, retired, or reserve) are directed to contact the bureau about alternate requirements.

Firearms and Baton Permits

Firearms—an individual who seeks a firearm permit will need fourteen hours of training, consisting of eight hours of classroom instruction and six hours of range. Among the topics are moral and legal issues, weapon handling, and emergency procedures. The course must be taken through a bureau-certified facility or instructor. Prospective students may call (916) 322-4000 for a list of providers. Ultimately, the individual will need to pass both a written exam and a range test.

The armed guard must maintain continued competency. Although the permit is issued for two years, the permit holder will need to requalify twice during each of the two years.

The bureau notes that the firearms permit does not authorize concealed weapons. Concealed weapon permits are issued at the local level. The bureau-issued firearms permit is mandatory, though, for security guards who carry guns.

Baton Permit—some California security guards carry batons. In order to be authorized to carry one, a security guard must have eight hours of training from an approved trainer. The bureau has provided a list of training facilities (www.bsis.ca.gov/forms_pubs/online_services/verify_license.shtml).

Background Check Requirements

Applicants must have fingerprint-based criminal background checks processed by the California Department of Justice (DOJ) and the FBI. California residents can expedite the process by using Live Scan electronic fingerprint processing services. The bureau has provided Live Scan service forms (http://www.bsis.ca.gov/forms_pubs/livescan/index.shtml); the prospective security professional will select the form designated for his or her license type. The Office of the Attorney General has provided a list of Live Scan locations, organized by county (https://oag.ca.gov/fingerprints/locations). The FBI and DOJ fingerprinting fees together total forty-nine dollars; fees can be paid on-site. An additional fee may be due to the vendor; the amount is variable.

Applicants who need hard cards are directed to call 800-952-5210.

The Application Process

Security guard applicants submit their applications after completing the initial eight hours of training. They may receive application forms from their training facility or employing agency. The security guard application can also be submitted online; applicants must first read the instructions and updates (https://www.bsis.ca.gov/industries/guard.shtml). Applicants who use the online system must also elect to use Live Scan fingerprinting services. Background check processing is typically the last step. After the fingerprints clear, a screen print will be available that can be used as an interim permit; once this is in hand, the security guard can be placed on duty (http://www.bsis.ca.gov/forms_pubs/guard_fact.shtml).

The security guard application fee is fifty dollars; the online convenience fee is one dollar. The firearm permit entails payment of an additional eighty-dollar fee.

School Security Guard Requirements

School security guards must receive state-mandated training if they provide school security services for twenty or more hours a week (http://www.bsis.ca.gov/industries/syllabus.shtml). They may or may not be under bureau jurisdiction, depending on their employment circumstances (http://www.bsis.ca.gov/consumers/faqs/school_security_guard.shtml).

Additional Information

Registration information is available from the California Bureau of Security and Investigative Services. The bureau has provided fact sheets for security guards (http://www.bsis.ca.gov/forms_pubs/guard_fact.shtml) and proprietary security officers (PPSO, PSO)(http://www.bsis.ca.gov/forms_pubs/ppso_fact.shtml). Individuals with questions about security guard registration may call (800) 952-5210 or email bsis at dca.ca.gov. Additional contact information is available online (http://www.bsis.ca.gov/about_us/contact_us.shtml).

Professional organizations do not issue licenses but serve as additional resources. Security professionals may wish to contact the California Association of Licensed Security Agencies, Guards, and Associates (http://www.calsaga.org) and their local chapter of ASIS International.

COLORADO

Concealed carry honored in all states except California, Connecticut, District of Columbia, Hawaii, Illinois, Maryland, Massachusetts, Minnesota, Nevada, New Jersey, New York, Oregon, Rhode Island, South Carolina, and Washington and **with restrictions** (must be twenty-one years of age) in Alaska, Arizona, Florida, Kansas, Kentucky, Maine, Michigan, Oklahoma, Pennsylvania, and West Virginia.

The State of Colorado does license security guards (https://www.denvergov.org/Government/Departments/Business-Licensing/Business-Licenses/Security-Services/Security-Guards). Those who carry firearms will apply for permits from their local governments. Multiple jurisdictions within Colorado license security guards. Colorado Springs licenses private security officers while Denver licenses "merchant guards" (https://www.denvergov.org/Government/Departments/Business-Licensing/Business-Licenses/Security-Services/Security-Guards).

The companies that employ security guards may also be subject to various laws and regulations. (http://www.denvergov.org/businesslicensing/DenverBusinessLicensing Center/BusinessLicenses/MerchantGuardCompany/tabid/441673/Default.aspx).

In many cases, the responsibility of the security guard is to meet the standards of the employer. Some employers choose to set requirements well above those that are required by law. A security guard may be hired by a company that provides security services to clients or may be hired directly by a business to patrol or provide other security services. Some security officers work in the public sector.

All prospective security guards can expect thorough background screening. Other requirements vary a good deal from one industry or employer to the next.

Background and Experience Requirements

A prospective security guard can expect a background check at the employment level. Employers may check for more than just criminal convictions.

They may, for example, examine the applicant's driving record. A drug test may also be required as a condition of hire.

Employers often state that the applicant must hold a high school diploma or GED. Some require, or at least state a preference, for education beyond this level. In some cases, the employer will consider either an academic degree or relevant work experience (for example, law enforcement or military work).

Military or law enforcement experience is highly valued for some types of security position.

Academic and Physical Skills

Job ads may cite various academic skills, for example, the ability to write reports. The security officer may need to read items such as procedural manuals and maintenance instructions. He or she may need to know or learn particular software applications.

Employers may cite physical abilities: for example, ease walking and standing and ability to lift forty or even one hundred pounds. They may mention specific items that might need to be carried (for example, fire extinguishers).

Various certifications and licenses, though not universally required, are important for particular positions. Security positions can include patrolling by car or even parking. In many cases, a security guard will be expected to have a driver's license.

Employers may also seek a first responder or EMT certification.

Differing Expectations for Security Guards Who Use or Do Not Use Force

Some job ads state that there will be no use of force and that the guard instead serves as a "visual deterrence." The guard may respond to suspicious activities by alerting others.

In some cases, though, the security officer will be expected to carry a firearm or know how to apply restraints. An individual may need to be at least twenty-one to receive consideration for an armed position. Legal mandates are more stringent.

Some other security jobs, for example, those at hotels, emphasize customer service.

Local Security Licenses

The Office of Economic Development and International Trade advises Colorado guards to check with local authorities about requirements.

Information about local licensing may be available from the city clerk.

Colorado Springs security guard license applications are available online from the city clerk's office (https://coloradosprings.gov/city-clerk/page/security-license). An applicant will need to submit a fingerprint card. Applicants may go in person to submit applications at the Police Operations Center.

Denver merchant guard applications are also available online (https://www.denvergov.org/Government/Departments/Business-Licensing/Business-Licenses/Security-Services/Security-Guards). The applicant must have a letter of hire. He or she must present character references. The licensing agency will carry out a name-based background check through the Colorado Bureau of Investigations (CBI). The applicant must have a physical examination. There is a separate application process for armed status. A training certificate must be presented. The individual must have an FBI background check.

Security Guard Jobs in the Public Sector

Security personnel may be hired in the public sector in any of multiple roles.

Positions with the Colorado job classification "safety security officer" are found in state agencies, including mental health facilities. Professionals who are employed in this capacity are expected to have either sixty semester hours of college coursework or two years of relevant law enforcement experience. Additional requirements include being at least twenty-one, having a driver's license, and not having disqualifying felony convictions.

Those with the classification "security" have a differing set of expectations. These professionals provide building security and manage parking access. College education is not necessarily expected. Prior experience as a parking attendant may be valued.

Information about jobs in the public sector is available from the Colorado Division of Human Resources (https://www.colorado.gov/pacific/dhr/classdescriptions).

Additional Information

Information about security guard state licensing requirements is available from the Colorado Office of Economic Development and International Trade (https://www.denvergov.org/Government/Departments/Business-Licensing/Business-Licenses/Security-Services/Security-Guards).

Professional associations may serve as an additional resource. Colorado boasts several local chapters of ASIS International.

CONNECTICUT

Concealed carry honored in all states except California, Colorado, Delaware, Georgia, Hawaii, Illinois, Louisiana, Maryland, Massachusetts, Minnesota, Nevada, New Mexico, New Jersey, New York, North Dakota, Oregon, Pennsylvania, Rhode Island, South Carolina, Washington, and Wyoming and **with restrictions** (must be twenty-one years of age) in Alaska, Arizona, Kansas, Kentucky, Maine, Michigan, Oklahoma, and West Virginia.

Connecticut regulates the security service industry. In order to be hired as a security guard by a security service or business, an individual must hold a security guard certification ID. Security guards must be registered by the security service that employs them; armed guards must be registered whether they work for a security service or a proprietary entity.

In order to be hired as a security guard, an individual must have reached the age of eighteen. In order to be hired as an armed security guard, he or she must have reached the age of twenty-one. The applicant will need to demonstrate appropriate training and acceptable legal background.

Individuals can also be licensed in private security. Requirements for the private security service license are set higher. The private security licensing also entails payment of significantly higher fees.

Security Guard Certification and Registration Requirements

To receive a certification card, an individual must complete training approved by the Commissioner of Emergency Services and Public Protection. The eight-hour course covers first aid, public safety, use of force, basic criminal justice, and laws and regulations concerning search and seizure.

The eight-hour course may be waived on the basis of equivalent training completed in the National Guard or armed services. A veteran of the armed services must present qualifications within two years of discharge in order to have the course requirement waived.

Certification is also dependent on clearing a criminal background check. The applicant cannot have been convicted of a felony or sexual offense; some other offenses would be disqualifying.

Security Guard Application Process

The student can expect to be fingerprinted at course completion; the licensing agency will expect two sets, printed on the required forms.

Several fees will be due to the State of Connecticut Treasurer. The background check entails payment of two separate fees, one for $50 and the other for $14.75. Certification costs $100.

The instructor will sign the required application form. The individual is expected to provide a copy of his or her Connecticut driver's license and, if applicable, naturalization papers.

Required materials will be submitted to the Special Licensing and Firearms Unit.

Instructions are available on the website; prospective security guards should visit the "forms" section and click "Administrative Directives for Security Officer's Training Certification ID Card."

Employers must ensure that their security guards are registered. The registration form can be downloaded from the website of the Connecticut Department of Emergency Services and Public Protection.

Firearms Endorsement Requirements and Application Process

The firearms permit endorsement requires completion of an additional course. The course is to be one that has been approved by the Commissioner of Emergency Services and Public Protection; the department has published a list of instructors (http://www.ct.gov/despp/cwp/view.asp?a=4213&Q=494628&desppNav_GID=2080&desppNavPage=%7C#firearms_permit). A prospective permit holder will also receive a list when he or she makes an application request. The prospective armed guard will learn firearm safety and range training. The individual will need to pass a range test to qualify.

Students can expect to receive permit applications from their instructors; the instructor will sign that training requirements have been met. Applicants may also request forms by calling (860) 685-8160.

The armed security guard will need to complete a refresher course each year.

Private Security Service License Requirements and Application Process

In order to receive a private security service license, an individual must be at least twenty-five years of age. He or she must have either 1) five years of security experience at the supervisory level or 2) ten years of experience as a police officer. The applicant cannot, however, be a current police officer. Pertinent education may substitute for up to a year of the required experience; this is at the discretion of the licensing agency.

The professional must take out a liability insurance policy that covers $300,000. It will also be necessary to post a $10,000 performance surety bond.

The licensing agency will require evidence of education of least the high school level; general equivalency can be accepted.

The applicant will need four reference letters. The original copies are to be sent directly to the licensing agency.

The applicant will also need to provide a credit bureau report, a three-year driving record, and a copy of his or her current driver's license.

Applicants who have served in the military must provide documentation showing the type of discharge. The licensing agency can accept a DD-214 or NGB-22.

Applicants who are in psychiatric care will provide a letter from the psychiatrist or psychologist addressing license suitability.

An out-of-state licensee will provide verification of credentialing.

The licensing agency will need two passport-style photographs; specifications are found in the application directions.

A background check is required. The applicant may not have felony convictions. Some misdemeanor convictions are disqualifying.

The private security license application requires notarization. Private security service applicants can expect to be scheduled for oral interview.

The initial license fee is $1,450. The two-year renewal fee is $625. Fees are subject to change.

Additional Information

Licensing information is available from the Connecticut Department of Emergency Services and Public Protection (http://www.ct.gov/despp/cwp/view. asp?a=4213&Q=494628&desppNav_GID=2080&desppNavPage=%7C). Prospective security guards are invited to call (860) 685-8046 with their questions. They may email dps.spec.licensing at po.state.ct.us if they cannot access the form that they need.

DELAWARE

Concealed carry honored in all states except California, Connecticut, District of Columbia. Georgia, Hawaii, Illinois, Louisiana, Maryland, Massachusetts, Montana, Nebraska, Nevada, New Jersey, New York, Oregon, Pennsylvania, Rhode Island, South Carolina, Washington, and Wyoming and **with restrictions** (must be twenty-one years of age) in Alaska, Arizona, Colorado, Florida, Iowa, Kansas, Kentucky, Maine, Michigan, Minnesota, Oklahoma, Texas, Virginia, West Virginia, and Wisconsin.

Delaware's private security employees are licensed by the Delaware Department of Safety and Homeland Security. An individual qualifies after completing training, passing a competency test, and going through a background check process. A person must be at least eighteen to work as an unarmed guard and at least twenty-one to work as an armed guard. The department-issued private security license is not offered to current law enforcement employees.

The department issues a number of other licenses, including armored car guard.

Training and Examination Requirements

The prospective security officer must take a sixteen-hour course. The department has provided a list of approved instructors with contact information; a link is found on the "Professional Licensing" page of the department website (https://dsp.delaware.gov/security-guards/).

The graduate will need a training certificate signed by his or her instructor.

License is by examination. The candidate will need to score at least 75 percent on the security guard certification test. The department has published a study guide that includes content outline and sample questions. The examination covers the following:

- laws
- regulations
- use of force (including verbal force)

- ethics
- emergency services / first response
- communication / report writing
- asset protection / safety / fire
- National Terrorism Advisory System

The examination is administered by Del Tech. It is offered at four campuses, located in Dover, Georgetown, Stanton, and Wilmington. A prospective security guard can visit the Delaware Tech Workforce Development and Community website to see a list of upcoming dates and times (http://go.dtcc.edu/pro). The department has also provided a link to campus fliers.

The exam currently costs forty-nine dollars. Registration can be carried out online. The candidate may instead call 302-857-1400 for the Terry Campus, 302-259-6329 for the Georgetown Campus, or 302-454-3956 for the Stanton/George campuses.

Background Check Requirements
A security guard applicant may not have been convicted of a felony or disqualifying misdemeanor, either in Delaware or another state. Disqualifying misdemeanors are described in Title 24, Chapter 13. They include those involving theft, drugs, or moral turpitude. An individual would also be disqualified on the basis of dishonorable discharge from the military.

The applicant will need to have a fingerprint-based criminal background check. Fingerprints can be made in Kent County or New Castle County. The department has posted hours of operation for each site. The New Castle service is by appointment only; applicants may call 302-739-2528. Currently, no appointment is necessary to have fingerprints made at the Kent location. However, applicants may want to visit the department website to confirm; they may call 302-739-5871 for directions.

Armed Security Guard Requirements
A security guard who will carry a firearm must have a commissioned security guard license. In most cases, an individual will need to complete a forty-hour

course under an approved instructor. Former law officials are among those who might be exempted based on prior training.

The armed guard must have been trained in the particular type of firearm that he or she is using. The list of approved instructors displays the particular type of weapon the instructor is approved to teach. It includes not only guns but items such as chemical spray, handcuffs, and nightstick. A security guard is not to use any items that he or she has not been certified to use.

The security guard license does not authorize a security guard to carry a concealed weapon.

The Application Process

Prospective security guards may submit their applications either before or after training; school policies vary. However, applicants should be aware of maximum time lines imposed by the licensing agency. Fingerprints are valid for only thirty days.

Applications can be downloaded from the department website (https://dsp.delaware.gov/security-guards/). The department will require training and testing certificates.

The applicant must pay a nonrefundable eighty-nine dollar fee. The department notes that it typically takes at least two weeks for fingerprints to clear and that applications should wait to make status inquiries until at least this much time has elapsed.

An approved licensee will receive a security guard identification card.

Other Licenses Issued by the Professional Licensing Section

Requirements for armored car guards are the same as those for commissioned security guards; an individual must be at least twenty-one (http://delcode.delaware.gov/title24/c013/index.shtml).

To receive a security guard business license, an individual must be at least twenty-five. There are three eligibility pathways: Former police officers are eligible provided they attended police academy. An individual without police experience can achieve eligibility by attaining a management position at a security agency and accruing four years of experience. He or she may instead demonstrate five years of investigative experience.

To be eligible for an armored car guard license, an individual will need four years of experience at the managerial level working for an armored car agency.

Professionals who go into business in either capacity will need to take out insurance policies and post surety bonds.

Additional Information

Private security employee licensing information is available from the Delaware Department of Safety and Homeland Security. Licensure and practice are governed by the Private Investigators and Private Security Agencies Act (http://delcode.delaware.gov/title24/c013/index.shtml).

The Delaware Chapter of ASIS International is a state professional organization (https://delawareasis.com/).

DISTRICT OF COLUMBIA

Concealed carry honored in all states except Alabama, California, Colorado, Connecticut, Delaware, Florida, Georgia, Hawaii, Illinois, Louisiana, Maryland, Massachusetts, Minnesota, Montana, Nevada, New Jersey, New Mexico, New York, North Carolina, North Dakota, Oregon, Pennsylvania, Rhode Island, South Carolina, Texas, Utah, Washington, and Wyoming and **with restrictions** (must be twenty-one years of age) in Alaska, Arizona, Kansas, Kentucky, Maine, Michigan, Oklahoma, and West Virginia.

DC security officers are certified by the Department of Consumer and Regulatory Affairs (DCRA) in cooperation with the Security Officers Management Branch (SOMB). Security officers receive the same designation whether they work for security agencies or provide services directly to an employer.

To be license eligible, one must meet health and background screening requirements. Certification also depends on completing mandatory training and passing an examination. Some aspects of the certification process are handled by a third party organization, Pearson VUE.

Security guards may receive temporary certification before all requirements have been met.

The District of Columbia recognizes a related occupation "special police." Special police have limited scope. They may work for corporations. Requirements are slightly higher than for security officers. Special police may be authorized to carry weapons. In this regard, there is some similarity between the DC "special police" designation and the "armed security guard" or "commissioned security guard" designation recognized in some other jurisdictions. DC special police, though, may be appointed to assist with special events like elections. Some special police are designated as campus security.

Eligibility Standards for Security Officers

Security guards must be at least eighteen years of age and competent in the English language; they must be able to read and write the language as well as speak it. A prospective security guard who is not a US citizen will need a valid work permit.

The security guard may not be addicted to drugs or alcohol and may not have a debilitating mental disorder or physical condition that could result in loss of control during extreme situations; epilepsy would be an example of the latter. The prospective security guard is to have a physical and provide documentation from his or her physician; results are to be from some point during the prior ninety-day period.

The prospective security guard can expect a drug test. An applicant who tests positive for any drug will need to provide documentation from a prescribing physician.

The candidate will also need to have an FBI background check. A criminal history is not always disqualifying. The nature of the crime, the amount of time that has elapsed, and the applicant's rehabilitation and motivation are among the factors that may be considered.

Applicants who have arrest histories will need to provide the disposition.

Background check results will be made known to the agency or employer.

Training and Examination Requirements for Security Officers

The security guard will need at least twenty-four hours of preassignment training. Preassignment training must include terrorism awareness, emergency procedures, and customer service. Terrorism awareness includes responding to unknown substances and unattended packages. Emergency procedures include first aid and evacuation.

The security guard must have an additional sixteen hours of training during his or her first ninety days on the job. Thereafter, the security officer will need to do eight hours a year of in-service.

The candidate must pass the Security Officers Examination. Examination information is found on the "District of Columbia Security" page of the Pearson VUE website (http://www.pearsonvue.com/dc/security). Candidates may call PSI at (800) 733-9267 to schedule. Examinations are administered at the Department of Consumer and Regulatory Affairs (DCRA) Occupational and Professional Licensing Administration office.

Requirements for Special Police

DC special police must be at least twenty-one years of age. They must be citizens of the United States. Those who will be carrying firearms must have range testing. The employing agency will need to specify the particular firearm(s) the individual can use.

Special police who have military backgrounds must document the type of discharge.

Special police, like security officers, must have health and drug screenings. They are not currently required to pass a written examination.

The Application Process

The hiring process and certification process are closely related. Individuals may receive applications from their employing agencies.

Applications, supplemental forms, and instructions can also be downloaded from Pearson VUE (http://www.pearsonvue.com/dc/security). Pearson VUE has provided an instructional document that outlines which documents are to be submitted to Pearson and which are submitted directly to the DC government.

The application itself will be submitted to Pearson VUE. Pearson VUE will require a copy of an ID, a birth certificate or passport, two small photographs, and documentation of name changes. Pearson VUE will also receive documentation from the physician of physical and mental fitness. Applicants for the special police will submit their DD-214 (if applicable) to Pearson VUE.

Information release forms and arrest affidavits are among the documents that will be provided directly to the governmental agency. Both require notarization.

Fingerprinting is typically carried out at the SOMB office (though a nonlocal applicant may instead submit two fingerprint cards through the mail). The applicant will provide other required documents when he or she shows up at the SOMB office. In addition to the information release form and arrest affidavit, the applicant will provide 1) drug screening results and 2) examination results or range test results and an approved gun list (if applicable).

The licensing agency notes that candidates may in the future apply online.

The licensing process entails payment of several fees. Thirty-five dollars is paid to the DC Treasurer; this covers the criminal history check. A security officer applicant will pay $103 to Pearson VUE; this includes a $65 application fee and $38 license fee.

An approved security guard will receive a certification card.

Additional Information

Security guard regulations are contained in Chapter 21 of Title 17 of the state code; special police regulations are contained in Chapter 6A-11. Some additional information is available from the Security Officers Management Branch (http://mpdc.dc.gov/page/security-officers-management-branch-somb).

Detailed information about the examination and application process is available from Pearson VUE. Applicants with questions may call Pearson VUE at (888) 204-6293.

ASIS International-National Capital Chapter is a professional organization for security professionals (http://www.asis-capital.org).

FLORIDA

Concealed carry honored in all states except California, Connecticut, District of Columbia, Hawaii, Illinois, Maryland, Massachusetts, Minnesota, New Jersey, New York, Oregon, Rhode Island, and Washington and **with restrictions** (must be twenty-one years of age) in Alabama, Alaska, Arizona, Colorado, Georgia, Indiana, Kansas, Kentucky, Louisiana, Maine, Michigan, Nebraska, Nevada, New Mexico, North Carolina, Ohio, Oklahoma, Pennsylvania, South Carolina, Tennessee, Texas, Virginia, West Virginia, Wisconsin, and Wyoming.

Florida security guards are licensed by the Florida Department of Agriculture and Consumer Services Division of Licensing. Security guards must be licensed unless they fall under exemption categories described in the state statute. The basic security officer license for individuals is "Class D." A security officer who carries a firearm will also need a "Class G" firearm license.

Florida also licenses professionals who provide management services for security agencies. These professionals may hold a "Class M" or "Class MB" manager license; some security agency / branch officers will also need a Class G firearm license.

Basic Eligibility Requirements

Licensees must meet certain basic requirements. They must be at least eighteen years old and must be citizens or hold other appropriate work eligibility documentation. They must be mentally competent and free of addictions.

The licensee will need to have an acceptable legal background. A criminal history is not disqualifying in all instances. An individual convicted of a felony might be found eligible if ten years has passed since he or she completed supervision. However, an adverse legal history could be disqualifying even without a felony conviction. Standards are described in the application instruction file.

A noncitizen who will carry firearms must document permanent residency and provide evidence of having lived in the state for at least ninety days.

Class D Security Guard Training Requirements

A prospective security officer will complete a program that meets standards described in the state administrative code (https://www.flrules.org/gateway/ChapterHome.asp?Chapter=5N-1). It may be taken through a department-licensed training program or school.

The curriculum is divided into two parts. The first is twenty-four hours. The second is sixteen hours. Competency will be assessed by examination.

Additional Requirements for a Class G Firearms License

In most cases, a security guard who will carry firearms will need to complete a twenty-eight-hour course to earn his or her Class G license. The course will be taught by a professional who holds a Class K firearm instructor license.

The course will teach a state-mandated curriculum (http://www.freshfromflorida.com/Divisions-Offices/Licensing/Private-Investigation/Private-Investigation-and-Firearms/G-License-Classroom-and-Range-Requirements). Legal aspects of use will comprise twelve hours. Safety and mechanics will comprise another eleven hours; this portion will culminate in a written test. Up to eight hours will be credited for firearms qualification; this portion will include practical exercises and qualifying rounds.

Some individuals will be exempted from taking the mandated twenty-eight-hour course based on training they received as law enforcement officers or correctional offers. Those who qualify for firearm instructor licenses can also be exempted.

License holders will need to requalify each year. The armed security officer will be qualified for a particular type of firearm (http://www.freshfromflorida.com/Divisions-Offices/Licensing/Private-Security-and-Firearms).

The Application Process

Applicants may request applications or download them from the website (https://licensing.freshfromflorida.com/forms/FormsRequest493.aspx). The application file includes a copy of relevant state statutes.

The applicant will need to provide a small photograph; a sample is included in the application instruction handbook.

The licensing agency will require documentation of having met training requirements.

The applicant will need to have a fingerprint-based criminal background check. He or she may opt to have fingerprints made electronically using Live Scan technology. The department has provided lists of sheriff's offices, regional offices, and private vendors that provide the service (http://www.freshfromflorida.com/Divisions-Offices/Licensing/Private-Investigation/Submitting-Fingerprints-Electronically/Submitting-Fingerprints-Electronically-for-Chapter-493-Licenses). Costs may vary. Regional offices currently charge forty-two dollars. Sheriff's offices charge approximately thirty-five dollars, though the cost may be higher at some locations. Applicants are invited to call (850) 245-5691 with questions they may have about the process.

The department can also accept fingerprints submitted on inked cards. Instructions are included in the application packet.

Applicants who have been licensed as security officers in other states will provide the name of the state and the period of licensure.

Applicants with histories of drug or alcohol abuse will provide references as well as evidence of rehabilitation. Those who have been diagnosed with mental illness are directed to provide documentation of fitness from a Florida psychiatrist or psychologist.

The applicant will sign a waiver, allowing the licensing agency to carry out various investigations that could be necessary, including an examination of school records.

A security guard pays a $45 license fee. The firearm license fee is $112. The application form requires notarization.

Security and Firearm Instructor Licenses

A Class DI instructor licensee will need to hold licensing as a security guard for at least three years to achieve eligibility unless he or she has other qualifying education or experience.

The licensing agency can accept a degree at the bachelor's level or higher in a related field such as education or criminal justice; an associate's degree is qualifying if combined with a year of security officer licensure. A professional can also qualify based on military law enforcement or security experience or on completion of a law enforcement training program, provided that the training was at the required level. A security professional who is licensed at the managerial level (Class M or MB) is eligible if he or she can also demonstrate some licensed management experience.

Individuals can be qualified to teach in certain limited roles based on training in fields such as nursing, emergency medicine / paramedicine, or firefighting.

A Class K firearms instructor must 1) pass a department-administered examination or 2) demonstrate firearm instructor certification from the Florida Criminal Justice Standards and Training Commission or a federal law enforcement agency or 3) earn a National Rifle Association Private Security Firearm Instructor Certificate (http://www.freshfromflorida.com/Divisions-Offices/Licensing/Private-Investigation/Private-Investigation-and-Firearms/K-License-Proof-of-Training-Required).

Additional Information

Licensing information is available from the Florida Department of Agriculture and Consumer Services Division of Licensing (https://www.fdacs.gov/Divisions-Offices/Licensing/Private-Security-Licenses). *The Security Officer Handbook* provides a detailed description of requirements (https://licensing.freshfromflorida.com/forms/FormsRequest493.aspx). The Division of Licensing can be reached by telephone at (850) 245-5691.

GEORGIA

Concealed carry honored in all states except California, Connecticut, Delaware, District of Columbia, Hawaii, Illinois, Maryland, Massachusetts, Minnesota, Nebraska, Nevada, New Jersey, New Mexico, New York, Oregon, Rhode Island, and Washington and **with restrictions** (must be twenty-one years of age) in Alaska, Arizona, Colorado, Florida, Kansas, Kentucky, Louisiana, Maine, Michigan, Oklahoma, Pennsylvania, South Carolina, Virginia, and West Virginia.

Georgia security guards are under the jurisdiction of the Georgia Board of Private Detectives and Security Agencies. Armed security guards must register with the state. They will undergo thorough background checks.

Unarmed guards do not have to register but must meet training requirements set by the state.

Professionals who operate security agencies must also meet requirements set by the state.

Training Requirements for Unarmed Guards
Training requirements are described in state rules and regulations (http://rules.sos.state.ga.us/cgi-bin/page.cgi?g=GEORGIA_BOARD_OF_PRIVATE_DETECTIVE_AND_SECURITY_AGENCIES_%2Findex.html&d=1). An unarmed private security guard will complete a program of at least twenty-four hours. The following topics will receive coverage:
- private security role
- legal aspects
- observation and patrol
- security resources
- incident response
- first aid overview
- customer service

The instructor will be a professional who is certified by the state. Typically, this is someone who has supervisory experience or law enforcement experience. A person may find instructors by doing a licensee search; he or she can get started by selecting "online services."

Additional Requirements for Armed Guards

An armed guard must complete at least fifteen hours of additional education (http://rules.sos.state.ga.us/docs/509/3/10.pdf). The instructor will be board-licensed.

A handgun course will include the following:
- liability issues
- use of deadly force
- types of handgun
- ballistics
- range training

The individual will initially need to pass two tests. One is a written exam, the other a test of firing range. Both must be passed with scores of at least 80 percent. In the case of the firing test, two strings will be fired. The highest score will be the qualifier. Prospective armed guards must qualify with the type of weapon that they will be carrying on the job.

If the employee will carry a shotgun or concealed weapon, the employer must make a special request, detailing duties and providing justification. Training requirements for shotguns are also described in administrative rules.

The Armed Guard Application Process

Armed guard registration is agency specific. The registration application will be submitted by the employing agency, but the prospective armed guard will need to complete much of the application. The licensing agency will require a five-year employment and address history.

An applicant who has a criminal or disciplinary history will need to submit certified documents, such as court dispositions or agency orders.

The licensing agency will seek a copy of the training certificate. The employer will also affirm, in a notarized statement, that the individual has had the required security guard training.

The application package includes additional forms that require employee notarization.

The registration package can be downloaded from the board website (http://sos.ga.gov/cgi-bin/plbforms.asp?board=31).

It costs seventy dollars to register an armed security employee.

Application status can be monitored online (https://secure.sos.state.ga.us/PLB_appStatus).

Criminal Background Check Process

The applicant will be required to have a fingerprint-based background check. He or she will have fingerprints made through the approved vendor, Cogent. Cogent has provided a map of electronic fingerprinting locations. Registration can be carried out online (https://www.aps.gemalto.com/ga/index.htm).

Applicants who are unable to visit an electronic fingerprinting site will need to submit their fingerprint cards to Cogent for processing (https://www.aps.gemalto.com/ga/index.htm). It will be necessary to preregister.

Requirements to Operate a Security Business

A professional who wishes to operate a security business must apply to the board for licensure. There are several eligibility pathways (http://rules.sos.state.ga.us/docs/509/2/02.pdf). The individual may qualify with four years of experience in law enforcement or two years of managerial or supervisory experience in the security industry. The board will also accept a degree at the baccalaureate level in criminal justice or acceptable related field. If the degree is not specifically in criminal justice, the licensing agency will review the coursework.

The individual will need to pass a prelicensure examination. The candidate will first submit a license application. If approved, he or she will receive registration information from PSI. The examination is currently $125 (https://candidate.psiexams.com/catalog/fap_test_details.jsp?testid=1790&prev_page=/catalog/fap_test_catalog_details.jsp).

The licensing agency will require one of the following: a surety bond, liability insurance policy, or certified financial statement indicating net worth of at least $50,000. This is not due until post examination. Details are found in the application packet.

A partnership, corporation, or other association can be licensed as a security business. There will, however, need to be an officer who meets requirements set by the state (http://sos.ga.gov/plb/acrobat/Laws/31_Priv_ Detective_and_Security_43-38.pdf). The designee will complete the application.

The License Application Process

Application materials can be found on the board website (http://sos.ga.gov/ cgi-bin/plbforms.asp?board=31).

An individual who has held a supervisory position with a security agency or in-house supervisory operation will need to provide a notarized letter from his or her employer.

An applicant/designee who is applying on the basis of academic degree will need to provide certified transcripts.

There is an application fee of one hundred dollars and a license fee of five hundred dollars. Applicants are advised to read the requirements before submitting materials.

Fingerprints can be made before application submission. The ORI number is included in the application packet.

Applicants are advised to provide email addresses.

Additional Information

Information about security guard requirements, including license exemptions, is available from the Georgia Board of Private Detectives and Security Agencies (http://sos.ga.gov/index.php/licensing/plb/42). The board can be reached by telephone at 404-656-2881. The Investigative and Security Professional Association of Georgia Inc. (https://sos.ga.gov/index.php/licensing/plb/42) is an additional professional resource.

HAWAII

Concealed carry honored in all states except California, Colorado, Connecticut, Delaware, District of Columbia, Georgia, Illinois, Louisiana, Maryland, Massachusetts, Minnesota, Montana, Nevada, New Jersey, New Mexico, New York, North Dakota, Oregon, Pennsylvania, Rhode Island, South Carolina, Washington, and Wyoming and **with restrictions** (must be twenty-one years of age) in Alaska, Arizona, Kansas, Kentucky, Maine, Oklahoma, and West Virginia.

Hawaii's security guards are under the jurisdiction of the Board of Private Detectives and Guards, a part of Hawaii Professional and Vocational Licensing (PVL).

The licensing agency makes a distinction between individuals who are in business as security guards or are the "principal guard" of a firm and those who are merely employees. The former are licensed, the latter registered. Both are subject to state requirements. Licensed security guards must meet experience requirements.

Professional and Vocational Licensing has provided a list of job positions that are subject to registration requirements as well as a list of positions that are exempt (http://cca.hawaii.gov/pvl/boards/private/act_208_guard_employee/).

Requirements for Security Guard Employment Registration
Hawaii requires guards employed by security agencies to be at least eighteen and have a high school diploma or equivalent education. They will need to clear criminal background checks (https://cca.hawaii.gov/pvl/boards/private/act_208_guard_employee/security-guard-training/initial-8-hour-training/). A prospective registrant cannot have a current psychiatric disorder that would negatively impact his or her ability to practice the profession.
The prospective guard will need to complete an eight-hour board-approved course before beginning service. PVL has provided a list of approved instructors (http://cca.hawaii.gov/pvl/boards/private/act_208_guard_employee). Training may be provided directly by the security company.

The following topics will be covered:

- laws and rules
- patrol
- screening of entrants
- incident investigation and documentation
- fire procedures
- evacuation procedures
- use of force
- arrest and evidence
- court testimony

Security guard employees will need to meet a continuing education requirement during each renewal period.

Security guards who will carry guns must obtain an additional permit.

Requirements for Security Guard Licensure

In order for a sole proprietor or principal to be licensed as a guard, he or she must demonstrate four years of qualifying work experience. The licensing agency can accept experience earned as an employee of a government agency or private employer or under the supervision of a licensed guard. The licensing agency can also accept experience as a police officer.

The licensee will need to pass an examination and go through an oral interview process; this step is subsequent to application. The written test covers laws and rules as well as security guard knowledge. The examination is administered in Oahu. Upcoming examination dates are available online (http://cca.hawaii.gov/pvl/boards/private/application-deadline-examination-dates/).

The licensing agency has provided a link to study materials; this is found in the "publications" section. The minimum score is 75 percent. Reexamination is permitted. However, a mandatory ninety-day wait time will be imposed after two failed attempts.

Hawaii requires licensees to maintain bonds through authorized sureties.

Background Check Requirements

Hawaii requires background checks of both licensees and registrants. Background checks are processed by the Hawaii Criminal Justice Data Center and the FBI.

Applicants will have their fingerprints processed by the approved vendor, Fieldprint. They begin the process by registering; registration can be carried out online. Fieldprint has provided a list of fingerprint locations within Hawaii (http://fieldprinthawaii.com/SubPage_2col.aspx?ChannelID=230).

The Guard Employee Application Process

Registration applications can be downloaded from the PVL website (http://cca.hawaii.gov/pvl/boards/private/application_publications/).

Currently, security guard employees may use any of multiple documents to document high school education or equivalency. The following may be accepted:

- high school transcript
- copy of high school diploma or college degree
- military DD-214
- statement from the Department of Education

Prospective registrants who cannot produce other documentation may submit a notarized statement from an employer, past or present, documenting four years of work experience that utilized the required academic skills. The employer will need to verify, among other things, that the individual has the ability to write factual reports. The applicant can download a "Statement of Educational Background" form from the PVL website.

Applicants who have psychological or psychiatric conditions will need to submit a status letter from a health provider as well as an explanation of the disorder.

Those with criminal histories will need to provide supporting documentation, including letters of recommendation. Those with disciplinary histories will need to provide explanation.

Detailed instructions are provided in the application packet.

Fees for registrants are prorated according to the stage in the renewal cycle.

Applications are to be mailed or hand-delivered to the board office in Honolulu.

The Security Guard Application Process

Guard applications are also posted on the PVL website.

At this level, the board will expect one of the following to verify high school or equivalency:

- high school transcript
- copy of high school or college diploma
- letter from the Department of Education verifying equivalency

Prospective licensees will have their qualifying experience verified through a notarized employer statement. They will note whether they will be a principal or sole proprietor. A principal may later file for change of status if circumstances change.

Individuals with psychological or psychiatric conditions will need to provider a letter of recommendation from an employer; this is in addition to the explanatory materials and health-care status letter required at the employee level.

Individuals who answer "yes" to questions about adverse legal or professional history or unlicensed activity will need to provide supporting documentation. Those with criminal records are directed to provide letters of recommendation.

Applicants should be aware that there is a separate application process for security agencies.

The application package references laws and rules that the individual is expected to be familiar with.

License applicants should include a fifty-dollar application fee and fifty-dollar examination fee. They should submit materials at least thirty days before a scheduled board meeting.

Additional Information

Information about security guard requirements is available from Professional and Vocational Licensing (http://cca.hawaii.gov/pvl/boards/private). Licensure is governed by statute and rule (http://cca.hawaii.gov/pvl/boards/private/statute_rules/).

Requirements are subject to change. The licensing agency notes that individuals are subject to the requirements that are in place at the time of application. Applicants with questions about licensing requirements can call (808) 586-3000.

IDAHO

Concealed carry honored in all states except California, Connecticut, District of Columbia, Illinois, Maryland, Massachusetts, New Jersey, New York, Oregon, and Rhode Island and **with restrictions** (must be twenty-one years of age) in Alaska, Arizona, Colorado, Delaware, Florida, Kansas, Kentucky, Louisiana, Maine, Michigan, Minnesota, Nebraska, Nevada, Oklahoma, Pennsylvania, South Carolina, Virginia, Washington, West Virginia, and Wisconsin.

The state of Idaho does not license armed or unarmed security guards. Individual municipalities, however, do have regulations in place. Security guards in cities such as Boise and Lewiston answer to a city authority as well as an individual employer.

Prospective security guards can expect to meet some standard requirements regardless of whether they are licensed. The minimum age is eighteen; this is the standard nationwide. Employees typically have background checks. Employers also look for a high school diploma or several years of meaningful work history.

City Security Guard Mandates

Multiple Idaho cities regulate the security industry. They use different titles for security personnel. Requirements vary slightly from city to city.

Boise licenses patrol services and patrol agents (http://cityclerk.cityofboise.org/licensing/patrol-services/Prospective). Security guards must be at least eighteen. They cannot have recent convictions for felonies or for misdemeanors involving dishonesty or theft; any sentence must have been completed at least three years in the past. Individuals who provide security for special events are exempt from licensing requirements but must have background checks. Security services must be covered by insurance policies and bonds. Agents must hold bonds if they are not covered by employer bond.

Idaho Falls licenses private patrol services and private patrol persons (http://www.idahofallsidaho.gov/city/city-departments/city-attorney/city-code.html). Like many jurisdictions, Idaho Falls makes some individuals exempt from licensure. In Idaho Falls, guards employed by "interstate or intrastate carriers" are among those exempt. The minimum age for licensees is twenty-one. Patrol persons must be citizens. Individuals are ineligible if they have been convicted of felonies or of other crimes involving "moral turpitude." Security services and patrol persons are to have their services guaranteed through bonds and insurance policies.

Lewiston licenses security guard services and individual security guards. The license service must provide a list of employees and carry out background checks.

Security guards in other municipalities may want to check with their city clerk.

Requirements Set by Security Agencies

Even in situations where the main responsible party is the employer, expectations make their way down to the level of the individual employee. Services may have a good deal of financial investment in the conduct of employees. They may have insurance policies that cover employees and contractors.

Many large security agencies operate across state lines; they may set standards far above those of local statutes and ordinances. A high school diploma or GED is typically the minimum educational level. Prospective hires may need to have comprehensive physicals and undergo drug screenings. Employers may cite a number of physical and verbal/communication skills.

Job expectations can vary a good deal. In some positions, security officers have frequent interaction with the public. Employers may value customer service experience. Many positions favor those with military, police, or corrections experience. An individual with a degree in criminal justice may also be given consideration.

Requirements for Public Sector Employment

State workers may patrol campuses or oversee security at special events. Although the public sector represents only a portion of security jobs, state job descriptions give some sense of what is required or desired in the security industry.

Idaho boasts multiple security classifications, including security officer and senior security officer. Security officer is the entry-level position, though some positions may require experience as a dispatcher. A security officer is expected to have some knowledge of security procedures. He or she should also have the ability to write reports. Human resources cites a number of physical skills that may be necessary, such as carrying incapacitated persons and standing and walking for up to eight hours. The department notes that some positions may require background checks and psychological evaluations. CPR certification is required, if not before hiring, within six months after.

A senior security officer position, unlike a security officer position, may require an individual to earn firearm qualifications or qualifications for "less lethal weapons." Some positions will be open only to individuals with law enforcement training. Requirements will depend on the particular position.

A security officer supervisor is expected to understand safety issues as they relate to large building complexes. A candidate is expected have had some experience training others as well as carrying out other duties, such as writing reports and making oral presentations.

The Idaho Division of Human Resources website provides information about general expectations in the public sector (https://www.governmentjobs.com/careers/idaho). Additional information is available when there are job vacancies.

Expectations for Armed Security Guards

Requirements for armed positions can be particularly stringent. An armed security officer typically has to be at least twenty-one. He or she must go through a comprehensive background check. The security agency may require personality testing.

A recent ad for an armed security officer in Boise listed multiple eligibility avenues, including military or security experience, an academic degree, or completion of the Police Officer's Standard Training (POST) course but noted that successful candidates from the past have had considerable military or police experience. Firing range was to be assessed by testing.

ILLINOIS

Concealed carry honored in all states except California, Colorado, Connecticut, Delaware, District of Columbia, Florida, Georgia, Hawaii, Louisiana, Maryland, Massachusetts, New Jersey, New Mexico, New York, North Dakota, Oregon, Pennsylvania, Rhode Island, South Carolina, Washington, and Wyoming and **with restrictions** (must be twenty-one years of age) in Alaska, Arizona, Kansas, Kentucky, Maine, Michigan, Oklahoma, and West Virginia.

Illinois recognizes security professionals in a variety of roles, including employees of security contractor agencies, employees of proprietary security forces, and private security contractors. Requirements vary according to employment circumstance. Some state mandates apply to professionals in multiple categories while others apply to only one.

Requirements are particularly stringent for private security contractors. They hold licensing as opposed to registration. In order to be license-eligible, security professionals must have supervisory experience. The licensing process is more expensive; licensees are required to carry insurance policies and pay higher fees.

An employee or guard who will be carrying a firearm will need an additional credential: a firearm control card.

Training Requirements for Security Guard Employees

Illinois has a basic training requirement for employees of security agencies (whether armed or unarmed) and for employees of proprietary security forces (when armed). The worker will need twenty hours of basic training during his or her first thirty days on the job (http://www.ilga.gov/commission/jcar/admincode/068/068012400F05050R.html).

Guards employed by private security contractor agencies will need an additional eight hours of training within their first six months.

Attaining a Permanent Employee Registration Card

An individual who is working in an unarmed capacity may be as young as eighteen years old. He or she must meet fitness requirements. A criminal history is not always disqualifying. The division will consider a number of factors (http://www.ilga.gov/commission/jcar/admincode/068/068012400F05250R.html).

The individual will submit the application along with background check materials and a fifty-five-dollar fee. A photograph will be required unless the applicant is granted an exception for religious reasons. Application materials and instructions are available online (https://www.idfpr.com/renewals/SecurityCont.asp).

Requirements for a Firearm Control Card

Armed security employees must be at least twenty-one.

A security employee who will carry a firearm will need to complete a forty-hour training course.

The prospective armed security employee can expect a written test and range test.

The Illinois firearm training requirement can be waived on the basis of law enforcement training. If the training was completed out-of-state, the professional will need to submit a detailed description.

An individual who holds Illinois firearm instructor registration can also be granted a waiver.

Firearm control card application materials are available from the IDFPR (https://www.idfpr.com/profs/SecurityCont.asp). There is a seventy-five-dollar application processing fee.

Background Check Requirements

Background checks are required for contractor licensure and for employee registration.

In-state candidates have their fingerprints made electronically through the Illinois State Police. The division has provided a vendor list (https://www.idfpr.com/LicenseLookUp/fingerprintlist.asp). Out-of-state candidates should request a fingerprint card from the Illinois State Police. They may call 1-800-560-6420.

An out-of-state candidate who uses hard copies will need to submit a certifying statement; the form is found in the application packet.

Private Security Contractor Requirements

Private security contractors must be at least twenty-one years of age. They must have supervisory experience, though business or police-related education may substitute for a portion of the usual experience requirement.

Without qualifying education, a professional will need three full years of experience at the supervisory level. The licensing agency can accept experience with a contract security agency or a security fleet that has at least thirty individuals registered. The licensing agency can also accept supervisory experience in 1) the security unit of a corporation that has at least one hundred employees or 2) a military police / security unit or law enforcement unit; the latter category may include political subdivisions, such as the public defender's office.

The licensing agency may credit security supervisory experience accrued in another state if it is determined to be substantially equivalent.

The licensing agency can credit two years of experience for a baccalaureate degree in police science or a field related to police science. An individual with a business degree can also be credited with two years of experience. If the business or police science degree is at the associate level, the professional can be credited with one year. A nondegree police science (or related) program may be credited as a year if it is judged to be comparable to an associate program.

The applicant cannot have been convicted of a felony during the prior ten years. Additionally, he or she must be judged to have good character. Applicants can be disqualified on the basis of criminal history even if they have not been convicted of a felony during the prior decade. However, the process is not automatic. Various factors may be taken into account.

The contractor will need to take out a liability insurance policy. The amount is established in the administrative code (http://www.ilga.gov/commission/jcar/admincode/068/068012400C02000R.html).

The prospective contractor will need to pass an examination with a score of at least 70 percent (http://www.ilga.gov/commission/jcar/admincode/068/068012400C02000R.html). The security contractor examination includes state and federal law, security practice, and license and practice requirements. A study guide is available online (https://www.idfpr.com/renewals/SecurityCont.asp).

The examination is taken after application. It is available from Continental Testing Service (CTS). Individuals can visit the CTS website to find the date of the next available examination (http://www.continentaltesting.net/ProfDetail.aspx?Entity=2&ProfID=26). The fee is listed as $298.

The Private Security Contractor Application Process
A prospective contractor may download application materials from the website (https://www.idfpr.com/renewals/SecurityCont.asp). The applicant will select either the "experience" application packet or the "education and experience" education packet. The applicant may submit an application online through CTS.

The experience form is to be included in a sealed envelope.

A security professional who is using the education and experience pathway will need to have the educational form completed by a school official. The completed form is to bear the school seal (or notary seal/signature).

A professional who has held private security licensure in another state will need to have a form filled out by the state(s) of licensure.

The licensing agency no longer issues licenses by endorsement; candidates must, in all cases, pass an examination (http://www.idfpr.com/News/2013/DetAlrmEndorsementNotice08092013.pdf).

The license fee is five hundred dollars. An individual who has passed the required examination has the option of deferring licensure and fee payment.

Additional Information

Licensing and registration information is available from the Illinois Department of Financial and Professional Regulation (https://www.idfpr.com/profs/SecurityCont.asp). Individuals with questions may call 1-800-560-6420 or use the IDFPR email contact form (https://www.idfpr.com/PROFS/EMAIL/prfgrp04.asp).

INDIANA

Concealed carry honored in all states except California, Connecticut, Delaware, District of Columbia, Hawaii, Illinois, Maryland, Massachusetts, Minnesota, Nebraska, Nevada, New Jersey, New Mexico, New York, Oregon, Rhode Island, South Carolina, and Washington and **with restrictions** (must be twenty-one years of age) in Alaska, Arizona, Colorado, Florida, Iowa, Kansas, Kentucky, Louisiana, Maine, Michigan, Oklahoma, Pennsylvania, Texas, Virginia, West Virginia, and Wisconsin.

Security guard employees are not required to hold licensing. However, they will need to be fingerprinted by the employing agency. The agency must have fingerprints on record. The licensing agency has stated that the "qualifier" or licensee is civilly responsible for employee conduct.

To head a private security business in Indiana, one must be state licensed. The Indiana Private Investigator and Security Guard Licensing Board has set a high set of standards for the responsible party of a security agency, whether proprietor or manager. The professional must have either 1) a baccalaureate degree in a field related to criminal justice or 2) two years of qualifying experience.

Security guard licenses do not authorize the use of firearms. Individuals are directed to the Indiana State Police with questions about the carrying of firearms (http://www.in.gov/pla/3087.htm).

Education and Experience Requirements for Private Security Licensees
A licensee will need to have reached the age of at least twenty-one. He or she must meet education or experience requirements. The professional may qualify on the basis of a criminal justice or related degree accredited by the Commission on Accreditation of Criminal Justice Programs or by any of six regional accrediting institutions.

The professional may also achieve eligibility through two years (four thousand hours) of qualifying experience. There are multiple security and investigations-related options. If the experience is in private security, it will need to be at the management or administrative level. The board can accept experience in a security agency or a proprietary security fleet that has at least twenty employees. The board may consider experience in cases where there were fewer employees; experience will need to be judged to be equivalent. The board can also accept experience earned in the following roles:

- private investigator
- manager or supervisor of a private investigation company
- sheriff's investigator
- investigator for the US Department of the Treasury or the US Department of Justice
- claims investigator
- armed forces criminal investigator
- military or security police
- attorney or investigator for an attorney
- law enforcement officer
- railroad police or investigator

If the agency is a partnership, at least one partner must be qualified. If it is a corporation, at least one officer must meet the requirements. This individual may be referred to as the "qualifier."

Background Check Requirements

Prospective licensees can expect thorough background screening. Felonies are disqualifying. Misdemeanors are disqualifying if they are determined to have "direct bearing" on the ability to practice the profession.

All applicants will need to have a fingerprint-based background check carried out by the Indiana State Police. Fingerprints are to be processed by the approved vendor, MorphoTrust. There are electronic fingerprinting sites located throughout the state; the list is organized by region (http://www.l1enrollment.com/locations/?st=in). Candidates can register online (http://www.identogo.com/FP/Indiana.aspx). They may instead call (877) 472-6917.

The applicant will also need to provide a background check, or CBC, from each state, county, and city of residence for the prior seven years. In the case of military applicants, a DD-214 can be accepted. The applicant will, however, need to provide CBCs for postdischarge residences.

The licensing agency has provided detailed instructions about the background check process (http://www.in.gov/pla/3089.htm).

Liability Insurance Requirements

The licensee will need liability insurance. The policy is to cover at least $100,000 in damages (http://www.in.gov/pla/3467.htm). The licensing agency notes that an applicant does not have to obtain the policy until after application acceptance. However, the license cannot be issued until the certificate of insurance is in hand.

The Application Process

Application materials can be downloaded from the website of the Professional Licensing Agency (http://www.in.gov/pla/3766.htm).

The experience verification form is to be completed by an employer. In the case of military experience, a DD-214 will suffice. Academic education is verified through official transcripts.

The applicant will attach a passport-quality photograph to the application. Applicants who answer "yes" to legal or professional history questions will need to provide notarized statements. Court documents must also be provided (if applicable).

Applicants who have held other professional licenses during the prior ten years are asked to provide official license verification; this is the case even with out-of-state licenses in unrelated fields, such as real estate.

The agency licensing fee is $300. It may be prorated to $150 depending on the stage of the current renewal cycle.

Application materials are to be sent to the following address:
Indiana Professional Licensing Agency
Attn: Private Investigator and Security Guard Board
402 West Washington Street, Room W072
Indianapolis, IN 46204

Applications cannot be reviewed without the required fee, background check results, and documentation of required experience. The completed application should arrive no less than a week before a scheduled board meeting; the licensing agency has published a list of upcoming meeting dates (http://www.in.gov/pla/3088.htm). The application will first be reviewed for administrative completeness by a customer service representative. If there is missing documentation, the applicant will receive email documentation.

The board may attach any of the following statuses to an application: approved, approved pending, tabled, or denied. "Approved pending" means there is something that must be submitted prior to issuance. If it is "tabled," there are concerns, and the applicant may be asked to appear before the board.

It will be necessary to submit a new application for an existing security agency if there is a new qualifier.

Additional Information
The Indiana Private Investigator and Security Licensing Board is under the banner of the Professional Licensing Agency (http://www.in.gov/pla/pisg. htm). Licensing staff can be reached by telephone at (317) 234-3022 or by email at pla10 at pla.in.gov.

IOWA

Concealed carry honored in all states except California, Connecticut, Delaware, District of Columbia, Hawaii, Illinois, Maryland, Massachusetts, Minnesota, Nevada, New Jersey, New Mexico, New York, Oregon, Rhode Island, South Carolina, and Washington and **with restrictions** (must be twenty-one years of age) in Alaska, Arizona, Colorado, Florida, Kansas, Kentucky, Maine, Michigan, Nebraska, Oklahoma, Pennsylvania, and West Virginia.

Iowa security officers are under the jurisdiction of the Department of Public Safety. Professionals who operate security agencies are licensed. Employees of security agencies are issued identification cards upon verification that they meet state mandates.

Both licensees and employees must meet character and background requirements. Additionally, licensees must take financial responsibility for business operations and conduct.

Security officers who will carry weapons must also obtain a firearms permit. For this, the Iowa legislature has set both general eligibility and training requirements.

Unarmed Security Officer Employee Requirements and Registration Process

A security agency employee must have a background check. There is a ten-dollar fee for registration. The application includes a temporary identification card, valid for up to fourteen days. The employee will later receive a state-issued permanent identification card. The employee identification card is agency specific. It is permissible for a security professional to be employed by more than one agency simultaneously. However, he or she will need to obtain a second identification card.

Armed Security Officer Requirements / Weapons Permit

A private armed security employee will need both a state employee identification card and a firearms permit. Iowa issues two types of firearms permit:

professional and nonprofessional. The professional permit is intended for private security personnel as well as employees in roles such as corrections and bank transportation; it authorizes the carrying of a weapon while performing work duties and traveling to and from the workplace. The licensing agency notes that it is permissible for a security officer with a nonprofessional permit to carry firearms but that employers may require the professional permit.

A professional permit can be issued to an individual as young as eighteen. For a nonprofessional permit, the age requirement is twenty-one. The permit may be denied on the basis of a criminal record or alcohol abuse. It is also denied when there is good cause (based on documented acts committed by the person) to believe that the weapon could be used to inflict harm on self or other.

The prospective permit holder will need to complete some form of training. There are a number of options described in Chapter 724 of the state code. One option is to complete a course offered by the National Rifle Association. The licensing agency can accept handgun safety courses designed for the public whether offered by colleges, police departments, or training schools, provided that they are taught by instructors who have been certified by an appropriate organization, such as the National Rifle Association or the Iowa Law Enforcement Academy. The handgun safety course may instead be one specifically designed for security guards or for investigators or special deputies. The Department of Public Safety can also accept small arms training completed in the military or firearms training intended for peace officers.

The licensing agency notes that range qualification is not mandated under state law but that firearm training courses may include range training. Individuals with permits may choose to use range qualification as an annual renewal option; the licensing agency stipulates that the qualification instructor be certified by an acceptable organization, such as the National Rifle Association or the Iowa Law Enforcement Academy. The other renewal option is to complete another firearms training course that would meet requirements for initial issuance.

The Firearms Permit Application Process

Firearms applications are available from the Department of Public Safety (https://dps.iowa.gov/divisions/administrative-services/weapons-permit). They may be submitted to the sheriff of the county of residence or to the Department of Public Safety, depending on circumstances; the licensing agency has stated that state employees applying for employment-based professional permits are to go through DPS.

A professional permit requires an employer signature and justification. Training can be documented by any of the following: a copy of a certificate of completion from an acceptable course; an affidavit from the school, organization, or instructor; or a military DD-214.

The applicant will sign a release authorizing the licensing agency to carry out required investigations, including those involving substance abuse and psychiatric treatment.

The Department of Public Safety has prepared a list of frequently asked questions about firearms permits (https://dps.iowa.gov/sites/default/files/administrative-services/weapons/faq_weapons.pdf). Some questions specifically reference private security officers.

Private Security Licenses

Licensees are individuals who operate security agencies. They must be at least eighteen. They cannot have histories of repeated violence and cannot have been convicted of felonies, aggravated misdemeanors, or crimes of moral turpitude. Other crimes are disqualifying if specifically referenced in the state code. Referenced crimes include fraud and illegal carrying of a dangerous weapon, among others.

Although peace officers are not issued private security licenses, they may, if authorized by the appropriate executive, engage in security business alone or in partnership with other peace officers.

Licensees must have bonds and insurance policies. The licensing fee is one hundred dollars.

Civil Service Security Guard Requirements

Governmental employees are among those exempted from credentialing. However, state and federal agencies set their own requirements. Iowa Human Resources has provided general job descriptions for state civil service (https://das.iowa.gov/human-resources/classification-and-pay/job-class-descriptions). There are no mandatory education or experience requirements for positions at the Security Guard I level. However, a commercial driver's license must be obtained after hiring. Human Resources notes that some agencies may expect guards to be at least twenty-one, hold citizenship status, and go through a background check process. An individual may qualify for Security Guard II status through experience and/or law enforcement education.

Additional Information

Information about security guard requirements is available from the Program Services Bureau of the Iowa Department of Public Safety (https://dps.iowa.gov/divisions/administrative-services/bail-enforcement-private-investigation-private-security). "Bail Enforcement / Private Investigative / Security Licensing" can be reached by email at piinfo at dps.state.ia.us or by telephone at (515) 725-6230. Weapons Permits can be contacted by email at wpinfo at dps.state.ia.us.

Prospective security guards should be aware that laws and regulations change periodically. Significant changes to Chapter 724, the law that governs firearms permits, went into effect in 2011.

KANSAS

Concealed carry honored in all states except California, Connecticut, District of Columbia, Hawaii, Illinois, Maryland, Massachusetts, New Jersey, New York, Oregon, and Rhode Island and **with restrictions** (must be twenty-one years of age) in Alaska, Arizona, Arkansas, Colorado, Florida, Idaho, Kentucky, Maine, Michigan, Mississippi, Missouri, New Hampshire, Oklahoma, Pennsylvania, South Carolina, South Dakota, Vermont, and West Virginia.

Kansas security guards draw their authority from local officials. In some cases, a security guard is not licensed. The security guard will instead need to meet the standards of the employer. The businesses itself, however, may be subject to various laws. Employers often set requirements beyond those required by law.

Security guards can expect to meet certain basic requirements. They will need to be at least eighteen years old. They will also need to merit public trust. Background checks are typically a very important part of the employment process; they may be comprehensive and include far more than just criminal history. The prospective employee may also be required to have a physical; this may include drug screening. Literacy skills are also important, as security guards often take notes and write reports. Some national agencies administer personality or skill assessments.

Requirements Set by Local Licensing Agencies

Kansas security guards can often look to their city clerk for information about licensing, though in some cases, regulation may be at the county level. Different jurisdictions use different terminology. They may reference licenses or permits. Some use alternative terms like "merchant guard."

Wichita issues private security permits. An individual must have drug screening before a temporary permit can be issued. The guard will need to complete a training program before a permanent permit can be issued. Information is available from the Wichita Police Department (https://www.wichita.gov/WPD/SupportServices/Pages/PSF.aspx).

Lenexa issues security guard permits (http://www.lenexa.com/police/faqs_securityguard.html). Individuals hired by security services are referred to as "security agents" in municipal code. Lenexa lists among the requirements reading and writing in English and notes that the security employees must have a driver's license if driving will be required. Applicants are disqualified on the basis of a felony conviction. A number of other crimes, including illegal drug possession, are disqualifying if they occurred within the prior five years. The background investigation is carried out by the employer. The city has set additional requirements for security services; services that employ armed guards must be insured.

Lawrence issues merchant guard licenses. Armed guards must complete a proficiency program; they are also subject to more stringent background checks. Additional requirements apply to professionals who run merchant guard businesses. Information is available from the City Clerk's Office (http://www.lawrenceks.org/city_clerk/forms).

Topeka issues private security guard licenses through its police department (https://www.topeka.org/cityclerk/licenses/). Interested individuals may call 785-368-9456. Applicants can expect a background investigation.

State Security Jobs

Public sector jobs represent a minority of the private security industry. However, civil service job descriptions can provide insight into employer expectations for competitive positions in both the public and private sector. Kansas civil service jobs are described on the website of the Kansas Department of Administration (https://admin.ks.gov/offices/personnel-services/compensation-and-classification/job-classifications/protective-service-class-specs). Among the security-related positions are capitol area guard and safety and security officer.

A capitol area guard provides security services at state facilities in Topeka. The minimum requirement is a high school education or equivalency. There are two levels of responsibility officially recognized in state job classifications. A Capital Area Guard II will have supervisory duties; the distinguishing requirement is experience.

A safety and security officer is responsible for other public areas; this may include college campuses. High school education or equivalency is also the minimum requirement for these positions. Some positions require a drug test. Some positions in the class group require a driver's license and/or emergency medical technician (EMT) or mobile intensive care technician credential.

Differing Job Expectations

Recent nationally advertised job postings set standards high for Kansas security guards. Duties and requirements vary a good deal from position to position.

Multistate "GS-4" placed an ad for a security officer in Elwood. The posting states that the background check is extensive and that an individual with a military background would need to produce a DD-214 as a condition of hire. An armed guard would also be required to pass a physical and a psychological evaluation.

A retail position placed by another national agency cites communication and customer service skills as important. Physical skills include bending, twisting, running, and lifting up to forty pounds. The hiring agency notes that the job requires constant walking and constant use of hands.

An ad for armed driver based in Topeka states that candidates need to be at least twenty-one years of age. Previous security guard experience and military backgrounds are both valued. The employing agency notes that the position may require a commercial driver's license, though it will not necessarily be in hand at the time of hiring.

KENTUCKY

Concealed carry honored in all states except California, Connecticut, District of Columbia, Hawaii, Illinois, Maryland, Massachusetts, New Jersey, New Mexico, New York, Oregon, Rhode Island, and Washington and **with restrictions** (must be twenty-one years of age) in Alaska, Arizona, Colorado, Florida, Kansas, Maine, Michigan, Oklahoma, Pennsylvania, South Carolina, and West Virginia.

Kentucky does not license security guards, armed or unarmed. However, some may be subject to local regulations. Louisville, for example, licenses armed security guards.

There are, however, generally accepted standards that many security agencies follow. Some Kentucky positions are very competitive and above the national standard.

General Security Guard Expectations

Some security jobs are advertised directly by local businesses. Others are contracted through security agencies. Standards are typically delineated in a contract between the security agency and the company requiring security services.

Unarmed security guards are generally expected to be eighteen or older. They need to have work authorizations; some organizations require that they be citizens or permanent resident aliens. Prospective security guards can expect their backgrounds to be scrutinized. However, different jobs will require different sets of attributes. A high school diploma or GED is a common though not universal requirement. Security guards must have a requisite level of physical fitness. The organization may specify, for example, the ability to walk for two hours without sitting. Often, companies cite lifting ability. This can vary a good deal; the organization may note that the individual should be able to lift weights up to twenty-five pounds—or up to one hundred.

Contract security companies may administer multiple assessments, inventorying skills, aptitudes, and personality traits. The Minnesota Multiphasic

Personality Inventory may be administered at employer request. The prospective employee may be required to have a comprehensive physical; this may include a drug test as well as vision and hearing screenings.

A large security agency will typically administer in-house trainings. Previous knowledge or experience may, however, be valued. Some companies note a preference for previous employment in law enforcement, the military, or other related fields. Some companies consider those who do not have this experience but have degrees in fields like criminal justice.

Kentucky Civil Service Security Positions

Some security officers work for governmental entities. Kentucky Human Resources cites multiple security-related state civil service roles (https://personnel.ky.gov/Pages/JobSpecs.aspx). At the lower levels, minimum educational standards are not specified. At higher classifications (for example, security shift supervisor), they are. For security shift supervisor, Human Resources cites high school education and two years of experience but notes that substitutions are allowable. Job descriptions do not reflect current openings. Actual standards may be higher.

Jobs located in Kentucky may also be under federal authority. Requirements may be quite high. One example is the Transportation Security Administration (TSA). A recent ad described a rigorous and competitive process with candidates taking computer-adapted tests designed to measure English language proficiency and the ability to interpret X-rays. Individuals who scored satisfactorily would go through other evaluations, including a joint mobility exam and an interview designed to measure decision-making ability and teamwork skills. Ultimately, candidates would be ranked as qualified, highly qualified, and best qualified. The Transportation Security Administration values national service experience.

Third-Party Certifications

Employers may also value third-party certifications. These are granted by private organizations and don't confer the legal right to work in jurisdictions where licensing is required. Certifications may be specific to a particular sector or work setting. Health-care organizations, for example, may cite International Association for Healthcare Security and Safety (IAHSS) basic officer certification as desirable for their security officers. IAHSS basic certification is granted on the basis of examination (https://www.iahss.org/page/trainingandcertifications).

Louisville Armed Guard Requirements

The city of Louisville licenses armed security officers (http://louisvilleky.gov/government/codes-regulations/armed-security-agencies-companies-guards). In order to qualify, one must be a US citizen and at least twenty-one years of age. The individual cannot have had misdemeanor convictions during the most recent two-year period. In many cases, a felony conviction is permanently disqualifying. An exception exists if the person has been granted a pardon or had civil rights restored and has explicitly been granted the right to carry a firearm pursuant to the Federal Gun Control Act.

The guard must have an acceptable mental health history. He or she cannot have been adjudicated incompetent. An individual who has been hospitalized for a mental disorder of substance abuse issues may be required to provide documentation of fitness from a doctor or clinical psychologist.

An individual will be denied licensure on the basis of dishonorable discharge from the military (https://louisvilleky.gov/government/codes-regulations/armed-security-agencies-companies-guards).

The prospective armed guard will complete a training program and go through an examination process. Training will cover the following:
- orientation and note taking
- fire prevention
- security officer legal basis/limitations
- security officer's use of arrest, force, search and seizure
- defensive tactics / alternatives to firearms usage
- crowd control
- first aid
- report writing
- firearms qualification

Armed Guards: Other Standard Setters

Those who need a license to carry concealed deadly weapons (CCDW) will find resources on the website of the Kentucky State Police (http://kentuckystatepolice.org/ccdw/ccdw-home/ccdw-faqs/). Training is required; individuals can contact their local sheriff's office to find about approved instructors in their area. There are also general eligibility requirements. Licenses are denied on the basis of felony convictions or misdemeanor convictions involving domestic violence.

The CCDW will not necessarily be a legal requirement. However, armed security officers may find that their employers expect them to meet standards at least on a par with CCDW. Employers may value law enforcement training or experience earned in the military.

LOUISIANA

Concealed carry honored in all states except California, Connecticut, Delaware, District of Columbia, Hawaii, Illinois, Maryland, Massachusetts, New Jersey, New Mexico, New York, Oregon, and Rhode Island and **with restrictions** (must be twenty-one years of age) in Alaska, Arizona, Colorado, Florida, Kansas, Kentucky, Maine, Michigan, Oklahoma, Pennsylvania, South Carolina, West Virginia, and Wisconsin.

Louisiana security guards are under the jurisdiction of the Louisiana State Board of Private Security Examiners. The board issues multiple credentials, including registration cards for employees and licenses for qualifying agents (principal officers).

Background checks are required of both registrants and licensees. The background check will be carried out by the Louisiana State Police Bureau of Identification.

Security Guard Employee Requirements

An individual must be currently employed to receive an ID card from the board. The minimum age is eighteen. Louisiana requires a total of sixteen hours of training: eight by the end of thirty days of employment and an additional eight by the end of sixty days.

The initial eight hours will include content in each of the following:
- statutes and rules
- emergency procedures
- security officer powers and limitations
- duties, field notes, and reports

A written test will be administered after the completion of each of the eight-hour segments. The passing score is 70 percent.

Law enforcement officers may take an examination after completing a shorter modular program. Individuals who have held registration in other states are also eligible provided that the state of registration had similar requirements. An individual who does not pass will be required to complete the full training.

An individual can contact the board for a list of licensed instructors.

Armed Security Officer Employee Requirements

A security officer who will be armed will need training with the particular weapon he or she will be using before beginning duties. There are a number of different weapons classifications. If there is a change in weapon, training will need to be completed again.

Security officers as young as eighteen are allowed to carry batons if properly trained. The preservice training will be at least eight hours and will be taught by an instructor licensed by the board. A written examination will be administered.

In order to be authorized to carry a firearm, a security officer must be at least twenty-one.

The initial training will include the following state-mandated topics:

- weapon handling
- dim-light firing
- safety and maintenance
- stress factors
- shoot, don't shoot program
- legal limitations

The trainee will also need to pass a marksmanship test. The armed security officer will need annual retraining. The retraining will culminate in a written test and a test of marksmanship.

The Security Guard Employee Application Process

The applicant will need to provide a set of fingerprints and documentation of work eligibility. He or she will sign the application.

The board licensee who employs the guard will assist in the application process; the employee can expect to receive a temporary registration card.

If a registered security guard changes weapon, it will be necessary to submit an application for status change. If the individual is employed by a second company, it will be necessary to submit dual registration.

Qualifying Agent Requirements

A qualifying agent will need to hold US citizenship. He or she must have three consecutive years of experience. The licensing agency will credit experience as a security employee or manager. Law enforcement experience can be with the US military or with a local, state, or federal authority. The individual will also need to possess a high school diploma or GED or have equivalent training, gained through employment.

Qualifying agents will need to meet fitness requirements. This includes not being dependent on narcotics or habitually drunk and not having been declared mentally incompetent by court declaration. The applicant cannot have been found guilty of 1) illegal possession or use of a weapon, 2) any felony, or 3) any crime that involved moral turpitude.

The prospective qualifying agent will need to pass an examination with a score of at least 70 percent. There is a fifty-dollar examination fee and ten-dollar administrative fee. A candidate who needs to attempt the examination again will pay a twenty-dollar reexamination fee and ten-dollar administrative fee.

The Qualifying Agent (Officer) Application Process

Qualifying agent applications are available for download from the board website (http://www.lsbpse.info/15_Agt_App/15_agt_app.html).

The applicant can get fingerprint cards from the board; these are not available for download. The two fingerprint cards will be included in the application package.

The licensing agency will need a five-year employment history and a list of any criminal convictions, excluding minor traffic offenses. The board will seek a résumé.

The applicant will need three letters of recommendation from people he or she has been acquainted with for at least five years.

An applicant who has been in the military is to provide a copy of DD-214 (or equivalent document).

An applicant who has ever suffered from drug or alcohol addiction or received treatment for mental illness is to provide explanation.

The prospective qualifying agent will need to confirm that he or she is covered under the company liability insurance policy.

Application, examination, and fingerprint fees are to be included in the application package.

The applicant is to attach a two-by-two photograph to the application and have the form notarized.

Applications are sent to the board office in Baton Rouge.

There is a separate security company application form. A security agency is required to carry liability insurance. The policy must meet standards described in the state statute.

Additional Information

Information about security officer licensing and registration is available from the Louisiana State Board of Private Security Examiners (http://www. lsbpse.info/). Credentialing is governed by law (http://www.lsbpse.info/8_ Laws/8_laws.html) and administrative code http://www.lsbpse.info/8B_ Rules_Regs/8b_rules_regs.html). The board can be reached by telephone at (225) 272-2310. Extension numbers for staff members are available online (http://www.lsbpse.info/7_Contact_Us/7_contact_us.html).

MAINE

Concealed carry honored in all states except California, Colorado, Connecticut, District of Columbia, Hawaii, Illinois, Maryland, Massachusetts, Minnesota, Montana, Nevada, New Jersey, New Mexico, New York, Oregon, Pennsylvania, Rhode Island, South Carolina, Texas, Washington, and Wisconsin and **with restrictions** (must be twenty-one years of age) in Alaska, Arizona, Florida, Iowa, Kansas, Kentucky, Louisiana, Michigan, Nebraska, Oklahoma, Virginia, and West Virginia.

Maine's private security guards are under the jurisdiction of the Special Investigations Unit of the Bureau of Maine State Police. The state has set requirements for contract security companies and employees who provide security services. These do not apply to proprietary security companies.

Security Guard Requirements

Employees of contract security companies must be citizens or resident aliens. They must have attained the age of at least eighteen. Additionally, they must meet general fitness requirements, including not having been adjudicated as incapacitated and not being a threat to self or others. A person is ineligible if he or she has an outstanding warrant or has received a dishonorable military discharge within the prior five years. Any crime that could be punished with a sentence of a full year is disqualifying. Some other crimes are disqualifying if the conviction was less than five years earlier; these are listed in Section 9412. Additionally, if the individual has, in the prior five years, received three or more convictions with maximum sentences of less than one year, he or she is ineligible. In many cases, even juvenile crimes are disqualifying.

The security agency will investigate the backgrounds of employees. New hires are reported to the state. This is the employer's responsibility. The commissioner will need basic information, such as addresses from the past five years.

The employer may need information normally kept confidential (such as records of involuntary commitment).

Security Agency Requirements

Those who head security agencies must meet similar character and legal requirements. Additionally, they must take financial responsibility for conduct. Licensees must have surety bonds.

Application materials can be downloaded from the website of the Department of Public Safety (http://www.maine.gov/dps/msp/licenses/pi.html). A prospective licensee must certify to having read "Laws Relating to Private Security Guards." The applicant will submit a recent photograph. He or she will sign a release form.

The release form notes that fingerprints will be required if there is any question as to identity.

Firearms Requirements

Maine has no licensing regulations for armed guards but has a complex set of laws regarding who can carry a firearm and when it can justifiably be used. The state police website includes a link to laws regarding the use of force in defense of persons and property (http://www.maine.gov/dps/msp/licenses/weapons_self_defense.html). Individuals who carry firearms are "strongly encouraged" to familiarize themselves with circumstances where deadly force is justifiable. Those with questions are advised to consult a lawyer.

The private security handbook specifically states that security guards who transport valuables are allowed to have firearms in their vehicles, provided that such weapons are not concealed.

The Kittery Police Department has noted that it is recommended that anyone who carries a firearm possess a concealed firearm even though "open carry" is legal in Maine (http://www.kitterypolice.com/concealed-weapons-permit-1.html).

A permit holder will need training in firearms safety. State law allows training to be completed from any of multiple sources.

Concealed weapons permits are also available from the state police (http://www.maine.gov/dps/msp/licenses/weapons_permits.html). In most cases, individuals go through their own city or town. The state police website includes a link to local jurisdictions.

A new law that went into effect in late 2015 allows many individuals to carry concealed weapons without a permit. A permit would be necessary in some cases, such as if the individual were under twenty-one. A permit makes concealed carry legal in some areas where it would not be legal otherwise. (Bureau of Human Resources, http://www.maine.gov/cgi-bin/bhrsalary/jobs)

Security companies may set much higher standards than those required by law. A recent posting for an armed security guard in Saco, Maine, stipulated that the individual would be at least twenty-five years of age, hold a high school diploma, and have six years of firearms experience, which could be in any of multiple fields, including military and corrections. The candidate was expected to have a weapons license and to pass a drug test postoffer.

Another ad, for a vault guard in Lewiston, sought an individual of at least twenty-one who had a firearms permit or ability to pass licensing requirements. Requirements were set somewhat lower: three months in a related field, such as cash handling (http://www.simplyhired.com/job/vault-clerk-job/brinks-co/c53igj56ig?cid=ysjjrapyagqxqnibvztesgawtpnpisia).

Notably, some ads are placed by major security companies with a multistate presence.

Civil Service

Some security professionals are hired into the public sector at the level of "watchperson." expectations are a high school diploma, a year of work experience requirements, and a class C driver's license; the latter is expected before permanent status is awarded. Expectations may be set higher for particular job vacancies.

A capitol security screener is expected to hold a high school diploma or equivalency and have two years of experience in security.

Additional Information

Information about security guard requirements is available from the Maine State Police (http://www.maine.gov/dps/msp/licenses/pi.html). The licensing agency can be reached by telephone at (207) 624-7210.

MARYLAND

Concealed carry honored in all states except California, Colorado, Connecticut, Delaware, District of Columbia, Georgia, Hawaii, Illinois, Louisiana, Massachusetts, Minnesota, Nebraska, Nevada, New Jersey, New Mexico, New York, North Dakota, Oregon, Pennsylvania, Rhode Island, South Carolina, Washington, and Wyoming and **with restrictions** (must be twenty-one years of age) in Alaska, Arizona, Kansas, Kentucky, Maine, Michigan, Oklahoma, Texas, and West Virginia.

Maryland security guards are under the jurisdiction of the Maryland State Police Licensing Division. The division recognizes multiple job roles, including corporate officer.

Security guards who will be armed must also apply for handgun permits. Requirements are more stringent.

Basic Security Guard Requirements

Security guard certification is not issued until such time as an individual is an employee or applicant (http://mdsp.maryland.gov/Organization/Pages/SupportServicesBureau/LicensingDivision/ProfessionalLicenses/SecurityGuardCertifications.aspx). The credential is dependent on 1) good character and 2) citizenship or legal authority to work in the United States. The security guard cannot have had a felony conviction; misdemeanor convictions that have a direct bearing on fitness are also disqualifying.

Certification is issued for three years at a time. A renewal applicant will again have a background check.

Armed Guard Requirements

An armed guard will need a handgun permit / wear-and-carry permit as a supplement to his or her security guard certification.

The individual will need to meet general fitness requirements and training requirements. The training program is to be approved by the Maryland State Police; a prospective student can search for qualified instructors on the State Police website (https://emdsp.mdsp.org/verification). The initial training will be at least sixteen hours. The prospective armed guard will need to shoot a qualifying round (http://mdsp.maryland.gov/Organization/Pages/SupportServicesBureau/LicensingDivision/Training/WearandCarryPermit.aspx).

Some individuals will qualify for exemption based on law enforcement, military, or National Guard experience. They may also qualify for exemption from "wear and carry" training if they have completed other acceptable training through a registered handgun instructor or are handgun instructors themselves.

Crimes involving dangerous substances are disqualifying. Misdemeanor convictions are disqualifying if the individual served a sentence of more than a year. Any criminal conviction is disqualifying if the individual could potentially have received a sentence of more than two years.

The permit may also be denied based on a history of instability or violence.

The applicant will also need to document the reason the handgun is needed. Employment as a security guard can be accepted as the reason. The employing agency will need to provide a letter documenting basic information, including the place the gun will be stored during off-duty hours. The employee will sign to verify knowledge of the applicable regulations and rules. A sample letter is linked from the "handgun wear and carry permit" page of the state police website (http://mdsp.maryland.gov/Organization/Pages/SupportServicesBureau/LicensingDivision/Firearms/WearandCarryPermit.aspx).

The permit must actually be in hand before the individual is authorized to carry the weapon; the licensing agency stresses that application submission does not grant authorization.

Requirements for Operating or Managing a Security Guard Business

Requirements are set higher for individuals who have their own security agency businesses or who act as representatives for security agencies. These professionals must be at least twenty-five years of age and must have three to five years of experience in a related field.

The licensing agency can accept five years of experience as a police officer if the individual has completed a program recognized by the Maryland Police Training Commission.

A professional who has worked as a detective for a police agency is eligible after three years. The time frame is also three years for an individual who has had training through the Maryland Police Training Commission and has worked in an investigative capacity for a governmental unit.

Fire investigators can attain eligibility after five years. They will need to have completed programs certified by the Maryland Fire-Rescue Education and Training Commission or the Maryland Police Commission.

Maryland correctional supervisors are eligible after five years, provided they have completed the requisite training.

The Security Guard Application Process

The applicant will need to have fingerprint-based background checks processed through the CJIS and the FBI. Fingerprints are now captured electronically using Live Scan. Authorized Live Scan providers can submit results directly to the Licensing Division. The Licensing Division notes that out-of-state individuals requesting gun permits are required to go through an authorized Live Scan provider. They may contact the state police for additional information. A list of providers is available online (https://www.dpscs.state.md.us/publicservs/fingerprint.shtml).

The background check fee is listed as $32.75. (The licensing agency notes that this is in addition to the fee charged by the vendor.) The applicant will need to provide an ORI number (http://mdsp.maryland.gov/Organization/Pages/SupportServicesBureau/LicensingDivision/Fingerprinting.aspx).

An individual applying for multiple certifications will only need to provide one set of fingerprints.

Application materials can be accessed from the website of the Licensing Division (http://mdsp.maryland.gov/Organization/Pages/SupportServicesBureau/LicensingDivision/ProfessionalLicenses/SecurityGuardCertifications.aspx). Applicants should make sure they have the most current version of the security guard application. There have been some changes. The form is now filled out electronically. The applicant will need to select the type of application; he or she will see different questions based on the selection. Once completed, the application can be mailed to the Licensing Division in Pikesville.

Some supplementary materials will be required.

The applicant must provide two passport-style photographs for each distinct certification application. Photographs are to be recent: taken within the thirty days prior to application. Photograph specifications are found in the application packet. The licensing agency notes that in cases where an individual is applying for more than one certification simultaneously, additional photographs may be required. An individual who is simultaneously applying for a handgun permit will need two photographs for the handgun application.

A prospective armed guard must include handgun qualification documentation.

The applicant will include the CJIS and FBI fingerprint cards.

Security guard registration costs $15. A handgun permit costs $75. A security guard agency application will cost $200 for an individual or $375 for a corporation.

Additional Information

Information about security guard requirements is available from the Maryland State Police (http://mdsp.maryland.gov/Organization/Pages/SupportServicesBureau/LicensingDivision.aspx). The Security Guard Section can be reached by telephone at 410-653-4623 or by email at msp.securityguard@maryland.gov. The Handgun Permit Section can be reached by telephone at 410-653-4624 or by email at msp.handgunpermits@maryland.gov.

MASSACHUSETTS

Concealed carry honored in all states except California, Colorado, Connecticut, Delaware, District of Columbia, Georgia, Hawaii, Illinois, Louisiana, Maryland, Minnesota, Nebraska, New Jersey, New Mexico, New York, North Dakota, Oregon, Pennsylvania, Rhode Island, South Carolina, Washington, and Wyoming and **with restrictions** (must be twenty-one years of age) in Alaska, Arizona, Kansas, Kentucky, Maine, Michigan, Oklahoma, West Virginia, and Wisconsin.

In Massachusetts, licenses are issued to security agencies, not to individual security agency employees. However, employees are subject to state mandates. In many cases, these amount to only basic eligibility requirements, designed to screen out truly unsuitable candidates. Actual standards set by employers may be much higher.

Security guards who carry firearms are legally held to higher standards. They must hold licenses—not security licenses per se but firearms licenses. In order to qualify for a firearms license, an armed security guard must meet general eligibility requirements and training requirements.

Unarmed Security Guard: Legal Mandates

By state law, individuals are not eligible to work for security agencies if they have been convicted of felonies or if they have held a license and had it revoked. Employees are required to provide their employers with information about their occupation during the prior three years. They must provide statements that they have not been convicted of felonies or crimes of moral turpitude. According to state law, the employer will retain the employee statement and provide it to the state police upon request (http://www.mass.gov/eopss/law-enforce-and-cj/law-enforce/prof-stds/cert-unit/ch-147-sec-22-30.html).

Massachusetts law does not mandate that security guards have reached the age of majority unless they will carry firearms.

Unarmed Security Guards: Employer Expectations

Employers are often far more selective than they are required by law to be. Age eighteen is the generally accepted industry-wide minimum around the nation; some employers place the minimum higher: age twenty-one. Many employers require that individuals have high school diplomas or GEDs.

Massachusetts security companies/licensees have a level of financial responsibility for the actions of their employees. They are required to take out five-thousand-dollar surety bonds that cover not only their own actions but those of their agents.

There are a number of regional and national security agencies contracted to fill positions in Massachusetts. They often specify that candidates have strong computer and English language / verbal skills. Some require that their security officers have previous experience in security or a related field (for example, the military). A bachelor's degree in a field like criminal justice may be accepted instead.

Civil service positions can also set standards quite high. Among the security-related roles cited by the Massachusetts Division of Human Resources are "Institution Security Officer I–Institution Security Officer IV." There is no minimum experience/education listed for those at the entry level. However, the division notes that a driver's license may be an expectation. Job classifications at and above the level of Institution Security Officer II require experience in police, law enforcement, or security and/or comparable education. An associate's degree in police science, criminal justice, or law enforcement might be accepted in lieu of experience at the Security Officer II or III level. To substitute for experience at the Security Officer IV level, one would need at least a bachelor's, though an associate's could be accepted for partial credit. Partial credit may also be granted for coursework taken toward a qualifying degree. Actual hiring requirements in the public sector (as in the private sector) will vary.

Armed Security Guard Requirements

A security guard who will carry a gun will need a firearms license. Massachusetts issues multiple types of firearm authorizations. A license to carry (LTC) is the one that is generally issued for handguns. In order to be eligible for an LTC, an individual must be at least twenty-one and must meet general fitness requirements. A person will be disqualified from obtaining based on "confinement" for mental illness unless a physician is able to certify that, despite the history, the individual is fit to carry a firearm. He or she will be disqualified based on a history of substance abuse or drunkenness unless five years have elapsed since treatment or confinement and a physician is able to certify that the condition is cured.

Felonies are disqualifying as are serious misdemeanors (those that can incur a sentence of two years). Certain other crimes are disqualifying, among them, those involving controlled substances.

The following approved courses are listed in the Code of Massachusetts Regulations (CMR):

- basic pistol course, home safety course, or personal protection course offered by the National Rifle Association
- Massachusetts Carry Permit Course offered by Smith & Wesson Academy
- Handgun Orientation Course offered by SIGS Arms Academy
- Basic Handgun Safety Course offered by the Massachusetts Chiefs of Police Association

The Massachusetts State Police routinely consider other courses; they can be approved following curriculum review. The state police website includes a list of approved courses (http://www.mass.gov/eopss/agencies/msp/archived-stories/2012/approved-basic-firearms-safety-course-list-updated.html).

Firearms application forms are available from the Executive Office of Public Safety and Security (http://www.mass.gov/eopss/firearms-reg-and-laws/frb/firearms-forms-and-applications.html); a security guard will check employment as the reason licensing is requested.

All initial firearms applications must be accompanied by certificates documenting completion of firearm safety or hunter safety courses.

Applicants who answer "yes" to potentially disqualifying questions will need to provide supporting documentation. In many cases, prospective licensees apply to their local police department.

Additional Information

Security agencies are licensed by the Certification Unit of the Massachusetts State Police (http://www.mass.gov/eopss/law-enforce-and-cj/law-enforce/prof-stds/cert-unit/). The Certification Unit can be reached at 978-538-6128.

Information about firearms licensing is available from the Executive Office of Public Safety and Security (http://www.mass.gov/eopss/firearms-reg-and-laws/).

MICHIGAN

Concealed carry honored in all states except California, Connecticut, District of Columbia, Hawaii, Illinois, Maryland, Massachusetts, New Jersey, New York, Oregon, and Rhode Island and **with restrictions** (must be twenty-one years of age) in Alaska, Arizona, Colorado, Florida, Kansas, Kentucky, Maine, Oklahoma, Pennsylvania, South Carolina, and West Virginia. The Michigan Department of Licensing and Regulatory Affairs (LARA) regulates the state's private security industry. Michigan has set high standards for the proprietors and managers who head private security agencies.

Requirements for Operating a Security Business

A potential licensee is to be at least twenty-five years of age and have education of at least the high school level; equivalency is accepted.

The individual will need two to four years of qualifying experience. The licensing agency will accept four years of experience as a security employee if it involves roughly the equivalent of four years at the supervisory level; supervisory experience is defined as experience above that of patrolman.

The applicant can also be qualified on the basis of having had three years of independent out-of-state experience.

Two years spent as a security employee or provider or as the security administrator of a business can be accepted if the professional also has a baccalaureate degree (or the equivalent of a baccalaureate degree) in industrial security or police administration.

The licensing agency will accept four years of experience as a police officer (whether for the US government or a city, county, or state government).

An applicant can be qualified with as little as two years of experience served in the military police or in an equivalent job classification while on duty in the armed services. However, the individual will need to document that he or she was able to demonstrate at least basic knowledge or entry-level experience in each of the following:

- physical protection and security
- enforcing regulations and guidelines

- site security operations
- overseeing correctional institutions and prisoners
- reconnaissance and surveillance

The military applicant will need to have been discharged under honorable/general conditions.

The prospective licensee cannot have a felony conviction on his or her record. Certain other offenses are disqualifying if the conviction occurred within the prior five years. These include, among others, fraud, illegal use or possession of a firearm, and impersonation of a police officer. The licensing agency can allow one alcohol-related offense but no more.

Additional disqualifiers include having been discharged dishonorably from the military or judged insane (without sanity having subsequently restored by court order).

The licensee will need either an insurance policy or a surety bond. According to current standards, the bond would need to be at least twenty-five thousand dollars. The insurance policy would need to cover twenty-five thousand in property damages, one hundred thousand for the injury or death of one person, and two hundred thousand for injuries affecting more than one person.

The Application Process
Application forms can be downloaded from the website of the Department of Licensing and Regulatory Affairs (http://www.michigan.gov/lara/0,4601,7-154-61343_35414_36748-339603-,00.html).

An applicant who is qualifying on the basis of military experience will need an affidavit from a commanding officer; the purpose is to document that the individual has basic knowledge or entry-level experience in all state-mandated areas.

If the applicant is seeking a fee waiver, discharge documents (for example, DD-214 or DD-215) will be required as well.

A sole proprietor or resident manager must provide two passport-style photographs.

A sole proprietor pays two hundred dollars for initial application (http://www.michigan.gov/lara/0,4601,7-154-61343_35414_60647_35470-114625-,00.html). The fee can be waived for veteran applicants.

The applicant must provide five reference statements from individuals who can attest to character, competency, and honesty (http://www.legislature.mi.gov/(S(qt3oht5puyedg3lad3rz4mu2))/mileg.aspx?page=getObject&objectName=mcl-338-1057).

He or she will also need the approval of the 1) prosecuting attorney and 2) the sheriff or chief of police; there is a space on the application form for their signatures.

A temporary license may, in some cases, allow a professional to commence operations sooner (http://www.legislature.mi.gov/(S(qt3oht5puyedg3lad3rz4mu2))/mileg.aspx?page=getObject&objectName=mcl-338-1057).

Hiring Expectations for Security Guard Employees

The Department of Licensing and Regulatory Affairs is no longer involved with the screening process of employees but suggests that employers use technology offered by the Michigan State Police Criminal Justice Information Center to carry out background checks (http://www.michigan.gov/lara/0,4601,7-154-61343_35414_60647_35470-356857-,00.html). Some employing agencies carry out comprehensive background checks that include credit history and Department of Motor Vehicles history. Some require drug screening as well. Additionally, some agencies administer assessments such as aptitude tests, skills assessments, or personality profiles.

The minimum age for employment may be eighteen or twenty-one, depending on the type of position. High school graduation (or GED attainment) is a typical expectation. Employers may specify computer literacy and/or English language literacy.

Law enforcement or military experience may be valued. The employer may seek knowledge of CPR and first aid.

Additional Information

The board is under the banner of the Department of Licensing and Regulatory Affairs (http://www.michigan.gov/lara/0,4601,7-154-61343_35414_60647_35470—,00.html). The Licensing Division can be reached by telephone at 517-241-9288.

MINNESOTA

Concealed carry honored in all states except California, Colorado, Connecticut, Delaware, District of Columbia, Florida, Georgia, Hawaii, Illinois, Maryland, Massachusetts, New Jersey, New Mexico, New York, Oregon, Pennsylvania, Rhode Island, Texas, Washington, and Wyoming and **with restrictions** (must be twenty-one years of age) in Alaska, Arizona, Kansas, Kentucky, Maine, Michigan, Oklahoma, South Carolina, and West Virginia. Minnesota security guards are under the jurisdiction of the State of Minnesota Board of Private Detective and Protective Agent Services. Protective agent services encompass a variety of businesses, including those that provide guards, security personnel, and armored car personnel (https:// www.revisor.mn.gov/statutes/cite/326.338). The professionals who run the security businesses, either as proprietors or "qualified representatives," must hold state licensing.

Security agency employees are not licensed but must meet requirements set at the state level. Requirements are higher for employees who will be armed.

Background Check Requirement for Employees

New hires must clear criminal background checks; this requirement applies to security guards employed by proprietary businesses as well as those employed by protective service agencies.

Felonies are disqualifying. Certain other offenses are disqualifying; these are described in the state statute (https://www.revisor.mn.gov/statutes/cite/326.336).

Employees will hold conditional status until the results have been processed and sent to the employer. Conditional employees may receive training but will not begin protective duties.

The employee must have at least twelve hours of preassignment training; this is to be completed within twenty-one days of employment (https://www.revisor.mn.gov/rules/7506.2600/). Required topics include the following:
- ethics
- communications

- security overview
- assessment and emergency response
- state statutes and administrative rules

The employee will be issued an identification card. The board has mandated that security agency employees receive continuing training.

Requirements for Armed Security Agency Employees

Training for armed guards will include the standard preassignment and continuing training as well as training in each of the following:
- firearms training
- training with weapons other than firearms
- alternatives to force
- standards for weapons and equipment
- first aid

Firearms training must include legal limitations on the use of force. Program elements are described in 7506.2300 of the state administrative code (https://www.revisor.mn.gov/rules/7506.2200/).

The board has provided a list of approved training providers (https://dps.mn.gov/entity/pdb/training/Pages/approve-training-providers.aspx); it includes both initial and continuing training providers.

Requirements for Sole Proprietors and Qualified Representatives

A protective agent license may be issued to a sole proprietor, partnership, or corporation. If the business is not a sole proprietor, there must be a qualified representative who serves as manager and supervisor. If the agency is a branch of an out-of-state business, there must be a Minnesota manager.

The sole proprietor or qualified representative must meet experience requirements. Minnesota requires fully six thousand hours of protective/security employment. Service may have been provided under a licensed protective agent or licensed private detective. The individual may have been employed in a protective, security, or investigative role with a sheriff's department, city police office, or investigative branch of the US government. Other employment may be accepted if the board finds it to be equivalent. In all cases, the licensing agency will expect the individual to have had experience with the following: security personnel supervision, security systems, and audits.

License holders, like employees, must meet training requirements.

Additional Licensing Requirements

Some requirements apply to all individuals who sign the application; this includes not only qualified representatives, Minnesota managers, and sole proprietors but (in the case of corporations) chief executive officers and chief financial officers. Each of these officials must have a background check. Each must provide five unrelated references with whom he or she has been acquainted for a minimum of five years; the board will supply forms for this purpose.

The licensing agency requires protective agent applicants to hold ten-thousand-dollar surety bonds. Additionally, they must either 1) carry insurance that meets board requirements or 2) otherwise demonstrate financial ability to respond to liability. Insurance must cover general liability, personal injury, and completed operations. The licensing agency can instead accept a net worth statement or irrevocable letter of credit. The minimum amount will depend on the number of employees.

The Application Process

Directions can be downloaded from the website of the Board of Private Detective and Protective Agent Services. However, the application itself must be requested from the board (https://dps.mn.gov/entity/pdb/Pages/general-licensing-information.aspx). The board will need to know whether the applicant is a sole proprietor, partnership, or corporation and whether the business will offer protective or investigative services. A twenty-five-dollar fee is to accompany the application request.

Applicants are invited to contact the board with their questions. Except in the case of sole proprietors, the application will have multiple signers. Each individual who signs will provide an employment and residence history. Each will supply a photograph and criminal history form as well as fingerprints and references.

Qualified representatives / Minnesota managers will provide experience documentation.

Licensing fees will vary. An individual will pay $800; a partnership, $1,600; and a corporation, $1,800. An applicant who is denied licensure will receive a partial refund.

Additional Information

Licensing information is available from the State of Minnesota Board of Private Detective and Protective Agent Services (https://dps.mn.gov/entity/pdb/contact/Pages/default.aspx). Statutes can be accessed from the board website (https://dps.mn.gov/entity/pdb/Pages/statutes.aspx). Administrative rules are found in Chapter 7506 of the state code (https://www.revisor.mn.gov/rules/7506/). The board can be reached by telephone at (651) 793-2666 or by email at mn.pdb at state.mn.us.

MISSISSIPPI

Concealed carry honored in all states except California, Connecticut, Delaware, District of Columbia, Hawaii, Illinois, Maryland, Massachusetts, Minnesota, Nebraska, New Jersey, New York, Oregon, Rhode Island, and Washington and **with restrictions** (must be twenty-one years of age) in Alaska, Arizona, Colorado, Florida, Kansas, Kentucky, Maine, Michigan, Nevada, Oklahoma, Pennsylvania, South Carolina, and West Virginia.

Mississippi does not license the private security industry. Mississippi's armed security guards, however, must hold state credentials. They receive their firearms permits from the Department of Public Safety, or DPS. In order to receive the credential, they must go through a background check process, both at the time of initial credentialing and at the time of renewal. State statute prevents individuals who have had felony convictions from receiving permits. The application includes background questions that provide further opportunity for screening.

Requirements for Mississippi DPS-Issued Security Guard Permit
Permit applicants must have fingerprint-based state and federal background checks. Fingerprint cards must be prepared by the Mississippi Highway Patrol / Department of Public Safety. They can be made at the DPS Headquarters in Jackson or one of the following Highway Patrol District Substations:
- Batesville
- Biloxi
- Brookhaven
- Greenwood
- Hattiesburg
- Meridian
- New Albany
- Starkville

Hours of operation are included in the application package; these vary from site to site.

The Permit Application Process

Permit application packets can be downloaded from the DPS website (http://www.dps.state.ms.us/firearms/firearms-permit-unit/security-guard-permits). Applications are processed in person at the Firearm Permit Unit in Jackson; applicants are directed not to mail them. The service is currently offered Monday and Thursday between 8:00 a.m. and 4:30 p.m.

The application includes qualifying questions about criminal history, mental illness, and addictions. Individuals who answer "yes" to screening questions will need to furnish details. An applicant who has had had a hospitalization due to mental illness, for example, will need to provide documentation from the treatment provider. An applicant who has had a crime pardoned or expunged will need to attach a copy of the order.

Applicants who have served in the military will need to provide information about the type of discharge.

The applicant will need to include a small photograph; it should be no more than thirty days old.

The applicant will sign an affidavit about domestic violence convictions. This form requires notarization. The information release form and affidavit do as well. Applicants who were born outside the United States are required to provide an additional notarized statement.

The applicant will pay a total of $132.00; this includes a $32.00 background check fee. The licensing agency accepts cashier's checks and some credit and debit cards (http://www.dps.state.ms.us/wp-content/uploads/SECURITY-GUARD-PERMIT-APP-2.pdf).

Permit Renewals

The security guard permit is issued for four years. The security guard will pay a fifty-dollar renewal fee and thirty-two-dollar background check fee. Retired law enforcement officers are not required to pay the renewal fee; they pay only the thirty-two-dollar fingerprint processing fee.

Mississippi Civil Service Job Descriptions

The Mississippi State Personnel Board has provided detailed job descriptions for security officers at multiple levels of service (http://agency.government-jobs.com/mississippi/default.cfm?action=agencyspecs). These were compiled by subject matter experts and are designed to reflect the needs of Mississippi's public sector. Although public sector jobs represent only a portion of the security guard industry, the descriptions may also provide insight into employer expectations in competitive positions in the private sector.

State job classifications include Security Officer I, II, and III as well as Security Officer Chief I, II, and III. Security officers at each level are expected to hold a high school diploma. Law enforcement training is an expectation for some positions.

The personnel board has listed typical physical requirements. Physical jobs can require lifting ability up to fifty or even one hundred pounds. Security guards typically need good visual acuity as well as peripheral and depth vision. Desired personal traits include service orientation, self-management skills, and accountability.

Management competencies are expected at the "Security Officer Chief" level. Among these are emotional maturity, results orientation, and macro-orientation.

State agencies expect individuals at the Chief Officer I level to have at least three years of job experience. At Chief Officer III, the expectation is five years.

Additional Employer Expectations

Some employers carry out drug screening as well as comprehensive background checks.

Employers often favor applicants with related experience. Some employers note that a military background is desirable. Some value various other types of experience, from firefighting to experience in a related service industry.

Employers sometimes cite computer and verbal/ written skills among the qualifications. Although high school education is adequate for many positions, some agencies seek employees with degrees at the associate's level or higher. They may seek various other trainings, for example, crisis intervention.

Additional Information

Information about security guard permits is available from the Firearm Permit Unit. The Firearm Permit Unit can be reached by telephone at (601)987-1593. The Permit Unit references Section 97-37-7 of state statute (http://www.dps.state.ms.us/firearms/firearms-permit-unit/security-guard-permits).

Requirements are subject to change. Bills have been introduced more than once that would create additional requirements for Mississippi's security professionals.

MISSOURI

Concealed carry honored in all states except California, Connecticut, District of Columbia, Hawaii, Illinois, Maryland, Massachusetts, Minnesota, Nevada, New Jersey, New York, Oregon, Rhode Island, and Washington and **with restrictions** (must be twenty-one years of age) in Alaska, Arizona, Colorado, Florida, Iowa, Kansas, Kentucky, Louisiana, Maine, Michigan, Nebraska, Oklahoma, Pennsylvania, South Carolina, Texas, Virginia, West Virginia, and Wisconsin. Missouri security guards are regulated at a local level. A number of cities, including St. Louis, Kansas City, and Columbia, license them. In some cases, a security guard may not hold licensing or registration and will instead answer directly to the employer. The expectations can still be high.

The following is a sampling of requirements, representing different Missouri cities and job roles.

St. Louis Security Guard Requirements

St. Louis recognizes four different types of security professional: watchman, courier, security officer, and corporate security advisor. All classifications except watchman are eligible to carry weapons if properly trained. Security officers and corporate security advisors both have limited police powers.

A watchman, whose basic duties are watching and reporting, may be as young as eighteen. Security personnel in other classifications must be twenty-one.

Some requirements are common to all license types. Licensees must be citizens or legal residents and must be free of felony convictions or chemical dependencies.

Security professionals do not receive licenses until there is an intent to hire.

Licensing information is available from the Private Security Section of the Metropolitan Police Department (http://www.slmpd.org/private_security.shtml).

Columbia, Missouri, Security Guard Requirements

Columbia, Missouri, licenses security guards who work for guard or watchman services. Licenses are issued as armed or unarmed. The minimum age is eighteen for unarmed guards, twenty-one for armed guards.

Licenses may be denied on the basis of felony convictions (if from the prior ten years) or of certain misdemeanor convictions (if from the prior five years). The licensing agency will consider mitigating factors, such as the individual's conduct in the time since the infraction.

A prospective armed guard will need to complete a written test, a test of skill and safety, and a firearm qualification course. Requirements are described in the city municipal code (https://www.municode.com/library/mo/columbia/codes/code_of_ordinances?nodeId=PTIICOOR_CH13LIPEMIBURE_ARTIIIARGUSEGU). Application forms are available from the Business License Office (https://www.como.gov/finance/business-licenses/armed-guard/).

Kansas City, Missouri, Security Guard Requirements

Kansas City issues Class A and Class B security licenses. Class A licensees have some powers that Class B licensees do not have, such as the power to detain suspects. Both Class A and Class B licenses can be issued armed or unarmed. Class A licensees include loss prevention agents and airport police, among others. Class B licensees include guards and armed couriers.

All prospective licensees must take a written test as well as go through a background check process. However, standards are not identical. All prospective licensees will need to know concepts such as liability issues, rules, crisis response, and interaction with the public. The Class A written test includes some additional concepts, such as patrol techniques and crime.

Class A licensees have additional requirements: the employer must vouch that the employee is both physically and mentally capable of apprehending and detaining without unnecessary show of force; the city will require annual confirmation of the employee's fitness.

Armed security personnel must complete firearms training and pass a range test; they must requalify periodically.

Applicants must meet fitness requirements. Many, but not all, criminal offenses are disqualifying. Dishonorable discharge from the armed forces is a disqualifier if service took place within the most recent ten-year period. Additionally, a prospective armed guard cannot have an order of protection in place.

Licensing information is available from the Kansas City Police Department (http://kcmo.gov/police/private-security-officers).

Public Sector Security Positions

Some security personnel are hired into civil service positions. The Missouri Division of Personnel recognizes several security-related roles, including Security Guard and Security Officer I, II, and III (http://oa.mo.gov/personnel/classification-specifications/s). There are multiple pathways to qualify as a security officer. Individuals can work their way up from security guard. They may also qualify based on law enforcement experience or other security experience, when combined with high school or equivalent education. Education can also be qualifying. The expectation at the Security Officer I level is thirty total units, with at least six units in criminal justice. At the Security Officer II level, the expectation is sixty total units, with at least nine in criminal justice.

The division has identified not only the minimum experience necessary to receive consideration but the traits necessary to be successful. Among the expectations at the guard level are walking outdoors during varying climate conditions, following a set patrol routine, and maintaining the proper demeanor (firm but tactful). Among the expectations at the office level are exercising independent judgment and coordinating security activities.

Some security officers will need a separate license to carry firearms.

General Standards

Employers may impose similar standards even when there is no licensing or state-mandated hiring process. Security guards typically go through a background check process. Sometimes there is drug screening as well. Guards must meet minimum age requirements: typically eighteen for unarmed positions and twenty-one for armed positions.

These are the fundamentals; other requirements will vary greatly according to job role. Even when an employer does not distinguish between different levels and types of unnamed security personnel, the employee typically will. Some positions will emphasize customer service. Some will value experience gained in law enforcement or the military.

Some employers cite specific physical abilities, such as the ability to lift twenty-five pounds.

MONTANA

Concealed carry honored in all states except California, Connecticut, Delaware, District of Columbia, Hawaii, Illinois, Maryland, Massachusetts, Minnesota, New Jersey, New Mexico, New York, Oregon, Rhode Island, South Carolina, and Washington and **with restrictions** (must be twenty-one years of age) in Alaska, Arizona, Colorado, Florida, Iowa, Kansas, Kentucky, Louisiana, Maine, Nebraska, Oklahoma, Pennsylvania, Texas, Virginia, West Virginia, and Wisconsin. Montana's private security guards are licensed by the Montana Board of Private Security. They must be licensed unless they fall under exemption categories identified in the state statute (http://leg.mt.gov/bills/mca/37/60/37-60-105.htm).

Security guards who will carry firearms must pursue a firearms endorsement.

The Montana board issues a number of other licenses, including resident manager. All contract security companies and proprietary security organizations are required to have an individual who serves in this role and who is typically present during weekday hours. Resident managers qualify through education and/or employment experience.

Montana Private Security Guard Requirements

Private security guards must be at least eighteen years of age (http://leg.mt.gov/bills/mca_toc/37_60_3.htm). They must be citizens or permanent US residents. They receive their licenses only after they have been employed by a contract security company or proprietary security organization.

The individual must meet fitness requirements. He or she must have good character and must not suffer from chemical dependencies or habitual drunkenness. An applicant will be disqualified on the basis of having been declared incompetent by a court or having been convicted of a felony offense or other crime involving dangerous weapons or moral turpitude. (Individuals are eligible if they have received pardons or had their competency fully restored.)

Training is required. A security guard can expect to receive the mandated training from his or her contract security company.

Armed Guard Requirements

A security guard who will carry a firearm will need an additional permit. He or she must complete a board-approved course. Training may be provided by a Montana Certified Firearm Instructor (CFI) or a Montana POST-certified instructor.

Board certified instructors teach a state-mandated curriculum, which includes firearm familiarization, safe handling, shooting judgment, issues regarding use of deadly force, and civil and criminal liability (http://www.mtrules.org/gateway/RuleNo.asp?RN=24%2E182%2E801). The prospective armed guard will take a written test and a proficiency test; the instructor will be responsible for determining competency.

Armed guards must requalify on a yearly basis.

Montana Resident Manager Requirements

A resident manager must meet experience requirements. The licensing agency can accept employment or vocational training.

The applicant must demonstrate two years of experience. Job experience can be obtained as 1) an employee in the field; 2) a sworn member of a police, investigative, or law enforcement department or agency; or 3) an administrator or supervisor in governmental or industrial security.

The Montana Law Enforcement Academy basic course is credited as six months of experience.

The board can instead accept four semesters of vocational training in security operations; to be credited for a semester of training, the student must take twelve credit hours.

A resident manager can also be licensed on the basis of combined experience, training, and education. In this instance, experience should account for at least half the requirement.

The prospective resident manager will be expected to pass a written test, though the requirement may be waived in some cases (http://www.mtrules.org/gateway/RuleNo.asp?RN=24%2E182%2E505). Applicants are scheduled for examination. The examinee is expected to score at least 70 percent on each portion. Retakes are permissible.

Background Check Requirement

Applicants must have criminal history checks carried out by the Montana Department of Justice and the FBI. The licensing agency notes that many law enforcement agencies can perform this service. Required information (including ORI number and reason for fingerprinting) can be found in the application packet. The background check carries a $27.25 fee; this is in addition to any fees that may be charged by the fingerprinting agency.

Fingerprint cards and fees are mailed to the Montana Department of Justice.

The Application Process

Application forms can be found on the website of the Montana Board of Private Security (http://bsd.dli.mt.gov/license/bsd_boards/psp_board/board_page.asp). There are separate application packages for security guards and resident managers.

The applicant will need to document age and citizenship or legal residency status. In the case of US born citizens, both these requirements can be satisfied with a copy of a birth certificate. The licensing agency will also require a passport-style photograph.

A security guard application package must include a copy of the training certificate. A guard who is requesting the firearms endorsement will also provide a copy of his or her firearms certification.

Resident manager applicants may use various documents, for example, copies of diplomas, transcripts, and certificates, to document qualifications.

A security guard applicant will need to provide a character reference. A resident manager applicant will need to provide three character references. References will mail the completed forms directly to the board office in Helena.

An applicant who has held an occupational license in another state must provide a verification form; this documentation is also to come straight from the source.

An applicant who answers "yes" to questions about adverse professional or legal history will need to provide supporting information. The licensing agency will require documents pertaining to charges and judgments or dismissals.

Application documents must be translated if they are in a language other than English.

The security guard application carries a nonrefundable fee of $100. The armed endorsement carries a $50 fee. A resident manager applicant pays a $175 application fee and $20 examination fee.

Staff review materials for administrative completeness and, in the case of routine applications, handle processing. The process takes about a month. Nonroutine applications are reviewed by the board; board review can extend the process by several months.

Applicants are invited to call the board or email their questions.

Private security licenses are renewed on an annual basis.

Additional Information

Licensing information is available from the Montana Board of Private Security (http://bsd.dli.mt.gov/license/bsd_boards/psp_board/board_page. asp). Licensing statutes (http://leg.mt.gov/bills/mca_toc/37_60_3.htm) are available online. Staff can be reached by telephone at 406-841-2300 or by email at dlibsdpsp at mt.gov.

NEBRASKA

Concealed carry honored in all states except California, Connecticut, Delaware, District of Columbia, Georgia, Hawaii, Illinois, Maryland, Massachusetts, Minnesota, Nevada, New Jersey, New York, Oregon, Pennsylvania, Rhode Island, and Washington and **with restrictions** (must be twenty-one years of age) in Alaska, Arizona, Colorado, Florida, Kansas, Kentucky, Maine, Oklahoma, South Carolina, and West Virginia.

Nebraska does not currently have a statewide licensing program for security officers. Prospective security officers answer to their employers.

Standards can vary a good deal, depending on job duties and budget; contract security agencies and governmental agencies often set standards quite high. A good background is fundamental. Prospective security guards may position themselves for success through trainings and voluntary certifications.

General Expectations for Security Officers

Nationwide, the expectation is generally that an unarmed security guard will be at least eighteen years of age and an armed security guard at least twenty-one. The most basic requirement is professional fitness. Employers often carry out a comprehensive background check; this may include a motor vehicle records check as well as a fingerprint-based criminal background check and an investigation into past employment. Many employers require drug and alcohol testing.

Some Nebraska employment ads are placed by major contract security agencies that have a regional or national presence. These organizations often have a well-established protocol for hiring. Requirements will vary depending on job duties. Some positions require candidate to take a personality assessment like the Minnesota Multiphasic Personality Inventory, or MMPI (https://www.pearsonassessments.com/store/usassessments/en/Store/Professional-Assessments/Personality-%26-Biopsychosocial/Minnesota-Multiphasic-Personality-Inventory-2/p/100000461.html). This is designed to identify candidates who have mental illness or other issues such as excessive anger. The candidate may need to have a thorough physical examination, including vision and hearing screening. The employer will want to know that the candidate can walk for long periods of time and display a reasonable amount of strength. The employer may also want to know that employees do not have serious conditions that could suddenly render them unable to respond.

Academic proficiency is also given consideration. Employers often cite verbal skills and the ability to write reports. A high school diploma or GED is a typical requirement. Some employers favor candidates with higher education. Coursework in criminal justice may be valued.

Law enforcement and military experience are often valued, especially if the job may entail doing more than just watching and reporting. Customer service experience may be considered as well. This is because many security officers interact with the public during daytime hours; they often spend more time giving directions than responding to emergency situations.

Training Expectations

The security industry has its own body of knowledge. States that license security guards typically require training in the following content areas:

- private security role
- legal limitations of power
- state rules and regulations
- access control
- emergency response
- writing notes and incident reports

The security company may have its own training program. However, the employer may also value previous knowledge.

Employers cite various third-party certifications. An employer may, for example, seek NFM Response to Resistance and PPCT Defensive Tactics training—if not before hiring within a specified time frame afterward. Some value voluntary credentials, such as certified protection officer (CPO). CPO certification is offered by the International Foundation for Protection

Officers. Certificate holders need to complete a specific curriculum. An individual will not achieve CPO certification until he or she has the equivalent of six months of job experience.

There are many trainings that are at least occasionally referenced. One recent posting for an Omaha security officer noted that the employee would need to obtain oleoresin capsicum (OC) foam deployment certification within a year of employment. In short, businesses have their own protocol for handling emergencies, and employers value both specific training and the ability to learn.

Nebraska Public Sector Job Expectations

State civil service job descriptions can provide a window into employer expectations (https://das.nebraska.gov/personnel/classcomp/jobspecs/P/pdf/P64831.pdf).

Nebraska security professionals are hired in several job classifications, including security guard. A minimum educational level is not specified for security guard positions. CPR certification and a driver's license are among the credentials that may be expected, though they are not necessarily a requirement in all positions. Required skills include the following:
- learning state and agency policies and procedures
- learning to operate electronic monitoring devices
- communicating with various groups, from visitors to government officials
- operating vehicles and equipment
- handling emergency situations calmly
- administering first aid and CPR

Higher level positions include security shift supervisor and security director. A security professional might attain the position of security shift supervisor through experience. While there is no minimum education level stated, candidates may need to take evaluations that measure, among other things, the ability to communicate through written and oral means.

Some security officers who work in Nebraska are under the authority of other governmental authorities. An example would be those who work for the Transportation Security Administration (TSA).

Candidates are expected to hold a high school diploma or GED or have a year of related experience. The hiring agency gives credit to those with national service experience, whether paid or volunteer. Candidates can expect multiple assessments as part of the hiring process. A candidate will take a computer-based test (CBT) that measures English language proficiency as well as ability to read X-rays.

NEVADA

Concealed carry honored in all states except California, Colorado, Connecticut, Delaware, District of Columbia, Georgia, Hawaii, Illinois, Maryland, Massachusetts, Minnesota, New Jersey, New York, Oregon, Pennsylvania, Rhode Island, South Carolina, and Washington and **with restrictions** (must be twenty-one years of age) in Alaska, Arizona, Florida, Kansas, Kentucky, Maine, Michigan, Nebraska, Oklahoma, and West Virginia.

Nevada security guards are under the jurisdiction of the Nevada Private Investigator's Licensing Board. Employees are registered and issued work cards.

The board also licenses private patrol officers; the board defines a private patrol officer as someone who furnishes workers, such as guards, patrol officers, and armored transport. Requirements and fees are higher. License applications may be submitted by individuals or corporations. A corporation must have someone on board who meets state requirements.

Nevada Security Guard Requirements
Security guards must be at least eighteen. They must meet character and citizenship/residency requirements. They may not have felony convictions. Additionally, they cannot have been convicted of crimes involving moral turpitude or illegal possession or use of dangerous weapons.

An individual who will be working for a board-licensed security company will need to pass the examination found in the application packet. It is based on state statutes and administrative code. The following topics are covered:
- rights of citizens
- powers of arrest
- limits of authority
- recognizing noncompliance with laws
- recognizing noncompliance with regulations

The board requires 100 percent. Retakes are permitted. However, this can delay the registration process. The board has made a study guide available. Candidates may download study guides or request print copies; print copies cost five dollars.

Armed Security Guard Requirements

In order to be authorized to carry a firearm, a security guard must be at least twenty-one. The individual will not be registered until such time as he or she has an employer.

The prospective armed guard must take a board-approved course. It is the employer's responsibility to arrange for training. The employer will also provide documentation to the board.

An individual who is certified as a firearms instructor or has worked as a peace officer may be exempted from the usual training requirements.

An armed guard is expected to fire qualifying rounds every six months.

The Security Guard Background Check Process

The Nevada board requires fingerprint-based criminal background checks. This step is carried out after application. The board has provided a list of private agencies that are authorized to provide fingerprinting services. The applicant is to bring his or her receipt when visiting a preferred location. Out-of-state candidates will need to provide fingerprints on FBI-approved FD-258 cards.

The board notes that the fee paid at the time of application covers the cost of background check processing.

An applicant may receive provisional status before the results of the background check are known.

The Registration Application Process

Security guard applicants may download their application forms or apply on-line; they may begin by selecting "work cards/ registered employee services."

The licensing agency will require the following:

- two forms of identification (driver's license or ID and Social Security card or birth certificate)
- a passport-style photograph
- exam
- work authorization or permanent resident card (noncitizens only)

Some supporting documents can be uploaded to the online system or, if this is not possible, sent by mail, email, or fax. The board does not, however, recommend faxing photographs.

Individuals who opt to print and mail their applications may send them to either the Carson City or Las Vegas address.

The application fee may be eighty-five dollars or ninety-five dollars depending on the method of fingerprint submission; the processing fee is reduced for those who utilize electronic services.

There is a forty-four-dollar fee for an expedited work card. The board has provided a list of frequently asked questions (http://pilb.nv.gov/).

Private Patrolman Requirements and Application Process

In order to be eligible for a private patrolman license, an individual must have at least five years of experience in the security industry; this is defined as ten thousand hours.

The applicant must pass an examination. The minimum score is currently 75 percent. In the case of corporations, it is the qualifying agent who will be tested.

The examination is administered in Carson City and Las Vegas. Currently, it is available four times per year. The board has published a list of upcoming examination dates. Applications are to be in at least a month before the intended examination. The board will send confirmation to approved candidates. Those who have not yet received confirmation are asked not to attempt to attend an examination session.

A prospective licensee will have state and federal background checks; he or she will need to submit two fingerprint cards and a $51.25 fee. In cases where the applicant has lived in California, it will be necessary to carry out an additional background check through the California Department of Justice (CDOJ). This will entail submission of a third fingerprint card and an additional $32 fee; the fee will be made out to CDOJ. The application packet includes current fingerprinting information and fees.

Corporation members/officers will also submit fingerprint cards and identifying documentation; there is a separate brief application form that can be downloaded from the board website.

Qualifying experience can be documented by employers or supervisors. The board may accept documentation by another qualified individual; in this instance, the individual will need to justify his or her qualifications.

The applicant will also need to provide three references. The board will require a financial statement. Corporate entities must provide additional documentation.

The application package includes several documents that require notarization. The application is to be accompanied by a nonrefundable $100 examination fee and $750 background deposit. There is an additional application fee of $20 per person. Applicants with questions are invited to call the board.

Application materials are sent to the Carson City office; the address is included in the application packet.

Additional Information

Credentialing information is available from the Nevada Private Investigator's Licensing Board (https://nevadapilb.glsuite.us/HomeFrame.aspx). Applicable statutes are found in Chapter 648 of the state code (https://www.leg.state.nv.us/NRS/NRS-648.html#NRS648Sec110). The board can be reached by telephone at (775) 687-3223 or by email at pilbinfo@ag.nv.gov.

NEW HAMPSHIRE

Concealed carry honored in all states except California, Connecticut, Delaware, District of Columbia, Hawaii, Illinois, Maryland, Massachusetts, Minnesota, Montana, Nebraska, Nevada, New Jersey, New Mexico, New York, Oregon, Rhode Island, South Carolina, Texas, Washington, and Wisconsin, and **with restrictions** (must be twenty-one years of age) in Alaska, Arizona, Colorado, Florida, Iowa, Kansas, Kentucky, Louisiana, Maine, Michigan, Oklahoma, Pennsylvania, Virginia, and West Virginia.

New Hampshire has an approval process for both armed and unarmed security guards who work as employees of security agencies. Unarmed security guards are not under department jurisdiction if they are hired directly by businesses: for example, if someone is hired directly by a store to serve as a watchperson (http://www.gencourt.state.nh.us/rsa/html/VII/106-F/106-F-2.htm).

Unarmed Security Guard Requirements

In order to work as an unarmed security guard, a person must meet general eligibility requirements. An individual could be denied based on criminal history or unprofessional acts.

Armed Security Guard Requirements

Armed security guards must complete a qualifying course, both initially and every year thereafter. They will need at least four hours of training that covers 1) firearms technique and safety and 2) laws and moral/ethical issues regarding use of force (http://www.gencourt.state.nh.us/rsa/html/VII/106-F/106-F-8-a.htm).

Firearms instructor schools operated by the following organizations have been accepted for qualification:
- National Rifle Association
- Smith & Wesson
- SIG Sauer
- Police Standards and Training Council
- FBI

Other programs can be accepted if they are determined to be equivalent by the Commissioner of Safety.

Candidates must provide identification to their instructors. The armed security guard will need to demonstrate accuracy. He or she can qualify with a score of 75 percent. Shooting expectations are detailed in the firearms proficiency certification form.

A security guard will need a shotgun familiarization course if his or her employer has shotguns.

The licensing agency notes that a pistol permit does not authorize the carrying of firearms by a security guard.

A security officer who does not pass the annual qualification can be permitted to work as an unarmed guard if he or she is otherwise entitled.

The individual may be reexamined.

The Registration Process for Armed and Unarmed Guards

Unarmed guards have criminal history records checks; armed guards have criminal records checks and fingerprint-based criminal background checks. They are directed to call (603) 223-3873 to schedule their fingerprinting appointments.

Employee applications are available on the website of the Department of Safety (http://www.nh.gov/safety/divisions/nhsp/ssb/permitslicensing/pluda.html). Applications are to be brought in person to the Department of Safety Building at 33 Hazen Drive in Concord. The public counter (Room 106) is open on weekdays between 8:15 a.m. and 4:00 p.m.

Armed guard status is dependent on receipt of a form DSSP 158, signed by the firearms instructor.

An applicant who answers "yes" to questions about criminal background, mental illness, addictions, protective orders, or actions against licenses will need to provide explanation.

The applicant will include names and addresses of three references. References will be sent questionnaires if there are questions about the applicant's character; the process is detailed in the state administrative code.

Fees for unarmed guards total forty dollars; this includes background check fees. For armed guards, there is an additional $26.50 fingerprinting fee.

Approved employees receive state-issued identification cards.

Individual Security Guard Requirements and Application Process

An individual who is licensed as a security guard must have a surety bond worth fifty thousand dollars (http://www.gencourt.state.nh.us/rsa/html/VII/106-F/106-F-9.htm). An applicant will need to provide evidence of a bond that is concurrent with the licensing period.

Licenses are denied on the basis of felony convictions or on records of violent misdemeanors or crimes involving theft or dishonesty.

An individual applicant pays a $150 fee plus $35 in criminal records and investigative background check fees.

Private security guards are issued identification cards upon approval.

New Hampshire Public Sector Security Officer Requirements

Some New Hampshire security officers are hired into the public sector. Human Resources has provided a set of general requirements for security officers at Levels I through IV (http://www.admin.state.nh.us/HR/classindex_a_d.htm).

The expectation at the Security Officer I level is a high school diploma or equivalency and a year of related experience. Experience could be earned in any of various job roles, including law enforcement, corrections, or military. Additional experience beyond the high school level may substitute for the year of experience. The individual is expected to have a driver's license.

Positions at the Security Officer II level are open only to candidates who are twenty-one or older. Candidates are expected to pass a physical. Some departments impose additional requirements.

In general, at the highest levels, there is an expectation of college coursework and police training.

Additional Information

Information about security guard requirements is available from the Permits and Licensing Unit of the Division of State Police (http://www.nh.gov/safety/divisions/nhsp/ssb/permitslicensing/index.html). Statutes (http://www.gencourt.state.nh.us/rsa/html/NHTOC/NHTOC-VII-106-F.htm) and administrative code can be accessed from the website of the Division of State Police.

The Permit and Licensing Unit can be reached by telephone at (603) 223-3873 or by email at PermitsandLicensing@dos.nh.gov.

NEW JERSEY

Concealed carry honored in all states except California, Colorado, Connecticut, Delaware, District of Columbia, Georgia, Hawaii, Illinois, Louisiana, Maryland, Massachusetts, Nebraska, Nevada, New Mexico, New York, North Dakota, Oregon, Pennsylvania, Rhode Island, South Carolina, Washington, Wisconsin, and Wyoming and **with restrictions** (must be twenty-one years of age) in Alaska, Arizona, Kansas, Kentucky, Maine, Michigan, Oklahoma, and West Virginia.

New Jersey security officers must meet requirements promulgated under the Security Officer Registration Act (SORA). Individuals who operate security agencies are licensed. Employees and subcontractors are registered as security officers. They must meet background and training requirements. Even off-duty police officers are, in many instances, subject to SORA. Security officers who are employed by businesses other than security services to serve their own internal purposes, however, are not subject to the same rules.

Armed security guards will need to hold pistol permits. The process is separate. In many cases, the application will be submitted to a local authority.

Security Officer Requirements

A security officer must be at least eighteen. He or she must have an acceptable legal background. There can be no criminal convictions of the first, second, third, or fourth degree and no convictions involving use, possession, or sale of controlled substances. Other convictions may be disqualifying if the superintendent determines that registration would be contrary to the public interest.

Once approved, the individual will need to complete a training program. It will include twenty-four hours of instruction and will be taught by a certified instructor. Training is to be completed within thirty days of employment.

Registration is renewed biennially. The security officer will need to take a sixteen-hour refresher course.

The Security Officer Application Process

New Jersey mandates that any employee regulated under SORA provide an "employee's statement." Employees will provide basic information, such as age, and will affirm that they have not been convicted of disqualifying crimes.

Application precedes fingerprinting and training. Applications are submitted online (https://eapps.njsp.org/applicant).

Background checks will be carried out by the State Bureau of Investigation and the Federal Bureau of Investigation. The applicant will find a fingerprinting form at the end of the application. The vendor is now Identogo by MorphoTrust. Applicants can find information on the "New Jersey" page of the MorphoTrust website (https://nj.ibtfingerprint.com/); however, they will not be able to schedule without the required form. This can be found in the application.

An individual who has been fingerprinted but is awaiting background check results may be granted a temporary permit.

There is a $75 application/certification fee.

Requirements for Armed Security Officers

Private security employees are specifically referenced in Chapter 54 of the State Administrative Code: "Firearms and Weapons." One of the requirements for obtaining a "pistol permit" is demonstration of need. If a security officer is to carry a handgun, the state police will need to know that he or she incurs threat of bodily harm while performing authorized duties and also that the weapon is needed to alleviate the threat of bodily harm to some person(s). Applications may be denied on the basis of criminal background, drug use, or mental illness.

The state requires a demonstration of safe handling and usage. There are many alternatives. The applicant may demonstrate that he or she has completed an appropriate course, test, or qualification. The instructor or provider does need to represent a reputable organization. An instructor may be qualified based on certification by the National Rifle Association or a police academy; other certifications may be accepted. A training course can also be accepted if it is determined to be substantially equivalent to the one that has been approved by the New Jersey Police Training Commission. Options are described in 13:54-2.4 of the Administrative Code.

The required application is SD 642. It can be downloaded from the website of the New Jersey State Police (http://www.njsp.org/info/forms. html#firearms). It is generally also available from police stations. Three references will need to sign the form; the purpose is to verify that the applicant has good character and can display self-control.

Handgun application materials are typically submitted to the chief of police of the local jurisdiction. However, in some cases, they are submitted to the Superintendent of the Division of State Police.

The applicant will provide evidence of required knowledge and a letter indicating the need to carry a firearm. The following are also required:

- four small photographs
- a consent to release mental health records
- a twenty-dollar fee

Requirements for Security Operators

Individuals who operate security agencies (proprietors, partners, officers) are also regulated by SORA. They must meet requirements beyond those required of security officers. Security operators must be at least twenty-five years of age. They must have five years of experience at an appropriate level of authority. In order to be accepted, experience earned through a security agency must be at the managerial or supervisory level. The licensing agency will also accept law enforcement experience. An individual who qualifies on the basis of law enforcement experience can no longer be connected with a law enforcement agency.

A security operator will need five character references from citizens whom he or she has known for at least three years.

A security agency must deliver a five-thousand-dollar surety bond.

Additional Information

Security officer registration information is available from the New Jersey State Police; the necessary documents can be found under "private detective information" (http://www.njsp.org/about/private-detective.html). The Private Detective Unit can be reached by email at pdu@gw.njsp.org.

NEW MEXICO

Concealed carry honored in all states except California, Connecticut, District of Columbia, Georgia, Hawaii, Illinois, Louisiana, Maryland, Massachusetts, New Jersey, New York, Oregon, Pennsylvania, Rhode Island, and Washington and **with restrictions** (must be twenty-one years of age) in Alaska, Arizona, Colorado, Florida, Kansas, Kentucky, Maine, Michigan, Oklahoma, South Carolina, Texas, West Virginia, and Wisconsin.

New Mexico security guards are under the jurisdiction of the New Mexico Private Investigations Advisory Board. The board registers security guards at multiple levels. In order to use devices that are regarded as nonlethal, a security guard must be at Level 2. The security guard must be at Level 3 to carry firearms.

Security Guard Eligibility Requirements
To be eligible for registration at Level I, an applicant must be at least eighteen years old. To be registered at Level 2 or 3, he or she must be at least twenty-one.

Level 2 or 3 security guards must hold high school diplomas or the equivalent. Additionally, Level 3 applicants must undergo psychological evaluation; the purpose is to determine if they have the mental stability to carry firearms.

Security Guard Training Requirements
All registered security guards must complete mandated training (http://www. rld.state.nm.us/boards/Private_Investigations_Exam_and_Education_ Schedule.aspx). New Mexico has a tiered system. The board has provided a list of approved training providers at each level (http://www.rld.state.nm.us/ boards/Private_Investigations_Requirements_and_Continuing_Education. aspx).

The individual must complete eight hours of training in order to be credentialed at Level 1. The basic curriculum includes the following: authority and responsibility, legal training, and management and preservation of incident scenes.

An additional twenty hours is required at Level 2. The following topics are covered:

- conflict management / verbal and written communication
- use of force / liability
- restraint and control devices
- defensive impact tools
- chemical agents

The Level 3 curriculum is sixteen hours. It includes the following:

- firearm safety rules
- weapon manipulation
- firearm retention and equipment
- storage devices
- ammunition and storage
- hazards of firearms in the home
- training family members
- locking devices
- types of sidearms
- marksmanship
- mental conditioning / tactics
- threat recognition / judgmental shooting
- powers of arrest / laws regarding firearms and deadly force

In order to be authorized to carry a firearm, an individual must qualify; the qualification must be carried out with the type and caliber weapon that the security guard will be carrying while on duty. Documentation must be provided by a recognized instructor; the instructor may be certified by the Law Enforcement Activities Division of the National Rifle Association or the New Mexico Law Enforcement Academy (http://164.64.110.239/nmac/parts/title16/16.048.0004.htm).

The student will need to shoot 80 percent on the qualifying round. He or she is allowed two attempts in direct succession. The armed security guard will requalify yearly.

Security Guard / Private Patrol Examination Requirement

Applicants must pass a jurisprudence examination, or test of laws and rules. The minimum passing score is 90 percent.

The examination can be found in the "forms" section of the board website. It is to be submitted with the application materials.

Background Check Process

New Mexico requires fingerprint-based criminal background checks. Applicants will use the approved vendor, Cogent. They can complete the registration process online (https://www.aps.gemalto.com/nm/index_NM.htm). An applicant will select his or her preferred New Mexico location from the map provided.

The Department of Public Safety no longer accepts "hard cards." However, Cogent offers a fingerprint scanning service (https://www.aps. gemalto.com/nm/index_NM.htm). Out-of-state applicants will initiate the process by registering with Cogent. They will have their fingerprints made on standard FD-258 applicant cards. The ORI number can be found in the application packet. The background check fee is forty-four dollars for both in-state and out-of-state applicants.

The applicant will include his or her Cogent receipt in the application packet. The board will receive background check results electronically.

The Application Process

Application forms can be downloaded from the board website (http://www. rld.state.nm.us/boards/Private_Investigations_Forms_and_Applications. aspx). Multiple supplemental documents will be required.

Applicants may use their driver's licenses or state-issued IDs to document age.

Applicants with "yes" answers to background or fitness questions will need to provide written explanation. Those who affirm a felony or misdemeanor charges will need to provide court documents.

The board will also require explanation of name changes. The applicant will need to attach two recent two-by-two photographs. The application packet includes a release form that requires notarization.

The licensing agency will require documentation of training certification. Level 2 and 3 applicants will provide documentation of their firearms or Taser certification.

Additionally, Level 2 and 3 applicants will include copies of their diplomas or equivalency documents.

A Level 3 applicant will provide documentation of positive evaluation from a licensed psychologist.

The application fee is fifty dollars for Level 1 or 2 credentialing and seventy-five for Level 3 credentialing.

Private Patrol Operator and Manager Licenses

An individual who is licensed as a private patrol operator is in business for himself or herself. Experience is required. The board will look for fully four thousand hours, accrued in the five-year period before application. At least one year is to have been spent in a supervisory role.

The professional will need to take out a liability insurance policy. The license application fee is four hundred dollars. To be licensed as a private patrol operations manager, a security professional must either be registered as a Level 3 security guard or licensed as a private patrol operator. He or she must provide employer documentation.

At the manager level, the application fee is three hundred dollars.

Additional Information

Information about security guard credentialing is available from the New Mexico Private Investigations Advisory Board (http://www.rld.state.nm.us/boards/Private_Investigations.aspx). The board can be reached by telephone at (505) 476-4650.

NEW YORK

Concealed carry honored in all states except California, Colorado, Connecticut, Delaware, District of Columbia, Florida, Georgia, Hawaii, Illinois, Louisiana, Maryland, Massachusetts, Minnesota, Nebraska, Nevada, New Jersey, New Mexico, North Dakota, Oregon, Pennsylvania, Rhode Island, South Carolina, Washington, and Wyoming and **with restrictions** (must be twenty-one years of age) in Alabama, Alaska, Arizona, Kansas, Kentucky, Maine, Michigan, Oklahoma, and West Virginia.

New York City—Concealed carry honored in all states except Alabama, California, Colorado, Connecticut, Delaware, District of Columbia, Georgia, Hawaii, Illinois, Louisiana, Maryland, Massachusetts, Minnesota, Montana, Nebraska, Nevada, New Jersey, New Mexico, North Carolina, North Dakota, Oregon, Pennsylvania, Rhode Island, South Carolina, Tennessee, Utah, Virginia, Washington, Wisconsin, and Wyoming and **with restrictions** (must be twenty-one years of age) in Alaska, Arizona, Kansas, Kentucky, Maine, Oklahoma, and West Virginia.

New York security guards are registered with the Division of Licensing Services. All security guards, armed or unarmed, must be registered with the division unless they fall under exemption categories outlined in the state statute (for example, current active status as a police officer).

In order to be eligible for registration, an individual must clear a criminal background check and meet general eligibility requirements, such as being of majority age. He or she must complete mandatory training. Training requirements are higher for armed security guards.

Eligibility Requirements
Security guards must be at least eighteen. They must be citizens or lawful residents of the United States. Their backgrounds must be free of felony convictions and crimes involving moral turpitude as well as other criminal offenses that are specifically referenced in state licensing law.

An individual may be denied registration on the basis of addiction to drugs or alcohol. He or she may be denied registration on the basis of 1) having been discharged from law enforcement or corrections for misconduct or incompetence or 2) having resigned under charge of misconduct or incompetence. The licensing agency will, however, consider the applicant's explanation for the discharge. In some cases, a waiver may be granted.

Security Guard Training Requirements
A security guard employee must complete eight hours of training before beginning duties. A certificate documenting preservice hours is to be provided to the division at the time of initial application.

The employee will receive an additional sixteen hours of training during his or her first ninety days on the job. The content of in-service hours will vary by job role and employer need.

In addition to preservice and in-service requirements, armed security guards must complete forty-seven hours of firearms training; prospective security guards typically enroll in training programs after receiving their basic security guard registration. A pistol permit is required.

Waivers and Exemptions for Peace Officers
Individuals with law enforcement training may qualify for training waivers. A former law enforcement agent may request a waiver for the eight hours of preservice training or the forty-seven-hour firearms training course. The officer will need to have at some point had training that was at least on a par with that required for security guards. A waiver may be granted to an individual who left law enforcement up to ten years prior. The former law enforcement officer may make a request by calling (518) 457-4135. The request can also be mailed. The waiver, if granted, is to be included in the application packet.

Current police officers are eligible for exemption without waiver. This is the case with some other peace officers. However, the division will still require some documentation. The application includes a summary of requirements for different categories of peace officer.

Continuing Competence Requirements

The division expects unarmed guards to complete eight hours of training each year (two eight-hour in-services during each renewal period).

Armed guards will complete sixteen hours of annual training: eight hours of in-service and an additional eight hours of firearms training.

Background Check Requirements

Employees are to have their fingerprints made prior to application. They will have them captured electronically, using the approved vendor, MorphoTrust. They must select a New York location. Scheduling can be carried out online; the applicant will need the ORI code found in the application packet. The individual may instead call MorphoTrust at 877-472-6915. The candidate will need to bring the request form found on the division website (http://www.dos.ny.gov/forms/licensing/1870-f-l-a.pdf). Two forms of ID will be required.

Security guard applicants must have background checks carried out by the Division of Criminal Justice Services (DCJS) and the FBI. The DCJS processing fee is currently $75.00 and the FBI fee, $14.75. Both fees are paid to MorphoTrust.

The vendor will provide two copies of the receipt; one is to accompany the application.

The New York Security Guard Application Process

Application materials can be downloaded from the board website (http://www.dos.ny.gov/licensing/securityguard/sguard.html). Application materials are available in English and in the following languages: Chinese, Haitian/Creole, Italian, Korean, Russian, and Spanish.

Applicants with "yes" responses to background questions are required to provide explanation.

The application fee is thirty-six dollars. Applicants who do not have a current New York photo ID or driver's license will need to visit the Department of Motor Vehicles (DMV) to have photos made. They will bring the inset from their application packet.

Application packets are mailed to the Division of Licensing Services in Albany.

The licensing agency requires notification of status changes. There is a separate form for this purpose.

Requirements for Private Patrol and Qualifying Agents

To go into business for oneself as a "watch, guard, or patrol agency," one must be at least twenty-five years of age. He or she must have two years of security (or equivalent) experience. Experience as a police officer or sheriff is creditable.

The licensing agency will require insurance. The applicant must provide signatures from five-character witnesses. He or she must pass an examination. The exam is offered approximately once per month; the licensing agency publishes an examination schedule twice a year.

If the business is a corporation, there must be a qualifying agent who has met the experience requirement. He or she will take the licensing examination.

A qualifier may provide services for his or her own company without separate registration as a security guard.

Additional Information

Information about security guard requirements is available from the New York State Division of Licensing (http://www.dos.ny.gov/licensing/securityguard/sguard.html). Call center representatives are available at (518) 474-7569. Licensees are expected to be familiar with the state licensing act.

NORTH CAROLINA

Concealed carry honored in all states except California, Connecticut, District of Columbia, Hawaii, Illinois, Maryland, Massachusetts, Minnesota, Nevada, New Jersey, New York, Oregon, and Rhode Island and **with restrictions** (must be twenty-one years of age) in Alaska, Arizona, Colorado, Florida, Kansas, Kentucky, Maine, Michigan, Oklahoma, Pennsylvania, South Carolina, and West Virginia.

North Carolina security guards are regulated by the North Carolina Private Protection Services Board. Some security guards will fall under exemption categories outlined in the state statute and will not need state credentialing; this is the case with governmental employees and with unarmed guards who are not agency employees but have been hired by a business to provide direct services.

Unarmed Security Guard Requirements
A security guard must be a citizen or resident alien at least eighteen years old. He or she must display good moral character. Administrative Code Title 12 Chapter 7 states that an applicant who has been convicted of particular criminal offenses during the prior five years will be considered to lack good moral character. Disqualifying offenses include those involving firearms, dugs, felonious assault, violence, larceny, burglary, breaking and entering, and moral turpitude.

Registration may also be denied based on a history of addiction or severe mental disease.

Unarmed guards must have at least sixteen hours of training. Training will cover the following concepts:
- legal issues
- the security guard in North Carolina
- patrol procedures
- emergency response
- communications

- deportment
- taking notes and writing reports

Training in "security officer legal issues" and "the security guard within North Carolina" together comprise four hours; this is to take place within twenty days of placement on post. The other required training is to take place within thirty days of the time the employee is hired in a permanent capacity.

The trainer is to be board-certified.

Armed Security Guard Requirements

An armed security guard employee must be at least twenty-one. The prospective armed guard must complete an additional course of at least twenty hours. The following content will be covered:

- legal limitations of security guard power and firearm usage / applicable statutes
- handgun safety
- handgun maintenance
- handgun fundamentals
- night firing

The course may be offered by the contract security company; the instructor will need to be board-certified.

The armed guard will need to qualify on an approved target course.

An armed guard who will carry a shotgun will need an additional four hours of training. He or she will need to qualify with the shotgun as well.

An armed permit holder will need to complete a refresher course and requalify before each annual renewal.

Background Check Requirements

North Carolina requires fingerprint-based background checks. Fingerprints are to be submitted on an FBI applicant card.

The applicant will also need to provide criminal record searches from counties where he or she has resided during the prior forty-eight months. In the case of in-state applicants, the search may be performed via the internet (if conducted through a North Carolina Administrative Office of the Courts Public Access User).

The Security Guard Application Process

An employee application form can be downloaded from the website of the Department of Public Safety (https://www.ncdps.gov/Index2.cfm?a=000003,003034,003059). There are different forms for different statuses, including unarmed guard and armed guard; the forms include a summary of required materials.

Prospective security guards must provide explanation if they have ever been convicted of felonies, misdemeanors, or traffic-related offenses.

Security guards must provide certificates of completion of security guard training and (if applicable) firearms training.

The Board will require a recent photograph; the photo is to be provided digitally in JPEG format. It may be submitted on CD or floppy disk or emailed to the following address: PPSASL-Photos at ncdoj.gov.

The applicant will sign an information release form. The initial registration fee for unarmed guard is $30; for armed guard, it is $45. The $38 fingerprint fee is also paid at the time of application. Application materials are sent to the board office in Raleigh.

Armed guard authorization is agency-specific. An armed guard who is employed by more than one company will need dual registration.

Employee registration is renewed on an annual basis.

Private Patrol and Qualifying Agent Requirements

An individual with management-, administrative-, or supervisory-level security experience can obtain a private patrol license; this authorizes self-employment.

The experience must be in a guard or patrol capacity. However, it may be accrued in a proprietary security organization, law enforcement organization, or branch of the US military.

If the experience was accrued in the military, the professional will need to demonstrate an occupational specialty as well as two years of recent experience.

If the applicant's background was in law enforcement or proprietary security, the licensing agency will look for three years of qualifying experience. The three years can be partially offset by postsecondary education. The board can credit 400 hours for an associate's degree, 800 hours for a bachelor's degree, or 1,200 hours for a graduate degree. Additional hours can be credited if the student completed concurrent coursework or training specifically focused on the private security industry: The director of the board may grant up to 100 hours of experience for training received in conjunction with an associate's degree, up to 200 for training received in conjunction with a bachelor's degree, or up to 300 for training received at the graduate level.

A military spouse who is credentialed in another jurisdiction on the basis of similar requirements may be eligible for licensing in North Carolina if he or she can demonstrate two years of recent experience. Education may substitute for a portion of the experience.

License applications should be requested from the Licensing Unit; the request may be made by telephone (https://www.ncdps.gov/index2.cfm?a=000003,003034,003051,003052). The applicant should be prepared to provide references. The licensing agency will seek county background checks representing the prior sixty months. The Department of Public Safety has provided instructions for in-state and out-of-state applicants. The applicant will pay a $150 application fee; this is in addition to the $38 fee for the fingerprint-based background check.

Additional Information

Licensing and registration information is available from the North Carolina Private Protective Services Board (https://www.ncdps.gov/Index2.cfm?a=000003,003034). The Licensing Unit can be reached by telephone at (919) 788-5320.

NORTH DAKOTA

Concealed carry honored in all states except California, Connecticut, District of Columbia, Hawaii, Illinois, Maryland, Massachusetts, New Jersey, New York, Oregon, and Rhode Island and **with restrictions** (must be twenty-one years of age) in Alaska, Arizona, Colorado, Florida, Iowa, Kansas, Kentucky, Louisiana, Maine, Michigan, Minnesota, Nebraska, Oklahoma, Pennsylvania, South Carolina, Tennessee, Texas, Virginia, Washington, West Virginia, and Wisconsin.

North Dakota security officers are under the jurisdiction of North Dakota Private Investigation and Security Board. All security officers must be credentialed unless they fall under exemption categories outlined in the North Dakota Century Code.

Those who work as employees of security agencies are registered. Those who work for proprietary companies have the option of being registered.

General Eligibility Requirements

In order to provide security services, an individual must have attained the age of at least eighteen. He or she must hold a high school diploma or the equivalent. The person cannot have a mental condition that would impact on the ability to practice competently. He or she cannot have been convicted of a disqualifying crime. Felonies are disqualifying as are certain lesser convictions including Class A or B misdemeanors that involve violence or intimidation. Any crime that must be listed in subsection 12.1-32-15 is potentially disqualifying; however, the board has the authority to license an individual despite a criminal conviction if it is determined that the crime does not impact negatively on the ability to carry out security duties and the individual has been rehabilitated to a sufficient extent.

However, registration can be denied on the basis of acts not specifically referenced in the state administrative code if the licensing agency determines that they reflect poorly on moral character and have some bearing on security guard practice.

Apprentice Security Officer Requirements

The entry-level credential is apprentice security officer. To hold apprentice status, an individual must complete twelve hours of classroom instruction or training (http://www.nd.gov/pisb/adminrules.html). In order to be credited, field training must be supervised by an experienced professional. This may be a commissioned security officer or a security professional who has two thousand hours of experience as a security officer or otherwise meets requirements described in section 93-02-02.1-10. Classroom instruction is to be supervised by a board-certified instructor. The initial training or instruction is to take place within thirty days of registration.

Security Officer and Commissioned Security Officer Requirements

In order to move up to "security officer" status, the security provider must accrue one thousand hours of work experience. He or she must also receive thirty-two hours of classroom instruction.

In order to move up to "commissioned security officer" status, the security officer must complete an additional three thousand hours of experience at the security officer level. He or she will need eighty hours of education.

Armed Guard Requirements

In order to be authorized to provide armed services, an employee must have reached at least "security officer" status (http://www.nd.gov/pisb/adminrules. html). A North Dakota armed guard must also complete training on a par with peace officers.

The board certifies firearms instructors. Board-certified instructors are professionals who have been certified as instructors by the North Dakota Peace Officer Standards and Training Board or the National Rifle Association or who have completed twenty-four months of internship under conditions acceptable to the board (http://www.nd.gov/pisb/faq.html).

The armed security officer will need to pass both a written exam and a shooting test.

Armed security officers must maintain continued proficiency. They must complete range qualification each year.

Security Provider Licensing Requirements

In order to be licensed for independent practice as a security service provider, a professional must have reached the "commissioned security officer" level or have fully four thousand hours of experience and eighty hours of instruction.

The prospective licensee must pass an examination; this step is typically completed after application. The exam is delivered in Bismarck. The candidate will need to be familiar with the current versions of state laws and rules. The board places limits on retakes. A candidate must wait thirty days after a failed attempt to apply for reexamination. If the candidate fails another attempt, he or she must wait a year. The board has made a study guide available for forty dollars.

Modified Requirements for Professionals with Comparable Training

There are various contexts in which the licensing agency will waive at least a portion of the training and experience requirements. As per 93-02-02.1-10 of the state administrative rule, credit may be granted for security work performed in other states that have comparable requirements, for security work performed for exempt proprietary businesses, or for law enforcement work. The licensing agency can also credit academic education in relevant subject areas.

The Application Process

Initial registration may take place before educational requirements have been met.

Application forms are available on the board website (http://www.nd.gov/pisb/forms.html). The applicant will also need to request fingerprint cards.

The applicant can also receive the necessary forms and materials by mailing a written request to the board along with twenty dollars.

Applicants are asked to attach all postsecondary transcripts. Applicants are to include two completed fingerprint cards. Those applying for licensure are also directed to include two passport-style photographs.

An employee can be issued a provisional registration card after all application materials, including fingerprints, have been submitted. The applicant will need to provide results from a criminal history records check. The permanent card will be issued after the results of fingerprint-based state and national background checks are in.

An applicant may incur multiple fees. The total fee for a security officer is $67 ($42 for background checks and $25 for registration). There is an additional $30 fee for armed status. A licensed security provider pays $42 for background checks, $100 for application and testing, and $130 for his or her license. This is in addition to the cost of a business license.

Licenses and registrations are renewed annually.

Additional Information
Licensing and registration information is available from the North Dakota Private Investigation and Security Board (http://www.nd.gov/pisb/). The board can be reached by telephone at (701) 222-3063.

OHIO

Concealed carry honored in all states except California, Connecticut, District of Columbia, Hawaii, Illinois, Maryland, Massachusetts, Minnesota, New Jersey, New York, Oregon, and Rhode Island and **with restrictions** (must be twenty-one years of age) in Alaska, Arizona, Colorado, Florida, Kansas, Kentucky, Maine, Michigan, Pennsylvania, South Carolina, and West Virginia.

Ohio security guards are regulated by Ohio Private Investigator Security Guard Services (PISGS). PISGS recognizes security professionals in various roles, including those who own security agencies, those who are hired to run security agencies, and those who are employed as guards. Those who are in the security business (whether sole proprietor, partnership, or corporation) are known as security providers. They are licensed. Officers may be designated as qualifying agents. Security guards who work as employees of security agencies are often referenced in statute simply as employees.

Licenses issued by Private Investigator Security Guard Services may be Class A, Class B, or Class C. If security is the only service provided, a Class C license will be issued.

Individuals must hold state credentials unless they are exempt under state statute. Individuals who are protecting the property of their own employers will not necessarily be defined as security providers under state statute (http://www.publicsafety.ohio.gov/links/PSU0004.pdf).

In order to carry firearms, one must hold a separate certification, also issued by PISGS. The firearm certification may be held by a licensee, qualifying agent, or employee.

One common requirement for all licenses and registrations is a background check.

The Background Check Process

All licensees and registrants must have fingerprint-based background checks. However, the process is not the same for all. Individuals who will carry firearms need to have background checks processed through the Bureau of Criminal Identification (BCI) and the FBI. Those who will not carry firearms need background checks only through the BCI. (If the employee or licensee will be carrying a firearm, the BCI is to be notified at the time of application.)

Applicants will use the approved vendor, Web Check. They can have the fingerprints made before application but should be aware that the Department of Public Safety can only accept background check results completed within the previous thirty days; they are advised to wait until they are ready to submit their materials. The licensing agency has provided a coupon that the applicant will fill out and bring to his or her chosen location (http://www.pisgs.ohio.gov/pisgs.stm).

Employee Registration

For employees, background is the primary qualifier. A criminal history is not always disqualifying. However, the individual cannot have been convicted, within the prior three years, of a felony or of any crime involving moral turpitude.

The employer will have the responsibility of ensuing that employees are registered. Employers may register employees using the online system. The licensing agency will require a passport-type photograph.

An approved security guard employee will be issued an ID card. Registration must be renewed annually.

Armed Guard Requirements

In order to be certified as a firearm bearer, a licensee or registrant must complete a program approved by the Ohio Peace Officer Training Commission (OPOTC).

The program will include twenty hours of training related to handgun usage. It may include additional training related to use of other firearms.

Prospective armed guards will certify that they have not been convicted of domestic violence.

Armed guards must requalify annually.

Qualifying Agent Requirements

A security agency must have at least one qualifying agent; this may be the owner or may be a person hired by the owner. There may be multiple qualifying agents. A qualifying agent will be required to submit a number of documents verifying character and qualifications.

The applicant must demonstrate integrity. The licensing agency will require five professional references. They are to come from individuals with whom the applicant has been acquainted for at least five years.

Recency is a factor in evaluating criminal history. The professional will need to have spent at least two years working in a related field. The time may have been spent providing services for a private security provider, a law enforcement agency, or another public agency. The licensing agency may accept experience as an attorney. Other experience may be accepted, including education in law enforcement or criminal justice. There are time limits. Education may be accepted if earned at any point during the prior ten years. It cannot, however, be used to fulfill the entire requirement. An individual who qualifies on the basis of education will still need two thousand hours of security work experience. Requirements are detailed in Administrative Code 4501:7-1.

Qualifying agents must pass an examination that covers the security business as well as state laws and rules. Candidates do not complete this step until after application. The examination is administered in Columbus. The licensing agency will send approved candidates email notification of available examination dates. The candidate should be familiar with Chapter 4749 of the state code and with the associated rules. The candidate is expected to pass the examination within ninety days of notification of approval. An individual may be allowed up to three attempts before the application is denied and reapplication is required. However, an applicant who fails to show up for a scheduled examination may be denied and required to reapply.

The Qualifying Agent Application Process

The security provider application and qualifying agent application are to be submitted together. They may now be submitted online. PISGS has provided a PDF guide. Individuals who opt for online application should obtain electronic copies of certain required documents. Various formats, including PDF, Word, and JPG can be accepted.

Applicants qualifying on the basis of security experience will need to document licensure in the state where experience was accrued.

Those who seek consideration of an academic degree should submit a copy of their certificate.

Those with military police backgrounds should submit a copy of the DD-214.

Those with law backgrounds should submit letters of good standing from the state's supreme court.

The licensing agency will require a two-by-two photograph. It can be digitalized if it meets specifications described in the online license guide.

Qualifying agents who seek adjunct firearm certification will provide a copy of their Ohio Peace Officer Training Academy (OPOTA) certificate. Those who hold status as peace officers will upload their recent score sheets.

The licensing agency will correspond by email. Applications are also available in print form on the PISGS website (http://www.pisgs.ohio.gov/pisgs.stm).

Applicants who seek firearm bearer certification will submit an additional form.

The licensing agency expedites processing for veterans and spouses.

Additional Information

Private Investigator Security Guard Services (http://www.pisgs.ohio.gov) is under the banner of the Ohio Department of Public Safety. The licensing agency can be reached by telephone at 614-466-0342.

OKLAHOMA

Concealed carry honored in all states except California, Connecticut, District of Columbia, Hawaii, Illinois, Maryland, Massachusetts, Minnesota, New Jersey, New York, Oregon, and Rhode Island and **with restrictions** (must be twenty-one years of age) in Alaska, Arizona, Colorado, Florida, Kansas, Kentucky, Maine, Michigan, Nebraska, Pennsylvania, South Carolina, West Virginia, and Wisconsin.

Oklahoma security guards are regulated by the Oklahoma Council on Law Enforcement Education and Training, or CLEET. Both armed and unarmed guards hold state licenses.

First-time security guards go through a state-specific training and testing program. Oklahoma has provisions in place for reciprocity.

Eligibility and Training Requirements for Unarmed Guards

To be eligible for an unarmed license, one must be a citizen or legal alien of the United States and at least eighteen years of age. Felonies and crimes of moral turpitude are disqualifying. However, provisions do exist for waiver.

Training is required unless the applicant has obtained sufficient experience in another jurisdiction. However, in some cases, the training will not be completed until after employment. An individual who has not already completed comparable training or qualified for exemption on the basis of work experience will need to complete training within 180 days. Unarmed guard training includes two phases, each consisting of twenty hours. The licensing agency has provided a list of approved trainers and the phases they are authorized to offer (http://www.ok.gov/cleet/Licensing/Training). Contact information is provided. Prospective students may call to confirm that information is current.

Ultimately, the student will need to pass an examination. In 2015, CLEET stopped offering the examination at its office in Ada. Examinations are available through Career Tech at forty-four Oklahoma testing centers. There is a twenty-five-dollar fee. Candidates are referred to the Career

Tech website for information about test sites (http://www.okcareertech.org/technology-centers).

Oklahoma peace officers, correctional officers, and reserve officers may provide evidence of equivalent training. Military police and full-time out-of-state police officers can also be considered for exemption from the usual training requirements. All professionals who believe they have had equivalent training will be required to submit training documentation at the time of application. The licensing agency may choose to waive the full unarmed course or a portion of it.

An out-of-state security guard may be granted an exemption from unarmed training if he or she has worked as a security guard full-time for at least one of the three prior years.

Additional Requirements for Armed Guards

Armed guards must be at least twenty-one. They must confirm employment and need to carry a firearm.

Armed guard training includes an additional thirty-two-hour phase (http://www.ok.gov/cleet/Licensing/Training/index.html). The candidate must pass a firearms test; this is in addition to the general test for unarmed guards.

Firearms training is not waived on the basis of prior training. An armed guard must have a psychological evaluation. This step is carried out before training. Results from psychological evaluations are valid for only six months. An individual who does not apply within the requisite time period will need to have another evaluation.

Full-time peace officers and active reserve officers may be exempted from psychological evaluation.

Insurance Requirements

The individual must hold an insurance policy or bond unless covered under his or her employer's insurance policy. An unarmed security guard would be required to have coverage of at least five thousand dollars and an armed guard coverage of at least ten thousand dollars. Currently, these figures constitute acceptable minimums for self-employed security guards who do not employ others. In cases where the applicant employs others, the policy must cover one hundred thousand dollars.

The Application Process

Prospective security guards will have their fingerprints made before application. They may obtain fingerprint cards from their local law enforcement office or submit an online request for fingerprint cards (http://www.ok.gov/cleet/Licensing/Security_Guards). Two fingerprint cards are to be included in the completed application package.

The applicant will also need to have records checks carried out by his or her local sheriff's department and police department. An applicant who has resided in Oklahoma for less than six months will need to obtain records checks from the previous place of residence; the application packet outlines options for obtaining the necessary documentation. An Oklahoma resident who has changed addresses within the prior ninety days will also need to provide records checks from previous municipalities.

Application packets can be downloaded from the CLEET website (http://www.ok.gov/cleet/CLEET_Forms/index.html).

The applicant will select one of four qualifications for licensure:
- conditional
- mandate training
- comparable training
- experience

"Conditional" is the status for employees who have not yet completed the required training. A conditional licensee must be sponsored by a security agency.

The application packet includes multiple documents that require notarization. One is a records release authorization. The applicant will also need to provide a notarized affidavit verifying lawful presence in the United States.

An applicant for unarmed guard will need to submit two passport-style photographs; an applicant for armed guard will need to submit three.

The applicant will submit either a letter of employment or evidence of insurance or bond.

An individual who has an arrest record will submit additional certified court documentation. If a court record does not exist, the individual will need a certified letter from the court affirming this.

The fee is $91 for an unarmed security guard license and $141 for an armed guard license. The fee includes fingerprint processing costs.

Application materials are sent to the following address:

CLEET Private Security

2401 Egypt Road

Ada, OK 74820-0669

Renewals and Upgrades

Security guard licenses are issued for three years. Eight hours of continuing education is required for renewal. The security guard will provide documentation of holding a current surety bond (unless covered under an employer's insurance policy).

Unarmed guards who have completed the requisite training and testing may file upgrade applications to change their status to that of armed guard. There is a fifty-dollar fee.

Requirements for Officers and Branch Managers

Officers and branch managers must be at least twenty-one. They must have good character.

Other Security Licenses Issued by CLEET

CLEET Private Security also issues temporary out-of-state licenses and special event licenses. In order to be eligible for the special event license, an individual must be employed by a security agency that is contracted to provide services for the event (http://www.oar.state.ok.us/viewhtml/390_35-5-4.htm).

Additional Information

Security guard licensing information is available from the Oklahoma Council on Law Enforcement Education and Training. Rules are available online (http://www.ok.gov/cleet/About_Us/Rules/index.html). Applicants should be aware that regulations change periodically. The licensing page includes contact information for multiple staff members. By dialing 405-239-5100, one can reach the main CLEET switchboard.

OREGON

Concealed carry honored in all states except California, Colorado, Connecticut, Delaware, District of Columbia, Georgia, Hawaii, Illinois, Louisiana, Maryland, Massachusetts, Minnesota, Nevada, New Jersey, New Mexico, New York, North Dakota, Pennsylvania, Rhode Island, South Carolina, Texas, Washington, Wisconsin, and Wyoming and **with restrictions** (must be twenty-one years of age) in Alaska, Arizona, Kansas, Kentucky, Maine, Michigan, Oklahoma, and West Virginia.

Oregon security professionals are licensed and certified by the Private Security Program. The program credentials both armed and unarmed security guards. Security agency managers are also licensed.

Security guards qualify by meeting general eligibility requirements and completing mandatory training.

Eligibility Requirements

Unarmed security professionals must be at least eighteen and in possession of a high school diploma, GED, or four-year degree. They must meet moral standards. The candidate can be disqualified on the basis of professional misconduct.

The department expects professionals to display the following values:

- honesty
- fair treatment of other people
- good character
- public trust
- respect for laws

The board has provided a list of disqualifying criminal offenses; a link can be found on the main page of the Private Security Program. Some crimes are permanently disqualifying. Others are disqualifying for a seven- or ten-year period.

Oregon has set additional standards for armed guards (http://www.oregon.gov/dpsst/PS/Pages/Armed-Security-Professional.aspx). They must be at least twenty-one years of age. The individual cannot have been committed to Oregon's Mental Health and Development Disability Services Division (or similar out-of-state service). He or she cannot have been banned from carrying a firearm as a result of mental illness or other issues and cannot have a civil restraining order in place that would preclude firearm possession in interstate commerce.

Security Guard Training Requirements
The prospective security guard must have English language skills, as the licensing agency mandates that training programs and assessments be completed in English.

The basic unarmed training curriculum is fourteen hours. Training is to be provided by a certified instructor. The board has provided a list of qualified instructors (http://www.oregon.gov/dpsst/PS/Pages/Armed-Security-Professional.aspx).

Armed security guards must complete a firearms course of at least twenty-four hours. The course will be taught by a certified firearms instructor. Ultimately, armed security guards will need to pass a gun-handling test and a firearm qualification as well as a written test.

Unarmed guards will complete renewal training during each two-year renewal period. Armed guards must requalify annually.

Security Manager Requirements
Oregon has provisions for licensure of supervisory managers and executive managers. Managers must meet licensing requirements for security professionals as described in Rule 259-060-0020. They must also meet manager training requirements. The manager course will be at least eight hours. It will include an assessment component. Managers need to score at least 85 percent to pass. The licensing agency recommends that candidates review statutes and rules beforehand. The course and exam together cost $250 for executive managers and $75 for supervisory managers.

Companies may employ one or more licensed executive managers. Executive managers must be at least twenty-one years of age. Management training is provided by the department or a designee of the department. Prospective executives can find a list of upcoming dates on the Department website (http://www.oregon.gov/dpsst/PS/Pages/Executive-Managers.aspx).

The Application Process

Security guards must have background checks processed by the Oregon State Police and the FBI. Fingerprints may be made and transmitted electronically by Fieldprint (http://www.fieldprintoregon.com/). Appointments can be scheduled online. There are sites located in many areas of the state. Applicants also have the option of utilizing out-of-state Fieldprint services (http://www.oregon.gov/dpsst/PS/Pages/fpfaq.aspx). The applicant will need to bring two forms of identification. Fieldprint can be reached at 888-472-8918.

Individuals may also request traditional fingerprint cards or Live Scan packets from the department; they may utilize local law enforcement agencies or trained providers to roll fingerprints and scan and print them. Completed fingerprint cards must be enclosed in tamperproof bags before submission. The person who rolls the fingerprints will need to sign an affidavit.

The fingerprint processing fee is $41.75 for security guards, $42.75 for managers.

Application forms can be downloaded from the website (http://www.oregon.gov/dpsst/PS/Pages/forms.aspx). The licensing agency will require several supporting documents. The applicant must sign a code of ethics form. The instructor will sign an affidavit verifying training.

An unarmed security guard may work under a temporary permit for a maximum of 120 days; board permission is required.

If there is a requirement that has not been met or documented, the applicant will receive a notice of deficiency. The requirement is to be met/documented within twenty-one days.

Initial certification carries a $106.75 fee. The executive manager licensing fee is $292.75. The supervisory manager licensing fee is $117.75.

Application materials are to be mailed to the Department of Safety Standards and Training in Portland.

A security professional who has qualified for an additional credential will need to again submit an application. Application status can be checked online using the IRIS system. Security guards who are currently certified as unarmed guards may work in an armed capacity while waiting for their ID cards to be issued; they will need to carry authorizing paperwork.

Additional Information

The Private Security Certification and Licensing Program is under the banner of the Oregon Department of Safety Standards and Training (http://www.oregon.gov/dpsst/PS/pages/index.aspx). The program can be reached by email at security.investigators at state.or.us or by telephone at (503)378-8531. Interested individuals can join the DPSST Private Security List Serve (http://www.oregon.gov/dpsst/PS/Pages/ListServe.aspx).

PENNSYLVANIA

Concealed carry honored in all states except California, Connecticut, Delaware, District of Columbia, Hawaii, Illinois, Maryland, Massachusetts, Minnesota, Nebraska, Nevada, New Jersey, New Mexico, New York, Oregon, Rhode Island, South Carolina, and Washington and **with restrictions** (must be twenty-one years of age) in Alaska, Arizona, Colorado, Florida, Kansas, Kentucky, Maine, Michigan, Oklahoma, and West Virginia.

Pennsylvania regulates the private security industry at the state level. However, an individual may submit materials to a local/ county authority.

Like other states, Pennsylvania distinguishes between individuals who run security agencies and those who are employed by them. The Private Detective Act of 1953 (as amended) covers requirements for watch, patrol, and guard businesses. It also sets minimum hiring standards for employees.

Armed guards must conform to a separate, higher set of standards.

Requirements for Security Businesses

A security business must be licensed. Practice must be covered under a surety bond. The state has set requirements that must be met by a sole proprietor or by at least one member of a corporation or partnership. The applicant must be at least twenty-five years old. He or she must have no fewer than three years of qualifying law enforcement or investigative/detective experience.

The qualifying member and other applicants (partners or members of the association) must be fingerprinted.

There may be minor procedural differences in credentialing from county to county. The following is from Monroe County (http://www.pabulletin. com/secure/data/vol35/35-38/1708.html). Applicants who are having trouble finding their local authority should recognize that security businesses are covered under a private detective act and that print/website materials may use the term "private detective."

Requirements for Security Guards as Employees

State law also governs hiring of employees. They are ineligible if they have been convicted of any felony or any crime specifically referenced in the act. Disqualifying crimes include, among others, possession or use of dangerous weapons, trading in stolen property, making or possessing burglar instruments, aiding prison escape, unlawful entry, picking pockets, and possession or distribution of narcotics. The ban is not in effect if an executive pardon has been granted.

The prospective employee must provide basic information, including a three-year work history with names of employers. The employer will ensure that the employee is fingerprinted.

Armed Guard Requirements and Application Process

The Lethal Weapons Training Act 235 covers requirements for armed security officers. By definition, "lethal weapons" includes weapons other than firearms that are designed to cause serious physical harm (for example, nightsticks). An armed guard will need to complete training mandated by Act 235. Completion of the academic module may result in "nonfirearms" certification (http://www.pacode.com/secure/data/037/chapter21/s21.12. html). Completion of academic and firearms modules will result in firearms certification, provided other requirements have been met.

Before the individual will be able to attend the training, he or she will have a background check, physical examination, and psychological examination. Standards (including uncorrected and corrected vision) are delineated in the Pennsylvania administrative code.

There are various exemptions available to current and former peace officers. These will vary according to individual circumstances. A recently retired municipal police officer who has at least twenty years of service may be eligible for waivers of initial training as well as physical and psychological evaluation. Exemption forms can be downloaded from the website of the Lethal Weapons Training Unit.

Other individuals may be considered for waiver based on recent comparable training (http://www.pacode.com/secure/data/037/chapter21/s21.14.

html). There are separate standards for academic and firearms waivers. Applicants will find ACT 120 waivers on the unit website.

Background Check Requirements

The background check will be carried out through the vendor, Cogent. Registration can be carried out online (https://www.dhs.pa.gov/providers/ Clearances-and-Licensing/Pages/default.aspx). The applicant may instead call 888-439-2486. The applicant will submit a total of $77.50 to Cogent. Some applicants, such as police officers who retired less than three years earlier, will pay lesser fees. There are fingerprinting sites located throughout Pennsylvania (https://www.dhs.pa.gov/providers/Clearances-and-Licensing/ Pages/default.aspx). A summary of the registration process is also found on the Cogent site (https://www.dhs.pa.gov/providers/Clearances-and-Licensing/Pages/default.aspx).

Out-of-state applicants are required to submit two passport-type photographs to the state police.

The Pennsylvania State Police website includes forms for the physical and psychological evaluation. In addition to measuring heart and lung function and carrying out other required tests, the physician will seek answers to all questions found on the form (for example, whether the prospective guard takes medication). The form must be submitted, no matter what the determination. The professional must be a physician (not a nurse practitioner or physician assistant) and must be licensed in Pennsylvania.

The psychological evaluation will be carried out by a Pennsylvania-licensed psychologist. It will include at least two components: an interview and history and a personality test. The state adopted personality test is the Minnesota Multiphasic Personality Inventory (MMPI). The psychologist is authorized to employ additional testing methods if necessary but will need to provide a thorough explanation as to their use.

A prospective armed guard will receive an approval or denial letter. The individual must complete training through an Act 235 school. The state police website includes a list of certified schools (http://www.psp.pa.gov/ lethalweapons/Pages/certified-schools.aspx#.Vdteh_lViko).

A thirty-dollar fee is due after training requirements have been met. Forms are available on the website of the Pennsylvania State Police (http://www.psp.pa.gov/lethalweapons/Pages/forms.aspx#.Vdf6rPlViko).

Application status may be monitored online (http://www.psp.pa.gov/lethalweapons/Pages/online-services.aspx#.VeMoyPlViko).

Additional Information

The text of the Private Detective Act is available online (http://www.legis.state.pa.us/WU01/LI/LI/US/PDF/1953/0/0361.PDF). The act is periodically amended. Further information about regulation of private security may be available from county courts.

Information about armed guard qualification is available from the Lethal Weapons Certification Unit (http://www.psp.pa.gov/lethalweapons/Pages/default.aspx#.VeMoVflVikq). The Lethal Weapons Certification Unit can be reached by telephone at (717) 346-4087 or by email at mpolethalweapcert@pa.gov.

RHODE ISLAND

Concealed carry honored in all states except California, Colorado, Connecticut, Delaware, District of Columbia, Georgia, Hawaii, Illinois, Louisiana, Maryland, Massachusetts, Montana, Nebraska, Nevada, New Jersey, New Mexico, New York, North Dakota, Oregon, Pennsylvania, South Carolina, Washington, and Wyoming and **with restrictions** (must be twenty-one years of age) in Alaska, Arizona, Kansas, Kentucky, Maine, Michigan, Oklahoma, Texas, and West Virginia.

Rhode Island security guards are under the jurisdiction of the Office of the Attorney General. The licensing agency distinguishes between individuals who are in business for themselves providing security services and those who are employed by security businesses. Security providers are licensed, while employers are registered.

Security professionals must clear criminal background checks. If they will be armed, they must meet additional requirements.

Unarmed guard requirements set by individual employers may be significantly higher than those mandated by state statute.

Employee Registration

The state legislature has set minimum employee standards that apply to all employees of security agencies with the exception of secretaries and other clerical workers. An individual with a known felony background is not to be hired.

The individual will need to provide basic information to the employer such as age, country of citizenship, and employment history for the prior five years. The applicant will affirm that he or she has not been convicted of a felony or crime of moral turpitude. The background statement is known as the employee's registration statement.

Background checks must be carried out. Licensees (employers) can request background checks from the attorney general's office for a five-dollar fee.

Employee application forms can be downloaded from the website of the Office of the Attorney General (http://www.riag.ri.gov/BCI/forms.php).

Armed Guard / Pistol Permit Requirements

Rhode Island requires individuals who carry handguns (whether concealed or open) to have pistol permits. This is the case for anyone who does not fall under an exemption category described in Chapter 11 of the state statute.

The minimum age is twenty-one. The individual must be qualified by a certified weapons instructor. Qualification standards are described in 11-47-15; relevant statutes are included in the application packet, which can be downloaded from the website of the Office of the Attorney General.

The office will carry out a criminal background check and may also check court records for restraining orders or records pertaining to mental illness.

An applicant must have fingerprints made. The application is to be accompanied by fingerprints, a photograph, and two forms of ID.

The individual must demonstrate that he or she has good cause to carry a firearm. The application packet states that anyone requesting a permit for employment purposes is to provide a signed, typed letter on company letterhead; a copy of the business license is to be submitted as well.

The application requires notarization. There is a forty-dollar fee; this is not paid until the permit is issued. Approved permit holders will receive notification in the mail. They will pick up their permits in person.

Requirements for a Security Business License

An individual who wishes to operate a security business must be at least eighteen and either hold citizenship or be a resident alien (http://webserver. rilin.state.ri.us/Statutes/TITLE5/5-5.1/5-5.1-8.HTM).

Licensees must have good moral character. They may not be dependent on narcotics or habitually intoxicated. They may not have any felonies in their backgrounds. They may not have had a similar license revoked or denied in any state.

Additionally, they may not have been declared mentally incompetent by a court (unless competency was subsequently restored).

Licensees must hold liability insurance (http://webserver.rilin.state.ri.us/Statutes/TITLE5/5-5.1/5-5.1-22.HTM).

The Security Guard License Application Process

Applicants must have fingerprint-based criminal background checks.

Out-of-state applicants are to have their fingerprints made on standard FBI FD-258 applicant cards. These will be mailed to the Rhode Island Attorney General's Office. In-state applicants will go through the Office of the Attorney General for their background checks. The Bureau of Criminal Identification has provided additional information, including a list of locations (http://www.riag.ri.gov/BCI/).

License applications can be downloaded (http://www.riag.ri.gov/BCI/forms.php). The applicant must provide five years of employment and address history.

An individual pays four hundred dollars for licensure. This is in addition to the thirty-five dollars that must be paid for the background check.

The applicant will need to present unexpired identification, such as a driver's license, passport, or state-issued ID.

Applicants with questions are invited to call 401-274-4400.

The license renewal period is two years.

License requirements also apply to partners or major corporate shareholders. They, too, must have fingerprint-based criminal background checks.

Rhode Island Civil Service Security Requirements

The Rhode Island Division of Human Resources has provided a description of security positions in the public sector (http://www.hr.ri.gov/classification/descriptions/jobspecs.php). The varying assessments, certifications, and expectations for experience may also be reflective of jobs in the private sector.

Civil service candidates must demonstrate some combination of education and experience, though there is some flexibility. "Public properties officer" is on the on low end with regard to expectations and pay. A high school diploma is not necessarily required, though the hiring agency does value military, police force, or corrections experience as well as previous experience working for protective agencies. The division notes that a physician statement is required.

Residence hall security officer is an example of a job where at least twelve years of education are expected. This type of position requires both a physical and a psychological evaluation. The security officer will need a first responder certificate, if not at the time of hiring within six months. First responder certificates come from the Rhode Island Department of Health.

Additional Information
Information about Rhode Island security licenses, permits, and registrations is available from the Office of the Attorney General (http://www.riag.ri.gov/BCI/). The licensing agency can be reached at 401-274-4400.

Licensure is governed by the Private Security Guard Act of 1987.

SOUTH CAROLINA

Concealed carry honored in all states except California, Colorado, Connecticut, Delaware, District of Columbia, Hawaii, Illinois, Maryland, Massachusetts, New Jersey, New York, Oregon, Pennsylvania, Rhode Island, and Washington and **with restrictions** (must be twenty-one years of age) in Alaska, Arizona, Florida, Kansas, Kentucky, Maine, Michigan, Oklahoma, and West Virginia.

South Carolina regulates security businesses and the security officers that they employ. Contract security businesses are licensed. Proprietary companies are licensed as proprietary security businesses if they seek the services of security officers who are uniformed, licensed, and/or have limited arrest powers. (Proprietary companies are free to employ gatekeepers or security officers provided they do not wear uniforms and are not granted regulated powers.)

Employees are issued registration. The chief executive officer or other designee is evaluated as part of the security business license application process.

Requirements for Security Officers in South Carolina

Security guard employees must be citizens at least eighteen years of age. They cannot use illegal drugs and cannot use alcohol in a way that negatively impacts performance; a drug test will be required. Security officers must demonstrate good character. They cannot have been convicted of felonies or crimes of moral turpitude. They cannot have been discharged from the armed forces for less than honorable reasons. A person who has been denied licensure for reasons other than lack of experience is ineligible for licensing.

The security guard will need to complete, at minimum, four hours of basic training. The standard basic training is completed through a certified training officer. The security officer may instead pursue alternate basic training. An alternate basic training program must be accredited by a recognized accrediting agency and approved by the South Carolina Law Enforcement Division (SLED). The security officer will also need two hours of orientation and training by a company trainer. A security officer who completes an alternative program will obtain an identification card identifying him or her as a certified private security officer.

An unarmed security officer may perform services for a limited time period pending registration. Security officer registration is renewed annually; the employee must continue to meet board standards.

A security officer may also be registered on a temporary basis for special events.

Requirements for Armed Security Officers

Armed guards must be at least twenty-one years of age and must be eligible to possess firearms.

They will need training in firearm safety and liability, both on and off duty. They will also need to demonstrate proficiency in the particular type of firearm that they will be using. A prospective armed guard will fire an approved qualification course; there are separate standards for revolvers and automatic pistols.

Requirements for Arrest Powers

A security officer may be granted the power to make arrests on the particular property he or she has been hired to protect. In order to be granted limited arrest powers, a security officer must have four hours of additional instruction. The course must cover, at minimum, legal issues and procedures and techniques. Instruction in legal issues must cover laws of arrest and search and seizure. The training officer will need to sign.

The Employee Application Process

Employee application forms can be downloaded from the SLED website (http://www.sled.sc.gov/PI.aspx?MenuID=PI).

The prospective security officer will provide a ten-year employment history. He or she will provide an arrest record (if applicable) that includes all incidents, including traffic citations; parking tickets are to be omitted.

SLED will need a copy of drug test results.

An applicant who has a serious medical or physical condition, including epilepsy or diabetes, is asked to submit a doctor's statement.

The applicant will sign a release authorizing various organizations to provide information to the licensing agency. The application form requires notarization.

The licensing agency will require fingerprints. The fee is $65 for an unarmed security officer and $110 for an armed security officer. A security officer who is originally registered as unarmed may upgrade for a $45 fee.

Applications are sent to the South Carolina Law Enforcement Division in Columbia.

Requirements for Proprietors and Chief Executive Officers

A sole proprietor or self-employed security officer must meet licensing requirements. In the case of a corporation, the highest executive officer or other designated officer must meet licensing requirements.

The professional must be at least twenty-one and have earned a high school diploma or the equivalent. He or she must meet the same character and fitness requirements that guards are required to meet.

Professionals who head contract security companies need two years of experience in security or law enforcement. Security experience may be with a licensed or SLED-approved company.

Experience is not listed as a statutory requirement for professionals who request licensing as a proprietary security business (http://scstatehouse.gov/code/t40c018.php).

The Business / Executive Officer Application Process

Executive officers submit their materials as part of the license application process. License applications are also available from SLED (http://www.sled.sc.gov/PI.aspx?MenuID=PI).

The applicant will submit two fingerprint cards. An applicant with a military history will submit DD-214.

The applicant will submit evidence of a ten-thousand-dollar bond.

In 2015, the licensing agency implemented a new policy requiring prospective licensees to submit photographs in digital form. Photos must be in JPEG format. They can be submitted in any of three ways; on compact disk, through email, or via Secure File Transfer Protocol (SFTP). Applicants who wish to use SFTP are directed to call the SLED technology help desk at (803) 896-8588.

Additional Information

Licensing and registration information is available from the South Carolina Law Enforcement Division. The division can be reached by telephone at (803) 737-9000.

Laws (http://scstatehouse.gov/code/t40c018.php) and regulations (http://www.scstatehouse.gov/coderegs/statmast.php) can be accessed online.

SOUTH DAKOTA

Concealed carry honored in all states except California, Connecticut, District of Columbia, Hawaii, Illinois, Maryland, Massachusetts, New Jersey, New Mexico, New York, Oregon, and Rhode Island and **with restrictions** (must be twenty-one years of age) in Alaska, Arizona, Colorado, Delaware, Florida, Iowa, Kansas, Kentucky, Louisiana, Maine, Michigan, Minnesota, Nebraska, Nevada, Oklahoma, Pennsylvania, South Carolina, Texas, Virginia, Washington, West Virginia, and Wisconsin.

South Dakota does not license security guards, though some local ordinances exist. The absence of licensing statutes means there could be security agencies in the state that impose standards lower than the norm. However, it doesn't mean that there are not employers setting very high standards.

In states that regulate the security industry tightly, registration often doesn't take place until after hiring. The first screening is done by the employer. Later, the state validates that some basic requirements have been met. In some cases, this amounts to little more than ensuring that a background check is carried out and that the guard has work authorization. When it comes to the more competitive positions, the employer is the driving force.

Basic Security Guard Expectations

There are some basic standards in effect in most of the nation: Security guards need to be at least eighteen years old. They need to have backgrounds that are free of felonies and of more serious misdemeanors, though some states do not penalize individuals for criminal activity that took place in the more distant past; the licensing agency may consider whether the applicant's record has been exemplary in the time since. Security officers must be free of addictions or potentially debilitating mental disorders. They must present US identification cards or demonstrate that they are authorized to work in the United States. Prospective security guards with military backgrounds may be required to produce a DD-214 indicating type of discharge.

Employers often cite physical skills, for example, the ability to walk several hours without a break or the ability to lift forty pounds. Serious medical conditions can be a disqualifier. Many positions are open only to individuals with driver's licenses, but this is not universal.

Security Guard Knowledge and Skill Base

Most states do require training, but the requirements vary a good deal. Unarmed guards could have a state-mandated training requirement anywhere from four hours to forty or more hours. South Dakota security guards do not have training mandates. However, some are hired by large security agencies that offer their own training programs. Security guards also have the option of pursuing training before hiring. A major security agency, posting recently for "event" security officers to provide services at the South Dakota state fair, noted that selected individuals would need knowledge of security operations or willingness to learn.

Though some security positions require very specialized training, there is a basic body of knowledge common to many security roles. Security officers who interact with the public do more than watch for illegal activity; they are also responsible for keeping people safe and orderly. In general, they

- know their role and the limitations of their authority
- understand how to interact with the public
- know how to take notes and write incident reports
- know emergency procedures
- know procedures, such as patrol and access control

Attaining More Competitive Positions

Some of the security agencies in South Dakota maintain a high profile nationwide. They often favor candidates who have past experience in security or have experience in related roles, such as corrections, law enforcement, or the military. However, higher education may also be considered.

Security agencies also seek oral and written communication skills—security officers are report writers. Although such skills are favored by most employers, large employers are more likely to carry out formal assessments. They may have a complex protocol for hiring. Before a security guard occupies a post, he or she will likely have drug screening. Depending on job duties and contractual requirements, the guard may also have a physical examination and a personality test, such as the Minnesota Multiphasic Personality Inventory.

One very competitive employer in the public sector is the Transportation Security Authority (TSA). Candidates who meet minimum requirements may be invited to take multiple assessments, including a computer-based test that measures, among other things, language proficiency. The physical is comprehensive and includes joint mobility and range of motion.

Local Security Guard Licenses
Rapid City licenses the security industry (http://www.rcgov.org/Finance/forms-and-applications.html). Security guards are required to have fingerprint-based criminal background checks.

Security guards in other towns and cities may be under the jurisdiction of local authorities.

Security guards should also be aware that laws change periodically and that there is a growing trend toward regulation nationwide.

Third-Party Certifications
Some employers seek candidates with certifications—or who are, at the least, willing and able to attain certification within a specified time period. The certification may be specific to a particular industry. For example, a recent posting at a health center in Sioux Falls noted that the candidate would need to be committed to obtaining basic certification through the International Association of Healthcare Security and Safety within a year. The certified health-care security officer (CHSO) credential is granted on the basis of examination.

The certified health-care protection administrator (CHPA) credential is a higher level certification available to administrators of health-care protection programs. Candidates must qualify for examination. They can qualify in various ways with some combination of experience, education, training, and professional membership (https://www.iahss.org/).

TENNESSEE

Concealed carry honored in all states except California, Connecticut, District of Columbia, Hawaii, Illinois, Maryland, Massachusetts, Minnesota, New Jersey, New York, Oregon, Rhode Island, and Washington and **with restrictions** (must be twenty-one years of age) in Alaska, Arizona, Colorado, Florida, Kansas, Kentucky, Maine, Michigan, Nebraska, North Dakota, Oklahoma, Pennsylvania, South Carolina, and West Virginia.

Tennessee regulates unarmed and armed security guards. The state also licenses contract security companies and proprietary security organizations. Organizations must have a qualifying agent or manager who meets state requirements.

Tennessee Private Protective Services makes some distinctions between guards or officers who work for security companies and those who work for proprietary organizations.

Requirements for Unarmed Guards Who Are Employed by Security Agencies

Unarmed security guard employees must be at least eighteen. They must be citizens or resident aliens and must meet character and fitness requirements set by the state.

An applicant cannot be habitually drunk or dependent on narcotics and cannot have a disability that would preclude performing duties.

An applicant is not automatically denied because of past criminal conviction. However, if the conviction is a felony or potentially disqualifying misdemeanor, the individual must have completed his or her sentence or probation no less than five years earlier.

Disqualifying misdemeanors include the following:
- shooting of a weapon
- violence
- sale, manufacture, or distribution of illegal substances
- shoplifting
- theft of property or services

Training is mandatory. The training may be provided by the contract security company. A prospective student can also find approved trainers by doing a license search through the website of the licensing agency. At least one training hour will be devoted to each of the following concepts:

- orientation
- legal power and limitation of power
- general duties
- emergency procedures

The student can expect testing. A state-certified trainer will provide a certificate verifying completion of requirements.

If the guard or officer will carry a device or weapon classified as "less than lethal," he or she will need training in the specific device. The instructor must be certified to offer the particular training. Less than lethal weapons include stun guns and chemical spray, among others.

Unarmed employees may be authorized to work temporarily following submission of the application and other required materials. Private Protective Services has provided a list of frequently asked questions (http://www.tn.gov/commerce/topic/prot-faqs).

Unarmed registration is renewed every two years.

Requirements for Unarmed Guards Employed by Proprietary Security Organizations

Unarmed guards employed by proprietary security organizations, unlike their counterparts employed by contract security companies, are prohibited from carrying any type of weapon (http://www.tn.gov/commerce/article/prot-get-a-license).

According to Tennessee code, it is "desired" that officers who interact with the public have training in emergency procedures and in security guard powers and limitations of power.

Requirements for Armed Guards in Tennessee

Armed guards must be twenty-one years of age. They have additional training requirements beyond those required for unarmed contract security employees. They will need to take an eight-hour course that includes legal limitations of firearms usage and firearms safety, maintenance, and handling. They will also need four hours of marksmanship training. This training culminates in a commissioner-approved target course.

Unarmed guards will need additional training for weapons or other devices that they may use.

An individual cannot work as an armed guard until he or she possesses, at minimum, a conditional card.

Armed guards must complete refresher / range training during each renewal period.

The Security Guard Application Process

Application materials can be downloaded from the website of the Department of Commerce and Insurance (http://www.tn.gov/commerce/article/prot-forms-and-downloads). They can also be requested via telephone at 615-741-6382 or 615-532-9130.

The applicant will need to submit three passport-style photographs. Those who answer "yes" to criminal history questions will need to provide additional supporting information.

You will need to submit fingerprints for a background check. Unarmed guards currently pay a fifty-dollar application fee and twenty-dollar registration fee. Armed guards currently pay a seventy-five-dollar application fee and thirty-dollar registration fee. An armed guard who needs a conditional permit will remit an additional fifteen dollars.

It typically takes four to six weeks to process an application.

Requirements for Qualifying Managers and Qualifying Agents

The qualifying manager of a proprietary organization will need a certificate of insurance. He or she will need to provide basic information to the licensing agency.

Requirements are more stringent for professionals who work as qualifying agents for contract security companies. The qualifying agent must be at least twenty-one and must have, in addition to a certificate of insurance, three credit references. He or she will qualify based on experience or examination. The licensing agency will accept three years of security experience at the supervisory, managerial, or administrative level; the work setting may be a contract company or proprietary organization. The licensing agency can also accept three years of law enforcement experience at the supervisory level; the qualifying experience may have been accrued in the armed forces.

A professional who chooses the examination pathway will be assessed on the following:

- physical security, administration, and personnel
- rules and regulations
- alarms, criminal justice, and procedures (including health and fire prevention)
- emergency procedures

The examination is administered by PSI. It is computer-delivered. The minimum passing score is 70 percent. The fee is currently $125. PSI has published a candidate handbook (https://candidate.psiexams.com/catalog/fti_agency_license_details.jsp?fromwhere=findtest&testid=3638). The candidate can use the application form found in the handbook or call (800) 733-9267. There are currently six test site locations: Chattanooga, Jackson, Johnson City, Knoxville, Memphis, and Nashville. Out-of-state candidates may submit a special request; this is found at the back of the candidate handbook.

Qualifying agents submit their documents as part of the agency application process (http://www.tn.gov/commerce/article/prot-forms-and-downloads).

The Background Check Process for Security Guard Applicants

In 2015, the licensing agency issued a statement requesting applicants use electronic fingerprinting services. The designated vendor is Identogo by MorphoTrust. There are sites throughout the state (http://www.l1enrollment.com/locations/?st=tn). Applicants may schedule online (http://www.l1enrollment.com/state/?st=tn). They also have the option of calling 855-226-2937. A thirty-eight-dollar fee is paid to MorphoTrust.

Out-of-state applicants will also use the approved vendor. However, they will have their fingerprints made on FD-258 "hard cards" and then sent to Identogo for scanning. The applicant may call to request cards. He or she will need the ORI number and other agency information. The licensing agency has provided detailed information about fingerprinting requirements (http://www.tn.gov/commerce/article/prot-fingerprinting-information).

Additional Information

Private Protective Services (https://www.tn.gov/commerce/regboards/pps.html) is under the banner of the Tennessee Department of Commerce and Insurance. The licensing agency can be reached by telephone at 615-741-6382 or by email at Private.Protective at TN.Gov. Additional contact information is available online (http://www.tn.gov/commerce/topic/prot-contact). Rules can also be accessed through the department website (http://share.tn.gov/sos/rules/0780/0780-05/0780-05.htm).

TEXAS

Concealed carry honored in all states except California, Connecticut, District of Columbia, Hawaii, Illinois, Maryland, Massachusetts, Minnesota, New Jersey, New York, Oregon, Rhode Island, and Washington and **with restrictions** (must be twenty-one years of age) in Alaska, Arizona, Colorado, Florida, Kansas, Kentucky, Maine, Michigan, Nebraska, Oklahoma, Pennsylvania, South Carolina, and West Virginia.

The Texas Department of Public Safety regulates both commissioned and noncommissioned security guards. Commissioned security guards are those who are authorized to carry firearms; they must meet more stringent training and eligibility requirements than noncommissioned guards.

The department also grants "Class B" licenses to security businesses. Officers who oversee security functions must meet standards set by the board. Although there may be multiple intermediate supervisors, only one individual will be designated as a manager for licensing purposes. (There may be additional "managers in waiting").

Eligibility Requirements for Security Guards

All security professionals must be at least eighteen years old. They must meet general fitness requirements. They cannot have been discharged from the military dishonorably or under any other conditions that would be viewed as prohibitive. They cannot be indicted or charged with felonies or Class A or B misdemeanors. They may not be registered as sex offenders in any state. They may not be mentally incompetent in the view of a court.

The individual will need to complete an approved training program at Level II. Required topics include 1) state law and board rule and 2) note taking and report writing. The program will culminate in a test (https://www.dps.texas.gov/rsd/psb/).

A security guard who has a current valid ID is eligible to transfer eligibility and work for a new employer. However, the employer will need to file an update (https://www.dps.texas.gov/rsd/psb/).

Requirements for Commissioned Security Guards

In order to be authorized to work as an armed guard, an individual must meet eligibility, training, and skill requirements. He or she must be, in the view of the licensing agency, capable of exercising good judgment. The licensing agency may determine that a person is incapable because of a serious psychiatric disorder or condition even if the condition is currently in remission or being managed by medication. However, an individual with a past diagnosis may be licensed if a psychiatrist provides a statement indicating that the person is indeed capable of good judgment. According to state statute, medical records may be required (http://www.statutes.legis.state.tx.us/Docs/OC/htm/OC.1702.htm).

A person may also be disqualified because of a chemical dependence, a restraining order, or a prohibition from possessing firearms. A person who has been convicted of two alcohol- or substance-related misdemeanors at the Class B level or greater is, in the view of the licensing agency, chemically dependent. Eligibility is discussed in depth in Section 1702.163 of the state statute.

Training must be completed through an approved school or instructor. The prospective commissioned guard will need to score satisfactorily on a test. An individual who completes training and demonstrates competence with firearms will be issued a Level III certificate.

Individuals who have current or recent experience as peace officers may be eligible for training exemptions; requirements are described in Rule 35.131.

The commission may be transferred under certain conditions. The board must be notified of new employment.

The Security Guard Application Process

The application may be submitted online or on paper (https://www.dps.texas.gov/rsd/psb/).

Applicants must have fingerprint-based FBI background checks. A twenty-five-dollar fingerprint fee is to be submitted with the application. The fingerprints themselves are submitted electronically, using

Fingerprint Applicant Services of Texas (FAST) and the approved provider Identogo by MorphoTrust (https://www.dps.texas.gov/rsd/psb/News/PSBWebFingerprintingInstr.htm). The applicant will register through Identogo (http://www.identogo.com/FP/texas.aspx). Identogo maintains electronic fingerprinting sites throughout Texas (http://www.l1enrollment.com/locations/?st=tx). The department has provided a form called a "FAST pass"; this should be brought to the appointment.

If fingerprints are made prior to application, the applicant should include a copy of his or her FAST receipt.

The licensing agency will need a copy of applicable training certificates. A noncitizen will need to provide an alien registration card or work authorization.

The registration fee, pocket card fee, and subscription subcharge total thirty-eight dollars for a noncommissioned security guard and sixty dollars for a commissioned security guard.

Requirements for Security Agency Managers

In order to be designated as the manager of a security company for licensing purposes, one must have at least two years of experience in the particular branch of security. (The security guard business is considered one branch of security. Among the others are armored car services and guard dog services.)

The manager will need to take an examination. This step is completed after application. The examination includes true/false and multiple choice questions (https://www.dps.texas.gov/rsd/psb/). Although it is open book, the candidate will work under time constraints. Prospective managers are advised to prepare by studying Chapter 1702 of the state occupational code / administrative rules.

The exam is administered in Austin at the Department of Public Safety Headquarters. The cost of examination is covered under the company fee. However, a one-hundred-dollar fee will be assessed if reexamination is required.

The exam is typically administered three to five times a month. The licensing agency expects that the examination requirement will be met within ninety days of fee payment. Otherwise, it may be necessary to file a new application.

A "manager in waiting" may also take the examination. In some cases, it is the owner of the business and not a hired manager who will meet experience and examination requirements.

Provisions for Veterans and Military Spouses

Texas has recently passed regulations approving alternative licensing procedures for military spouses (https://texreg.sos.state.tx.us/public/readtac$ext.ViewTAC?tac_view=4&ti=19&pt=7&ch=234&rl=Y).

The licensing agency will consider the experience and education of military members and veterans.

Additional Information

Private Security is under the banner of the Texas Department of Public Safety (https://www.dps.texas.gov/rsd/psb/). Private Security can be reached by email contact form (https://www.dps.texas.gov/contact.htm) or by telephone at (512) 424-7293.

UTAH

Concealed carry honored in all states except California, Connecticut, District of Columbia, Hawaii, Illinois, Maryland, Massachusetts, Minnesota, New Jersey, New Mexico, New York, Oregon, Rhode Island, and South Carolina and **with restrictions** (must be twenty-one years of age) in Alaska, Arizona, Colorado, Florida, Iowa, Kansas, Kentucky, Louisiana, Maine, Michigan, Nebraska, Oklahoma, Pennsylvania, Texas, Virginia, Washington, West Virginia, and Wisconsin.

Utah licenses both security officers and security agencies. The Division of Occupational and Professional Licensing (DOPL) recognizes three types of security officer: unarmed, armed, and armored car. Requirements include background check, training, and assessment.

The state also sets standards for qualifying agents: professionals who are responsible for the operations of security companies; these professionals may be proprietors or managers. Qualifying agents must meet examination and experience requirements. The qualifying agent and other managers and major shareholders are fingerprinted.

Requirements for Unarmed Security Officers in Utah

Prospective security officers must meet eligibility and training requirements. A prospective security officer will be denied licensure based on a felony, a misdemeanor that involves moral turpitude, or another crime that, when the duties of a security officer are taken into account, indicates that licensure would not be in the public interest. Disqualifying crimes are referenced in the state rule (http://dopl.utah.gov/laws/R156-63a.pdf). Other disqualifiers include chemical dependency, habitual drunkenness, or having been declared incompetent by a court of competence (unless competence has since been restored).

The prospective guard will need to complete a division-approved training program, consisting of required subjects and electives.

The basic program will include at least sixteen hours of required courses. It will cover the following:

- private security nature and role
- legal responsibilities
- state laws and rules
- situational response evaluations
- patrol techniques
- documentation and report writing
- use of force (including alternatives)
- community-police relations
- sexual harassment in the workplace

The program will include eight hours of electives. The following are among the topics that may be covered:
- CPR and first aid
- self-defense
- access control
- crowd control
- use of defensive objects

The program will culminate in an exam that includes concepts covered in the sixteen hours of basic training. The student will need to score at least 80 percent.

Unarmed guards are responsible for completing sixteen hours of continuing education.

Requirements for Armed Security Officers

An armed guard must be at least eighteen. He or she will complete an additional approved course. The course will include at least six hours of classroom instruction and six hours of range instruction. The student will need to pass both a final exam and a practical pistol course. The passing score is again 80 percent.

The armed guard will complete sixteen hours of continuing firearms training every two years. This is in addition to the general continuing education requirements. The armed guard should receive four hours of training every six months.

Requirements for Armored Car Security Officers

Armored car security officers must be at least twenty-one. They must complete a basic program and a firearms training program. Armored car licensing requirements are described in Rule 156-63b.

The Security Officer Application Process

Application forms can be downloaded from DOPL website (http://dopl.utah. gov/licensing/security_companies_guards.html). There is one security officer application; applicants will mark the application to show whether armed, unarmed, or armored car security officer licensing is sought.

The security officer application packet includes a form that must be signed by the basic classroom instructor and (if applicable) the firearms instructor.

The licensing agency will need to see a driver's license, an ID, or work authorization.

An applicant who answered "yes" to questions on the qualifying questionnaire will need to provide an explanation. In some cases, court and police records will be required.

There is a one-hundred-dollar security officer application fee. Applications may be mailed or hand-delivered; there are two addresses listed in the application packet.

The licensing agency will require fingerprint-based background checks carried out by the Utah Bureau of Criminal Identification (BCI) and the FBI. Fingerprints may be made at the DOPL office; there is no charge for this service. Applicants also have the option of having fingerprints made in advance and including two fingerprint cards in the application packet.

An interim permit can be issued more quickly than a license. An applicant who seeks an interim permit will need to provide a criminal history report that shows no record. The permit cannot be issued if the applicant has answered "yes" to any questions in the qualifying questionnaire (http://dopl.utah.gov/laws/R156-63a.pdf).

A security guard who wishes to upgrade from unarmed to armed will need to provide an additional background check as well as evidence of required training.

Requirements for Qualifying Agents

A professional who serves as qualifying agent for a contract security company must have six thousand hours of creditable experience. The professional must have had a position that required a level of responsibility. The licensing agency can accept supervisory, managerial, or administrative experience that was accrued within the security industry. The supervisory experience may instead be earned in law enforcement; duties may have been provided to a governmental or military entity but must be found acceptable to the division.

The qualifying agent will need to pass the Utah Security Personnel Qualifying Agent's Examination with a score of at least 75 percent. The following are among the topics covered:
- security business management
- qualifying agent liability issues
- workplace security
- retail security
- security officer training
- security officer supervision
- risk analysis and risk reduction

The prospective qualifier will take the examination before application. The examination is administered by PSI. PSI has provided a candidate handbook (https://candidate.psiexams.com/catalog/fti_agency_license_details.jsp?fromwhere=findtest&testid=1155). Candidates are allowed to register directly. There is a seventy-two-dollar fee. The candidate may register by internet, phone, fax, or mail. He or she will need to allow time for processing before scheduling the examination. The time frame will vary depending on registration method. The examination is currently offered in the following Utah metropolitan areas: North Salt Lake City, Ogden, Provo, and St. George.

If the qualifying agent leaves the agency, he or she must be replaced on the time frame mandated in the state statute (http://dopl.utah.gov/laws/58-63.pdf).

The Qualifying Agent Application Process

Qualifying agents submit their application materials as part of the licensing agency application process.

The licensing agency will seek a current résumé. Experience will be documented in two ways. The applicant will provide an employer form and W-2s or (in cases where there was ownership) tax returns.

Examination results are submitted directly to the licensing agency by PSI.

Additional Information

Licensing information is available from the Utah Division of Occupational and Professional Licensing (http://dopl.utah.gov/licensing/security_companies_guards.html). The licensing agency can be reached by telephone at (801) 530-6628 or (toll-free within the state) at (866) 275-3675.

VERMONT

Concealed carry honored in all states except Alabama, California, Colorado, Connecticut, Delaware, District of Columbia, Georgia, Hawaii, Illinois, Indiana, Iowa, Maryland, Massachusetts, Michigan, Minnesota, Missouri, Montana, Nebraska, Nevada, New Jersey, New Mexico, New York, North Carolina, North Dakota, Ohio, Oregon, Pennsylvania, Rhode Island, South Carolina, Tennessee, Texas, Utah, Virginia, Washington, Wisconsin, and Wyoming and **with restrictions** (must be twenty-one years of age) in Alaska, Arizona, Kansas, Kentucky, Maine, Oklahoma, and West Virginia.

The Vermont Board of Private Investigative and Security Services registers armed and unarmed security guards who work as employees; the board licenses independent practitioners and professionals who serve as qualifying agents for security companies. Security guards must complete state-mandated training while qualifying agents must meet experience and examination requirements.

Security Guard Training Requirements

Registrants must complete a training program. Some courses are delivered in-house by the security agency. In other cases, the student will enroll in a course by an outsider provider; the course must be board-approved. In order to receive a permanent registration card, an individual must complete forty hours of approved training. The following is the expected curriculum, though variances may be granted:

- role of security guards—two hours
- legal powers and limitations—four hours
- ethics and conduct (including board rules)—four hours
- patrolling and investigation—four hours
- communication and public relations—four hours
- observation and note taking—four hours
- emergency response—eight hours
- access control—two hours
- evidence—two hours

- statements—two hours
- report writing—four hours

The student can expect testing; the board approves security guard examinations and the criteria they use for passing.

In some cases, security guards may be exempted from the usual training requirements, all or in part. The licensing agency will consider the circumstances of those who have been employed long-term in the field, who have met similar educational requirements in another jurisdiction, or who have had equivalent training for other job roles; the latter could include military, law enforcement, or emergency medical technician. Individuals who have been granted a waiver may still be required to complete training in areas

Registration is renewed every two years. The first renewal period is typically shorter.

Temporary Security Guard Registration
The licensing agency issues part-time temporary registration to individuals who are completing educational requirements and awaiting FBI background check results. Temporary registrants must have supervisors readily available. In order to receive a temporary credential, the trainee must complete at least eight hours of training. This includes the following:
- security guard role—two hours
- legal powers and limitations—three hours
- ethics—three hours

A part-time employee (one who works less than eighty hours a month) will have a longer time period in which to complete the full training program. However, he or she will not receive permanent credentialing until such time as the full forty hours has been completed.

The board may credit up to ten hours of hands-on practical training toward the forty-hour requirement needed for permanent registration; practical training hours cannot be applied toward the eight-hour requirement for temporary registration.

Armed Security Guard Requirements in Vermont

An armed guard must be trained by a Vermont-licensed instructor. The student will have classroom instruction in safe handling of firearms and in legal responsibility. There will be at least twelve hours devoted to general firearm safety, use, and responsibility and at least four hours devoted to the particular weapon that will be used on the job. Classroom learning will be assessed through examination. The student will also need to shoot a qualifying range.

An armed guard will need to requalify during each renewal period. The requalification course is to be at least six hours.

Qualifying Agent Requirements

A security agency must have a qualifying agent who meets experience and knowledge requirements. In some cases, a security agency is headed by a sole proprietor who does not employ other security guards.

A prospective qualifying agent must demonstrate two years of work experience. The licensing agency will accept two thousand hours of experience accrued in the two-year period preceding application. Experience may be in the security industry or as a sworn member of a law enforcement agency (http://legislature.vermont.gov/statutes/section/26/059/03174).

The qualifying agent must pass an examination. Candidates can prepare by studying statutes and rules. The examination is administered at the board office. The Vermont licensing agency allows two examination attempts. A candidate who does not pass after two attempts must wait a year and then reapply.

Licenses are also renewed biennially.

Background Check Requirements

All registrants and qualifying agents are required to have criminal background checks performed by the Vermont Crime Information Center (VCIC) and the FBI. The applicant will initiate the process by signing a release form and having it notarized. The form will be submitted to the Vermont Office of Professional Regulation. The Office of Professional Regulation will then send an authorization certificate and a list of fingerprinting sites. A twenty-five-dollar fee will be assessed at the fingerprinting site.

The Application Process

Application forms can be downloaded from the Professional Regulation website (https://sos.vermont.gov/private-investigative-security-services/forms-instructions/). The application includes professional fitness questions and questions about child support, tax, restitution, and court fine status. Some applicants will need to attach supporting documents.

Security guards will need to have training documentation on file. Prospective qualifying agents will submit character references and documentation of experience.

Out-of-state licensees will need to provide a verification of licensure form to the state(s) of licensure.

The applicant will need to attach a two-by-two photograph to the application form.

The application fee is $60 for unarmed guards and $120 for armed guards. It is $150 for unarmed qualifying agents and $200 for qualifying agents who seek armed status.

Additional Information

The Board of Private Investigative and Security Services is under the banner of Vermont Professional Regulation (https://sos.vermont.gov/private-investigative-security-services/). A Board representative can be reached at 802-828-1134.

Regulations change periodically. The most current version of the rules went into effect in April of 2015.

VIRGINIA

Concealed carry honored in all states except California, Connecticut, Delaware, District of Columbia, Illinois, Maryland, Massachusetts, Minnesota, New Jersey, New York, Oregon, Pennsylvania, Rhode Island, and Washington and **with restrictions** (must be twenty-one years of age) in Alaska, Arizona, Colorado, Florida, Kansas, Kentucky, Maine, Michigan, Oklahoma, South Carolina, West Virginia, and Wisconsin.

Virginia security guards are under the jurisdiction of the Department of Criminal Justice Services (DCJS). Security professionals must be credentialed unless they are exempted under state code (http://law.lis.virginia.gov/vacode/title9.1/chapter1/section9.1-140/). Both armed and unarmed guards are registered. Virginia's armed guards have limited powers of arrest; they must complete significantly longer training programs.

Virginia also certifies high-level managers as compliance agents; each private security services business must have a professional in this role. A compliance agent must meet experience requirements.

Security Officer Requirements

An unarmed security officer must be at least eighteen years old and must be a citizen or legal resident of the United States (http://www.dcjs.virginia.gov/pss/howto/registrations/unarmedSecurityOfficer.cfm).

He or she must complete eighteen hours of entry-level core training. The program will include an orientation that covers general security officer duties, ethics, and applicable state code, as well as signs of terrorism. Core training will also include the following:

- law
- patrol, communication, and access control
- documentation
- confrontation management
- emergency procedures
- use of force

The course will culminate in a comprehensive written exam. Prospective students can search for private training schools on the department website (http://www.dcjs.virginia.gov/pss/trainingSchools/index.cfm).

Professionals with recent law enforcement experience may be exempted from completing the traditional Virginia curriculum (http://lis.virginia.gov/cgi-bin/legp604.exe?000+reg+6VAC20-171-450). They must be able to document having had entry-level training as well as five years of continuous experience. Security professionals who have worked continuously for at least five years in the field or who previously completed an approved training program that is at the level of current Virginia standards may also be eligible for exemption.

The individual will file a partial training exemption with appropriate supporting documentation.

Registration must be renewed biennially. The security officer will pursue four hours of in-service training in the core subjects.

Armed Security Officer Requirements

In Virginia, the minimum age for armed guards is the same as for unarmed guards: eighteen years of age (http://www.dcjs.virginia.gov/pss/howto/registrations/armedSecurityOfficer.cfm).

A professional who will be armed must pursue an additional endorsement. The total program (including the eighteen-hour core program) will be fifty to fifty-three hours. The security officer will have eight hours of coursework in arrest authority and twenty-four hours in handgun training. Some security officers will pursue three hours of shotgun training; this is required only if the security officer will have access to a shotgun at work.

The firearms student will need to pass a written test before completing range training (http://lis.virginia.gov/cgi-bin/legp604.exe?000+reg+6VAC20-171-300). The minimum score is 70 percent. In order to pass the basic handgun qualification, the student will need to score 75 percent.

The department has provided a list of firearms training schools (http://www.dcjs.virginia.gov/pss/howto/endorsements/firearms.cfm).

An armed security officer must have completed training and completed the registration process before he or she can work as an armed security officer (http://www.dcjs.virginia.gov/pss/faq/catView.cfm?category=Armed%20Security%20Officer/Courier).

The armed security officer will need to complete firearms retraining; this is in addition to the required in-service in the core subjects. Registration is issued for two years, but the firearms endorsement is renewed annually.

The Security Officer Application Process

Applicants must have fingerprint-based criminal background checks. This step may be completed before all requirements have been met for certification. However, the process will need to be completed in a timely manner, as the background check is valid for only 120 days. The prospective security officer will submit the fingerprint card along with the supplied fingerprint processing form, evidence of legal residence, and a fifty-dollar fee.

An individual who has ever been convicted of a crime (other than a minor traffic violation) will need to include documentation such as court records. The licensing agency will also seek supportive documentation, such as reference letters and evidence of rehabilitation.

The Department of Criminal Justice Services has provided an information page about the fingerprinting and background check process (http://www.dcjs.virginia.gov/pss/howTo/common/fingerprints.cfm); an applicant will find links to needed forms.

A student can expect his or her certified training school to send notification to the licensing agency when requirements have been met (http://www.dcjs.virginia.gov/pss/faq/catView.cfm?category=Training).

An applicant who is requesting consideration of alternate training will submit a training waiver credit form along with supporting documentation and twenty-five-dollar fee. This step can be completed well in advance of application for registration. However, an exemption is no longer valid after twelve months (http://lis.virginia.gov/cgi-bin/legp604.exe?000+reg+6VAC20-171-445).

Registration applications are available on the website of the Department of Criminal Justice Services (http://www.dcjs.virginia.gov/forms/section-Forms.cfm?code=8&program=ps).

A security professional may add categories between renewals by submitting an "additional registration category" form.

Compliance Agent Requirements and Application Process

Experienced professionals may be certified as compliance agents. Experience may be earned in security, law enforcement, or a related field (http://law.lis.virginia.gov/vacode/title9.1/chapter1/section9.1-139/). The requirement varies depending on whether prior experience was at the managerial or supervisory level. If experience was at the required level, three years will suffice. Otherwise, the licensing agency will require five years.

The compliance agent must attend a training session and pass an examination (http://lis.virginia.gov/cgi-bin/legp604.exe?000+reg+6VAC20-171-72). The minimum passing score is 80 percent.

The individual will initiate the process by submitting a training enrollment application and other application materials, including fingerprints and documentation of eligibility (http://www.dcjs.virginia.gov/pss/howto/certifications/complianceAgent.cfm). The training costs seventy-five dollars. A fifty-dollar application fee will be included with the application packet.

A prospective compliance agent who does not pass the examination on a first attempt may retake it. If he or she does not pass on a second attempt, it will be necessary to submit another application and attend the six-hour training session again.

Renewal depends on completion of in-service requirements. A security agency will designate a compliance agent as part of the application process.

Additional Information

Licensing and registration information is available from the Virginia Department of Criminal Justice Services (http://www.dcjs.virginia.gov/pss/programs.cfm). The licensing agency can be reached by telephone at (804) 786-4700.

Legislative code and regulations are available online (http://www.dcjs. virginia.gov/pss/code.cfm).

WASHINGTON

Concealed carry honored in all states except California, Colorado, Connecticut, Delaware, District of Columbia, Georgia, Hawaii, Illinois, Maryland, Massachusetts, Minnesota, Nebraska, Nevada, New Jersey, New Mexico, New York, Oregon, Pennsylvania, Rhode Island, South Carolina, and Wyoming **and with restrictions** (must be twenty-one years of age) in Alaska, Arizona, Kansas, Kentucky, Maine, Michigan, Oklahoma, and West Virginia.

Washington licenses both unarmed and armed security guards. Guards must meet eligibility and training requirements.

The Department of Licensing (DOL) also licenses professionals who operate security businesses. The primary responsible party may be termed the "qualifying principal" or "company principal." This may be a high-level officer. In some cases, it will be an owner. In the case of partnerships, both partners must meet eligibility requirements for principals.

Security Guard Requirements

Unarmed guards must be US citizens or resident aliens, eighteen years of age or older. The DOL notes that work authorization is not equivalent to permanent resident alien status and is not adequate.

Security guards are not actually registered until such time as they have an offer of employment.

Applicants may be denied licensure on the basis of criminal background, though not all crimes are disqualifying. Applicants are referred to the document "recommended sanctions" (https://www.dol.wa.gov/business/security-guards/sggetunarmed.html). According to this document, individuals with felony or gross misdemeanor convictions may eventually be considered for professional licensure, though in most cases, the time frame is seven to ten years.

A security guard must have at least eight hours of preassignment training by a licensed trainer. Training may be administered in-house. However, this is not always the case. Preassignment training will cover the following:

- basic security guard principles
- legal power and limitations
- accident prevention and safety
- emergency response
- report writing

The DOL has provided a study guide (https://www.dol.wa.gov/business/securityguards/sgpreassigntrain.html).

An individual with recent experience as a peace officer may be allowed to take the exam without completing the course (https://app.leg.wa.gov/rcw/default.aspx?cite=18.170.105).

The security guard will need to complete an additional eight hours of post assignment training. Post assignment training will cover the following:

- basic security guard role
- legal aspects
- conduct
- principles of communication
- access control
- observation and reporting of incidents
- safeguarding information
- evacuation process
- emergency response
- job assignment and post orders
- life safety awareness

Thereafter, the security guard will need to do four hours of refresher training each year.

Security guards may be issued temporary registration cards after they have completed preassignment training and made application.

Requirements for Armed Guards
Armed security guards must be at least twenty-one years of age (https://www.dol.wa.gov/business/securityguards/sggetarmed.html). An armed guard will

need both an armed guard license and a firearms certificate; these two authorizations are issued by different agencies.

The individual will first apply for an armed license. He or she will then seek out a trainer. A prospective armed guard must earn a certificate through the Washington State Criminal Justice Training Commission (WSCJTC). The WSCJTC has provided a list of instructors who can deliver the required eight-hour course (https://www.dol.wa.gov/business/securityguards/sggetarmed.html). At the conclusion of the course, the student will take a written test and one or more firearm qualifications. (The security guard will need to qualify with each type of firearm he or she will carry.)

After requirements have been met, the company will submit an application for a firearms certificate. The certificate is agency-specific. There is a one-hundred-dollar fee.

An armed guard who is not a US citizen will also need an alien firearms license (https://www.dol.wa.gov/business/firearms/faalien.html).

The armed guard must display continued proficiency with the weapon. Armed guard status is based on annual requalification. The firearms certificate does not require renewal.

A security guard who has a firearms certificate will need an "add/change" form, however, if there is a change in weapon. An employee who transfers directly from one company to another will also have an "add/change" form filed on his or her behalf.

The Security Guard Application Process

Security guard employees can expect their employing agency to take an active role in the licensing process.

Prospective security guards must have fingerprint-based criminal background checks. This step is to be carried out before license application. The fingerprint card is to be included in the application package.

An applicant who has been convicted of a crime other than a traffic violation will need to provide court records.

Application forms can be downloaded from the DOL website (https://www.dol.wa.gov/business/securityguards/sgforms.html). The company will submit the completed application.

Unarmed security guards have a $111 fee. There is an additional $10 fee for armed status, payable to the DOL. (This is separate from the firearms certification fee).

Requirements for Company Principal

The company principal must be at least twenty-one. He or she can be qualified through experience or examination.

The licensing agency can accept managerial, supervisory, or administrative experience, either in security or a related field. A candidate who qualifies by experience will need three full years of experience. A candidate who does not have the requisite experience will take an examination.

The candidate will take the examination at a Washington driver's license office. The fee is seventy-five dollars. Currently, the exam is offered at sites around the state; applicants will mark their first and second choice. A representative will later contact the candidate to schedule. Results will be available approximately ten days later. An unsuccessful candidate will receive information about reexamination.

Some principals also hold firearms certification. A principal who needs verification of firearms certification will pay a ten-dollar fee to the DOL.

All required application materials are available from the Department of Licensing (https://www.dol.wa.gov/business/securityguards/sgforms.html).

When a company application and principal application are submitted together, the fee is $350. When an existing company changes principal, the fee is $100.

Out-of-State Licensee

An out-of-state licensee will submit license verification. The licensing agency will also seek information about licensing and training requirements.

Additional Information

Information about security guard licensing is available from the Washington Department of Licensing (https://www.dol.wa.gov/business/securityguards/). The Private Security Guard Program can be reached by telephone at 360-664-6611 or by email at security at dol.wa.gov.

Information about firearms certification is available from the Criminal Justice Training Commission. The Criminal Justice Training Commission can be reached by telephone at (206) 835-7300.

WEST VIRGINIA

Concealed carry honored in all states except California, Connecticut, District of Columbia, Hawaii, Illinois, Maryland, Massachusetts, New Jersey, New York, Oregon, Rhode Island, and Washington and **with restrictions** (must be twenty-one years of age) in Alaska, Arizona, Colorado, Florida, Kansas, Kentucky, Louisiana, Maine, Michigan, Minnesota, Nebraska, Oklahoma, Pennsylvania, South Carolina, Texas, Virginia, and Wisconsin.

West Virginia licenses both private security guards and security firms.

Security guards who work as employees are generally not licensed. State code provides for exemptions for both individuals who are hired by licensed security firms and those who are hired to provide services directly to a single business (http://www.sos.wv.gov/business-licensing/licensing/Pages/ExemptionsforSecurityGuards.aspx). However, employees of licensed security companies must meet a stringent set of requirements. The focus is on character and background; training is left to employer discretion.

High-level supervisors (termed "qualifying agents") must also meet state mandates. At this level, security professionals must have training or experience.

Security Guard Employee Requirements

A security guard must be at least eighteen years old and either a US citizen or resident alien. The individual must have good moral character and meet fitness requirements. An employee cannot have narcotics addictions or be habitually drunk. He or she cannot be incompetent in the view of a court of competent jurisdiction. He or she cannot have had a felony conviction or any other conviction specifically referenced in Chapter 30 of the state code. Among the disqualifiers are possessing or distributing drugs, receiving stolen property, or illegally entering a building. Credentials will also be denied on the basis of unfavorable professional history. This would include having had a security guard or investigative license revoked or denied in another jurisdiction. Falsely representing oneself as a licensee is among the other disqualifiers.

Employees do not file applications with the state. However, the company will report its employees to the licensing agency. The employer will maintain a set of fingerprints and passport-style photograph on file. West Virginia code states that it is illegal for an employer to hire an employee who does not meet the requirements described in the state code.

Private Security Guard Requirements

A private security guard is someone who is not exempted on the basis of employee status but who provides security services personally and does not employ other guards. To be licensed as a private security guard, an individual must meet general eligibility requirements and also have a year of qualifying experience or training. The experience may be accrued in the security business or at a private investigative firm. The licensing agency can accept other experience deemed substantially equivalent; this may include law enforcement. A professional who puts in fifty thirty-two-hour weeks is considered to have accrued a year of experience.

Alternatively, the security guard can qualify on the basis of thirty semester hours of coursework in law enforcement, investigative studies, or a related field. The licensing agency can accept combined experience and training; an individual with fifteen semester hours of coursework would only need the equivalent of half a year of full-time experience.

The Private Security Guard Application Process

Application packets can be requested by telephone at (304) 558-8000. Applications are also available for download (http://www.sos.wv.gov/business-licensing/licensing/Pages/ApplyingforanIndividualSecurityGuardLicense.aspx). A candidate who downloads the application form will need to email the Licensing Division at "Licensing at wvsos.com" to request fingerprint cards. Fingerprints must be made on official West Virginia cards. Applicants must follow the fingerprinting instructions on the division website. However, they have the option of having their fingerprints made at any convenient law enforcement office, in state or out of state.

The prospective private security guard will need to take some steps in advance. The licensing agency requires five references on board-supplied forms; the completed references are to be included in the application packet. References are to come from individuals who have known the prospective licensee for at least five years.

Other documents, such as proof of qualifying experience, are to be included in the application package as well. Security or private investigative experience can be documented through sworn statements by principals; education can be documented through transcripts.

The security guard will also need to provide evidence of a surety bond of $2,500. The application includes a form to be used for this purpose; the form requires notarization.

A West Virginia resident pays a $150 fee; a nonresident pays $550. All but $50 can be refunded in the event the license is denied.

The application requires notarization. Private security guard applications are mailed to the Licensing Division in Charleston. Licenses are renewed annually.

Qualifying Agent Requirements
If the security service is a firm, there must be a qualifying agent. A qualifying agent is a supervisor who is responsible for daily operations. The qualifying agent must meet requirements on a par with those of private security guards.

The other officers and corporate members are not required to meet experience or training requirements. However, they will need to provide references and fingerprints.

Additional Information
Information about security guard requirements is available from the West Virginia Secretary of State (http://www.sos.wv.gov/business-licensing/licensing/pages/aboutInvestigatorGuardlicensing.aspx). Business and Licensing can be reached at (304) 558-8000.

West Virginia Code sets requirements for concealed weapons; the concealed weapons chapter specifically references employees who use such weapons (http://www.legis.state.wv.us/WVCODE/ChapterEntire. cfm?chap=61&art=7&section=4). An individual under age twenty-one can be issued a concealed firearms license if the weapon is required for employment. Training is required for anyone who carries a concealed weapon. Local authorities may have gun laws more stringent than those enacted at the state level.

WISCONSIN

Concealed carry honored in all states except California, Connecticut, Delaware, District of Columbia, Hawaii, Illinois, Maryland, Massachusetts, Minnesota, New Jersey, New Mexico, New York, Oregon, Rhode Island, South Carolina, Texas, Washington and **with restrictions** (must be twenty-one years of age) in Alaska, Arizona, Colorado, Florida, Kansas, Kentucky, Maine, Michigan, Oklahoma, Pennsylvania, and West Virginia.

Wisconsin regulates armed and unarmed security guards. They are termed "private security persons." An individual must be credentialed unless he or she is exempt under state law. An individual hired to provide security services directly to a business may be exempt. An individual who works for a security agency will be credentialed.

Security guards who will be armed will need firearms permits. Those who are in business for themselves must also apply for agency licenses. All credentials are issued by the Department of Safety and Professional Services.

Requirements for Private Security Persons

A security guard must meet character and fitness requirements. The guard cannot use drugs or alcohol in an excessive manner. He or she cannot have a mental or physical condition that would preclude competent practice. Felonies are permanently disqualifying unless a pardon was granted. An applicant could be denied a credential on the basis of a misdemeanor.

Additional Requirements for Armed Security Guards

An armed guard must hold a firearms permit. The firearms permit requires thirty-six hours of training. The instructor must be department-certified; the department has provided a list of potential instructors (http://dsps.wi.gov/Default.aspx?Page=c8b40b06-b361-4315-9475-a370a7a96a50).

The curriculum will include the following:
- safety rules, dangers, and firearm cleaning care, handling, and usage
- legal use of firearms
- moral and ethical issues

- lawful detentions
- criminal and civil liability

The trainer will sign a certification of proficiency.

Up to thirty hours of the initial training may be waived in some instances. In order to qualify for a waiver, the individual must have been authorized by another jurisdiction to carry firearms at some point during the prior five-year period; the authorization may have been as a security guard, private investigator, or peace officer. The professional must have had at least thirty hours of training that covered the essential elements, with the exception of Wisconsin law. He or she will need six hours of refresher training.

A temporary permit does not authorize armed service. A certificate of proficiency is good for one year. The armed guard will complete six hours of refresher training to demonstrate continued proficiency.

The firearms permit is agency-specific. A guard who goes to work for another agency will need a new permit.

The Background Check and Application Process
Wisconsin requires federal and state background checks. Prospective permit holders are to have their fingerprints made before application. They will use the approved vendor, Fieldprint (http://www.fieldprintwisconsin.com/). Fieldprint operates Live Scan (electronic) fingerprinting sites throughout Wisconsin. The individual must schedule in advance; this step can be carried out online. There is a $39.25 fee. The applicant will need to bring two forms of ID to the fingerprinting site.

Field print also operates sites in other states; out-of-state candidates can select from these. The applicant will need to enter the correct code. This is available on the DSPS website (http://dsps.wi.gov/Licenses-Permits/PrivateSecurityPermit/PSPlicense).

The application is to be submitted within fourteen days of fingerprint submission. The applicant will note the date of fingerprint submission on the application form.

Applications for private security persons are available from the Department of Safety and Professional Services (http://dsps.wi.gov/Licenses-Permits/PrivateSecurityPermit/PSPforms). Applicants may use the Online Licensure Application System, OLAS (https://olas.wi.gov/).

An applicant who has ever had a criminal conviction will need to submit Form 2252: Convictions and Pending Charges. The licensing agency will require a self-explanation as well as official court records and evidence of compliance with orders. An applicant with adverse professional history (for example, disciplinary action or lawsuits) will also need to attach supporting documentation.

There is a seventy-five-dollar credentialing fee. A private security person may be granted a temporary permit that authorizes unarmed service pending the results of the required background checks. The applicant must clear a criminal records check carried out by the Department of Justice. There is a ten-dollar fee for the temporary permit and an eight-dollar fee for the records check.

Private security permits are renewed biennially during even-numbered years.

The licensing agency must be notified of any changes in employment.

Requirements for Sole Proprietors

An individual who is in business for himself or herself will need a liability insurance policy in the amount of $100,000. If firearms will be used, they must be covered under the policy. The agency will need to compose a firearm policy and provide a copy to the licensing agency. If firearms are not used, the licensing agency may accept a bond in lieu of an insurance policy.

Applications are available from the Department of Safety and Professional Services (http://dsps.wi.gov/Licenses-Permits/PrivateSecurityAgency/PDAGYforms). An applicant for a security guard agency license will use the private detective agency license form; the DSPS notes that security agencies are statutorily licensed as private detective agencies.

The agency fee is also seventy-five dollars. Agency licenses are renewed biennially on odd-numbered years.

Additional Information

Information about security guard credentialing is available from the Wisconsin Department of Safety and Professional Services (http://dsps.wi.gov/Licenses-Permits/Credentialing/Business-Professions). The licensing agency can be reached by telephone at (608) 266-2112 or by email at DSPSCredSecurity at wi.gov.

Statutes and administrative code are available online (http://dsps.wi.gov/Boards-Councils/Administrative-Rules-and-Statutes/Private-Detectives-and-Private-Security-Personnel-Administrative-Rules-and-Statutes).

WYOMING

Concealed carry honored in all states except California, Connecticut, Delaware, District of Columbia, Hawaii, Illinois, Maryland, Massachusetts, Minnesota, New Jersey, New York, Oregon, Rhode Island, and Washington and **with restrictions** (must be twenty-one years of age) in Alaska, Arizona, Colorado, Florida, Kansas, Kentucky, Maine, Nebraska, Oklahoma, Pennsylvania, South Carolina, and West Virginia.

Wyoming does not currently license security guards. However, some security guards are subject to local law. Casper, for instance, licenses both individual security guards and the security companies that they work for.

Where there are no laws in place, requirements are set by the individual employer. Some security guards are hired directly by stores or other businesses. Many work for security agencies. Some agencies that hire in Wyoming operate across state lines. While requirements will depend on the contract, they can be quite high. Still other security guards work in the public sector. They may be hired to safeguard public properties and the citizens. Security guards may also be hired by federal agencies. An example would be those who work at airports. Public sector employees are subject to regulations set at the state or national level.

Even when there are legal mandates governing hiring, they often represent a minimum standard for public safety. The basic requirements for licensure as a security guard in Casper include a clear background check and signed information release form. The guard is not licensed until there is intent to hire. This is also the case in many states where registration is mandated at the state level. Once the employer has selected a preferred candidate, the state evaluates his or her background to make sure it meets standards. Training is usually required, but the state often does not actually require that it be completed until post hiring.

Requirements for Security Guards Hired by Major Contract Security Companies

Security guards are generally expected to clear criminal background tests and demonstrate acceptable work histories. Some contract security companies also check motor vehicle records and/or require drug testing. There may be a comprehensive physical examination. Security agencies may, at the request of a client, require assessments, such as the Minnesota Multiphasic Personality Inventory (MMPI).

Requirements for Security Guards in the Public Sector

Civil service jobs represent a small portion of the security guard industry. However, state job classifications typically follow a well-defined career ladder, and human resource agencies provide a set of generic job descriptions that may provide some insight into expectations in the private sector as well. Wyoming Human Resources lists multiple security-related positions, among them Security Guard I and Security Guard II (http://agency.governmentjobs. com/wyoming/default.cfm?action=agencyspecs). The educational expectation at the Security Guard I level is a high school diploma. A commercial driver's license is among the other requirements. At the Security Guard II level, the expectation is an associate's degree and progressive experience as a Security Guard I. The stated preference is for a degree in criminal justice. However, additional experience may substitute for education.

Among the highest-paid security-related public service roles is state hospital security guard manager. At this level, the educational expectation is a bachelor's degree. Criminal justice is listed as the typical degree. Again, some substitutions are allowable. A professional could be considered after three to four years climbing the ranks as a security guard.

Actual job postings may stipulate additional requirements. A recent job posting for state security officer in Cheyenne noted that candidates were to have knowledge of the security industry and that preference would be given to those who had experience in roles such as civilian or military police or corrections.

Armed Security Guard Expectations

Wyoming is an open-carry state and has, as of yet, set no specific eligibility or training requirements for armed security guards. However, employers may set standards at the generally accepted national standard. A recent posting on a local job board illustrates this. The candidate was expected to be at least twenty-one years old and hold a high school diploma or the equivalent. He or she needed to be willing to have a criminal background check and a drug test.

This is similar to what is required in many states. Drug use or excessive use of alcohol is typically listed as a disqualifier, though drug testing is typically not mandated at the registration or licensing level. One difference is that states that license or register armed guards do typically require training. Often this involves more than just training in actual handling and usage; the individual may be required to have instruction in legal limitations of powers and in moral and ethical issues. Training culminates with the prospective armed guard firing one or more qualifying rounds. The armed security guard generally needs to requalify on at least an annual basis.

A contract security agency will likely have its own training program in place. However, previous knowledge and training may be valued.

Some employers favor candidates with military or police backgrounds, as they have had comprehensive training that includes firearms usage. This experience may also be valued in situations where only nonlethal devices are used. A recent posting for a hospital security officer in Sweetwater County is a case in point: The individual was to know how to use handcuffs and restraints. Previous experience was valued but might be in security, military, or law enforcement.

CREDITS

All information in this book is credited to experience, education, guidance, literature, and advice from the following:

My wife, Jan Allyn Naetzker-Nolan, CMSW
AFIMAC
Blue Line Security of Wartburg, Tennessee
Brosnan Security
Harford Community College
International Foundation of Protection Officers
LaSorsa and Associates Executive Protection
Pac-Tac Protective Solutions
Reading Area Community College
Regius Security
SOC, LLC
Solid Ground Security Solutions of Maryville, Tennessee
Strom Engineering Corporation
Triple Canopy
US Air Force Noncommissioned Officers Academy
US Army Noncommissioned Officers Academy
US Department of State
University of Phoenix
Vinnell Arabia

ABOUT THE AUTHOR

Robert Nile Nolan is a native of West Virginia. He graduated from Parkersburg High School in 1969 and joined the United States Air Force as a vehicle operator/dispatcher in 1970. He quickly attained the rank of E-5 and attended the U.S. Air Force Noncommissioned Officers Academy. He was honorably discharged in 1977.

Robert joined the Army National Guard in 1980 as an Infantryman. Later, he became a Reconnaissance Platoon Sergeant at the rank of E-7. During his time in the military, he served as a Senior Instructor at a Noncommissioned Officers Academy, and was the Noncommissioned Officer in Charge (NCOIC) of a Counterdrug Task Force operating throughout New York.

During the events of 9-11-2001 he deployed to Manhattan, NY as NCOIC of a security team coordinating with Naval Intelligence and homeland security, deployed to JFK airport as acting First Sergeant overseeing military security, and deployed to the United States/Canadian border as NCOIC of a security team to assist the Border Patrol, Customs Agents and New York State Police. He also deployed to a nuclear power plant in Oswego New York as NCOIC of a security team to assist in the security and safety of the power plant.

Robert deployed to Iraq with the U.S. Army and filled the positions of night shift NCOIC of the Tactical Operations Center, NCOIC of the gym, and was attached to 1st ID, 125th Special Operations (Falcon Cell) as the NCOIC leading an elite team of U.S. Army Rangers and Iraqi Commandos into battle.

After retiring from the U.S. Army in 2007 with 26 years active duty, he contracted with Vinnell Arabia teaching Advanced Infantry Tactics to Royal Family Officers of the Saudi Arabian National Guard for 1 year. He then worked for Triple Canopy and SOC LLC as a Security Manager contracted to the U.S. Department of State for the American Embassy and USAID compound in Baghdad, Iraq for 5 years.

Robert is 71 years of age and resides in Tennessee with his wife Jan Allyn Naetzker-Nolan. He owns Shadow Security LLC and works on temporary security jobs for the camaraderie and to stay active in the security community. He is a Free Mason, a Shellback, and Life member of the Combat Veterans Motorcycle Association.

Education
Bachelor's Degree, Organizational Security Management and Supervision, University of Phoenix

Associate degree, Occupational Studies, Reading Area Community College, Reading Pa.

Certificate in Law Enforcement, Harford Community College, Bel Air, Md.

Certificate as Executive Protection Agent – LaSorsa and Associates

Certificate as Shift Supervisor - AFIMAC

Certificate as Tactical Security Officer – AFIMAC

Certificate as Technical Evidence Collection Specialist – AFIMAC

Certified Armed Guard for the state of Tennessee

Certified Battle Focused Instructor, U.S. Army

Certified Instructor for Protection Officer, International Foundation of Protection Officers

Certified Protection Officer, International Foundation of Protection Officers

Certified Security Supervisor Manager, International Foundation of Protection Officers

Certified Instructor for QPR Suicide Prevention Gatekeeper Program

U.S. Air Force NCO Leadership School

U.S. Army Primary, Basic, and Advanced NCO Leadership School

U.S. Army Ranger School

U.S. Army Combative Arms Instructor

Fluent in spoken Spanish

Military Awards & Commendations

1 Combat Infantryman Badge – Iraq 2003 to 2005

2 U.S. Army Commendation Medals

2 U.S. Army Achievement Medals

1 U.S. Army Humanitarian Service Medal

1 New York State Homeland Security Service Medal

1 Global War on Terrorism Expeditionary Medal

1 Global War on Terrorism Service Medal

1 Ranger Tab

3 National Defense Service Medals

1 Air Force Good Conduct Medal

1 Air Force Professional Development Ribbon

1 Armed Forces Reserve Medal with M Device

1 Commendation by Naval Intelligence for Homeland Security

1 Commendation by New York Adjutant General for Bodyguard Service

1 Plaque for Soldier of the Year

1 Plaque for Commanders Award

Numerous certificates of achievements and appreciation